The Political Economy of Germany in the Twentieth Century

The Political Economy of Germany in the Twentieth Century

Karl Hardach

University of California Press

Berkeley / Los Angeles / London

Original German edition: *Wirtschaftsgeschichte Deutschlands im 20. Jahrhundert,* by Karl Hardach. © Vandenhoeck & Ruprecht, Göttingen, 1976.

University of California Press
Berkeley and Los Angeles, California
University of California Press, Ltd.
London, England
© 1980 by The Regents of the University of California

Printed in the United States of America

1 2 3 4 5 6 7 8 9

Library of Congress Cataloging in Publication Data
Hardach, Karl.
  The political economy of Germany in the twentieth century.
  Translation of Wirtschaftsgeschichte Deutschlands im 20. Jahrhundert.
  Includes bibliographies and index.
  1. Germany—Economic conditions.   I. Title.
IC286.H3613   330.943'08   78-64754
ISBN 0-520-03809-6

Contents

Tables and Maps

Maps

Preface

In the nineteenth century, economics and historiography were the academic parents of economic history. The child has, however, emancipated itself in the meantime. It is neither a chronologically arranged study of economic facts nor is it history embellished with economics and statistics. In contrast to historical materialism, economic history is characterized by a dislike for all forms of intellectual one-sidedness and by the conviction that it is politics, not economics, which above all determines the historical process. The economic machine has a largely instrumental character and can serve many masters. This fact has become especially apparent in Germany in this century, as economic events—indeed the entire economic system—have to a large degree been formed by political decisions.

For this reason the political elements in the economic history of Germany since World War I have been particularly stressed in the present study. In addition to this, and beyond merely providing facts, an attempt is made to explain economic relationships. Instead of merely saying *what* took place in the economic realm, it is intended— when possible and necessary—to analyze *why* it happened. How did a particular economic event come about? Why was an economic measure taken? What were the reasons for its failure or success? Every historian knows that such inquiring as to how and why is open to many more snares and pitfalls than a simple, straightforward narrative of so-called historical facts. There is a difference between making an analysis of a historical process and a mere listing of historical data, between providing figures like a statistical yearbook and explaining how they come about. This does not mean that the reader will find only a few statistics here. On the contrary, the text, the footnotes and the tables in the appendix contain quite a lot of figures. Economic historians have, indeed, a penchant for quantifying. It is no accident that economic history traditionally sees itself as being "the most exact of all historical sciences" although, of course, the initiated know that many quantitative statements are even today not much more than the educated guesses of experts. Inexact figures, however, are still better than none at all.

This book cannot be a compendium treating everything, no matter how fleetingly, nor does it seek to be. The presentation of the main features in a relatively brief space has priority over completeness, which is hardly attainable anyway. For those interested in learning more about the economic development of Germany in the twentieth century, the bibliographies contain suggestions for further reading. Though much of the listed literature—a third of which is in the English language—goes significantly beyond the few aspects which could be touched upon in the cursory survey, no pretension is made to present a detailed bibliography. Since the debt owed to scholars whose works have been plundered for ideas and information is enormous, the publications used in preparing this book are also listed. In order to avoid, however, a sprawling undergrowth of references on all pages, no acknowledgements have been made in footnotes.

This volume is based on practical experience in university teaching and is oriented to its needs up to a point. Questions and problems posed to the author as an American college professor have influenced the content and the way in which it is portrayed. Given the widespread interest in economic processes nowadays, however, this book is not only addressed to students. It presupposes neither special economic nor historical knowledge and dispenses with technical jargon—as much as possible—in favor of more generally understandable language. A glossary of economic terms in the appendix may be helpful for understanding certain indispensable economic terminology.

This American edition follows a German one published in 1976. Germanisms in the author's manuscript were weeded out by Scotswoman Marlene Pitkethly while Ika Hülsenbusch supplied much technical help. Dr. Hans Joachim Landmesser assisted in preparing the index and the glossary and in bringing some of the tables up to date. Dr. Ulrich Nocken as a colleague gave valuable advice on Weimar, on which he is a specialist, and provided useful hints on other periods as well. All these good people, beyond the call of duty and friendship, did their best to make this a better book. Only the Teutonic stubbornness of the author thwarted their total success.

CHAPTER 1

Trends and Politics

The structure and development of the economies of the industrialized European countries in the twentieth century correspond in many important points. For the period since the Second World War this applies only to the Western states, but up to 1945 all of Europe (except the Soviet Union) had basically the same economic system: a more or less managed market economy. That meant two things: that the decisions on what, how, where and when to produce and to consume were taken by individual economic units; and that all economic decisions were taken with reference to prices which were determined by supply and demand for goods, services, and factors of production. The final result of this process tended to be a situation in which the economic activities of all economic units were coordinated, while the largest and most influential economic unit in the system, the state, influenced the total process to a certain extent but never fully controlled it. Geographic proximity, intensive business and cultural relations and firmly established trading and capital links also contributed to the similarities of economic institutions and economic policy objectives in the industrial countries with managed market economies. Thus the schoolboy-like claim, "you know the recent economic development of one nation and you know them all," though overstated, cannot be termed a totally misleading exaggeration. This similarity of the developed economies in structure and performance has encouraged scholars to classify them according to various criteria.

If the ratio of the net output of consumer-goods industries to that of capital-goods industries is used as a measure—as suggested by W. G.

Hoffmann—then by 1914 basically only the United States had reached the third stage of industrialization (where the two sectors of industry are approximately of equal importance), while the industrial countries of Europe were still in the second stage (where the ratio is about 2.5:1). By the late 1930s, however, most of Europe's industrial countries had reached or were very close to the third stage, and by the 1950s the United States, Britain and Germany could be said to have reached the fourth stage (where the consumer-goods industries are left far behind the rapidly growing capital-goods industries.[1] The classification of the industrialized countries according to the expenditure structure of an average household budget—as pioneered by J. Fourastié—is also congruous with this international trend towards greater uniformity. While prior to World War I less than half of the family budget was spent on food in the United States, as against more than half in the industrialized countries of Europe, the grocery bill in the same European countries in the 1950s no longer exceeded 50 percent, despite improved nutrition. More, however, was now being spent on durable consumer goods and services. These developments are quite compatible with W. W. Rostow's suggestion that, shortly before World War I, Germany had joined the earlier industrialized countries in reaching the end of the fourth stage of his economic growth model, called "the drive to maturity." According to Rostow, beginning in the 1950s, Germany and the other Western European countries encountered the not unequivocal joys of the final economic stage, "the age of high mass consumption." In general, the Western European nations can be said to have matched the qualitative lead which the United States held before World War I by the 1950s.

It is against the background of this international economic trend towards greater similarity of the industrial nations that some macroeconomic data in the development of Germany have to be seen. Today there are more Germans—in East and West—than ever before, despite the heavy population losses in two world wars (Table 1 in the appendix). The demographic deficit of World War I amounted to about 5.65 million (about 2.4 million military dead, 2.95 million who were never born, and 0.3 million due to increased general mortality), that of World War II to about 10.5 million (about 3.8 million military dead, 3.1 million civilian dead due to acts of war, including some 300,000 political victims, about 2.6 million unborn, and about 1 million due to increased general mortality). These losses affect the balance between the sexes, the age distribution, and the potential labor force to this day. Not only the wars but also a host of socioeconomic factors have

---

1. In this book Germany means either the Reich or the Federal Republic, thus avoiding the incorrect and inconvenient term "West Germany."

slowed down German population growth almost continuously in this century, and have nearly brought it to a halt, inasmuch as the decline in the birth rate has been much more pronounced than in the mortality rate (Table 2). The marriage rate—though open to significant short-term fluctuations—has been quite stable, and yet families blessed (or cursed) with many children have become more uncommon (Table 3). Nowadays a newborn child has a much better chance of living through the most dangerous period of its life, the first year, as the infant mortality rate fell by over 85 percent in the sixty years under consideration. At the same time the baby's chances of becoming a septuagenarian are much greater than they were half a century ago, when the average life expectancy was only about 45 years. The so-called weaker sex has managed to increase its longevity in comparison to the supposedly stronger sex in both absolute and relative terms, which must either reflect his inherent inferiority or her living on easy street (Table 4). Better nutrition and improved medical care are probably the most important reasons for the increased life expectancy, which explains why, despite war losses and declining birthrate, the population on the whole has increased. The proportion of employable age (between 15 and 65) has, however, remained remarkably stable since 1910 (Table 5).

Population density has almost doubled, mainly as a result of territorial losses and the consequent population shifts. At the same time the geographic distribution has changed dramatically (Table 6). The portion of the population living in places of less than 2,000 inhabitants has declined greatly—only half as many in the Federal Republic of Germany (FRG) as in the German Reich prior to World War 1—while the percentage of those living in small towns (up to 10,000) has only slightly increased. In the medium-sized towns (up to 100,000), the increase has been greater; but it is the cities which, in the Federal Republic at least, have gained the most. At the beginning of the sixties, in the so-called main agglomeration areas (with a population density of over 1,300 persons per square kilometer), over 40 percent of the total population was living on only 7 percent of the land area. By 1970, 60 percent of the Federal Republic's population and 54 percent of that of the German Democratic Republic (GDR) lived in cities and towns of over 10,000 inhabitants, compared with only 41 percent for the Reich in 1910. More Germans than ever before have become urbanites.

Corresponding to this, the occupational structure has changed considerably in the approximately six decades under consideration (Table 7). The percentage of those employed in agriculture (primary sector) has declined steadily, while the number of industrial employees (secondary sector) has constantly been on the rise. The Federal Republic, in particular, seems to be gradually entering the postindustrial phase of economic development, however, for the share of those employed in the service (tertiary) sector has recently been growing faster than that of industry, which remained almost unchanged throughout the 1960s.

This faster increase of employment in the service sector, with its lower demand for physical strength, was not the only factor which opened up new employment opportunities for women. The share of female employees in industry in the FRG also increased between 1950 and 1970 (Table 8). While in the United States Rosie the Riveter was asked and/or found it desirable to return to apron and apple pie after 1945, a similar course could not be taken in Germany. The preceding massacre of males provided vacancies and job opportunities for women, who owing to the deaths of male breadwinners had frequently become the providers for themselves and their families. Their integration into the labor force on all levels of employment has been much more thorough and smooth than in some other major industrial nations. Female employment in any case differed from sector to sector and also within the industries of a sector.

This is also true for the self-employed, whose importance has, not surprisingly, declined, especially in the industrial sector. Here the process of concentration has continued, particularly increasing the employment share of the large enterprises with over 1,000 employees (Table 9). No less characteristic is the increase in the number of salaried employees—the so-called white-collar workers—in the industrial sector (Table 10). The number of hours worked per week declined by a third between 1913 and 1969 (Table 11), and this was not only in the industrial sector. In the same period the standard of living in Germany improved considerably. Private consumption was characterized by an increased share spent on nonfood items in general, and for durable goods (e.g. household appliances, cars) and services (education, recreation, transportation) in particular (Table 12). Although the share of income spent on food was smaller, the quality of the food had risen. The amount of vegetable products in the overall diet has declined, while the proportion of animal foodstuffs has just as clearly increased (Table 13). The relatively smaller grocery bill is partly the result of the general rise in income, which while not eliminating the basic inequality in the distribution of income has tended slightly to better the relative position of the small and medium income groups (Tables 14 and 15). Of the European industrial nations which were belligerents in both world wars, Germany has enjoyed the highest per capita growth rate in terms of real national product, only slightly behind the neutral states (Tables 16 and 17). Of this greatly increased national product only a very minor portion is earned in agricultural occupations. Practically speaking, the Germans have ceased to be tillers of the soil (Table 18).

The decline of the self-employed in the industrial sector, mentioned above, was in part due to the greatly increased need for capital equipment in industrial production. It reflected the trend towards growing mechanization and automation of the production processes. This tendency was also visible in the changing structure of capital employment, with its greater emphasis on implements and machinery, as well as in the growing share of industrial investment. On the other hand, the very substantial investment in nonagricultural housing over the decades is an expression of the increasing urbanization (Tables 19 and 20).

The growth of cities is one of the many immediate causes of the expansion of the government's economic activity, though wars and changes in the distribution of political power in the nation are the two factors primarily responsible. In Germany, as in the other modern nations, the scope of public finances has grown more rapidly than the national income in the 20th century. Considered over a longer period of time, history appears in the case of Germany to bear out "Wagner's Law," or the tendency towards relatively rising public expenditures: on the eve of World War I less than one-sixth of the national income was claimed by the government; by 1970, however, this had risen to almost two-fifths (Table 21). In consequence of World War I, the government's share jumped from 15 to 25 percent, rising fairly steadily thereafter in the interwar years to 45 percent. After World War II, the government's share stood at a low 36 percent in 1950, staying at about this level, with only minor fluctuations, until 1970. As long as public expenditures accounted for only a relatively small percentage of the national income, purely fiscal considerations usually sufficed as a yardstick of how to allocate these funds, but as they increased, public spending became a frequently decisive factor in the economy and had to be considered from the overall economic point of view. The character of public finance has changed, as it has been put, from "the portion system" to "the control system."

While a clear statement can be made about the development of the government's share in the national income, this cannot be done regarding the contribution of foreign trade to national income (Table 22). The share of imports declined steadily from the early 1900s, reaching less than one-third of the pre–World War I level shortly before World War II. The post–World War II years saw an equally continuous rise of the share of imports in the national income, though by the late 1960s it had still not reached the level of 1910–1913. The movements of the share of exports in the national income were quite similar; since World War II it has increased at a greater rate, so that in the Federal Republic by the end of the 1960s it exceeded that of the German Reich in the pre–World War I period. From the early 1930s the share of exports tended to exceed the share of imports. Considerable changes have taken place in the proportions of the product groups (Table 23). The share of foodstuffs, for example, declined from 1913 (Reich) to 1970 (FRG) by one-half for imports and by two-thirds for exports. The decline in raw materials was even greater, while the share of finished products quintupled for imports, and for exports grew from 64 to 86 percent. The growing division of labor among the industrial countries led to a greater "Europeanization" of German foreign trade, a phenomenon which was further promoted by the Common Market (Table 24). The FRG's share in total world trade in 1970 was still below the 1913 level for the Reich as a whole (Table 25).

All these facts, and many others of a similar nature which one could cite, contain a wealth of problems and give rise to interesting questions of interpretation, but they remain essentially superficial, since they usually differ from the corresponding data for other Western industrial nations merely in degree. What is, however, typical of the course of economic events in Germany during the last half century or so, if not entirely unique, is the extent to which it has been determined by politics at the highest level. Though many an economic historian nowadays frowns on too close a relationship with political history, it is impossible not to view the fundamental political changes in Germany in recent decades as also being decisive turning points in the economic history of the country. To establish the evolution of this or that macroeconomic dimension, dear to the heart of the economist, is immensely useful, but entirely insufficient to provide an understanding of the course of economic affairs, since it leaves out the political, social and cultural framework within which economic history unfolds. Consequently a brief retrospective glance at Germany's checkered political career in the 20th century is imperative.

In order to see the subsequent years in proper perspective, one has to start with World War I—when the nineteenth century in reality ended—and its consequences. Revolution and demobilization, reparations and hyperinflation were not only causally connected with the Great War, but also of far-reaching impact upon economic events during the 1920s. The network of the world economic system, which had become rather frayed, even torn, during the war, was mended only gradually in the following years. That it was impossible to restore its old pattern was not realized for quite a while. During the second half of the twenties, the so-called golden years of Weimar, Germany again became a full-fledged member of the international political and economic community, participating in the advantages provided by a world economy based on extensive division of labor. That such membership involved severe risks soon became obvious, with the setting in of the worldwide economic crisis in the autumn of 1929. Few doubt nowadays that it was the conditions of the depression which largely contributed to the rise of Hitler, in addition to the unforgotten defeat in 1918 and the resulting tributary peace of Versailles, felt by many to be unjust. The demagogical tirades of the Führer would hardly have met with such a lively response if extraordinary economic circumstances had not prepared an unusually fertile soil in Germany for the Europewide phenomenon of fascism.

Although during the peace years national socialism, the German version of fascism, aimed in general at the creation of a new economic system that would be an alternative of capitalism and communism, combining so-called responsible economic self-administration with comprehensive guidance by the state, such attempts had to take a back seat to the solving of the more pressing problems of the day. Surmounting the domestic consequences of the world economic crisis, initiating rearmament, and developing safeguards against economic warfare—without significant upward pressure on prices and impairment of the standard of living—took priority until September 1939. During the first, "Blitzkrieg" phase of the war, the economy remained on what was virtually a peacetime footing. From the turn of 1941/42 on, two periods of increased and eventually all-out economic war efforts followed, resulting not only in the military and political collapse of the Reich in May 1945 but also in economic breakdown, since Germany herself eventually became a major theater of war.

Besides reconstruction, reparations, territorial losses and extensive displacements of population, the assumption of governmental power by the four Allies was the chief characteristic of the German economy during the immediate postwar period. The years from mid-1945 to mid-1948 were in the nature of an interim phase, with the temporary dismemberment of the national economy into four isolated zonal economies, their partial reintegration, and the eventual establishment of two fundamentally different economic systems in Germany. This was paralleled by a gradual return of decision-making powers to newly established German authorities, finally culminating in the foundation of the Federal Republic of Germany and the German Democratic Republic in 1949. From the beginning both states reflected in essence the social, economic and political systems—for better or worse—of their respective foster parents. The eventual integration of both states as full partners in the Western or Eastern bloc respectively during the Cold War further underlined these divergences. Mutual antagonism has characterized the relationship between the two states ever since, and the recent détente is yet a very tender plant, with unproven frost resistance. This much, however, seems clear: détente without defense is as much a delusion as the vain hope that increased economic ties form a sure basis for a better understanding among nations, or encourage the will to keep peace. History shows, for example, that Britain and Germany, which were each other's best customers in 1913, went to war a year later.

Bibliography

Andic, S., and Veverka, J. "The Growth of Government Expenditure in Germany since the Unification." *Finanzarchiv* 23 NF (1964).

Aubin, H., and Zorn, W., eds. *Handbuch der deutschen Wirtschafts- und Sozialgeschichte*. Vol. 2: *Das 19. und 20. Jahrhundert*. Stuttgart, 1976.

Bericht der Bundesregierung und Materialien zur Lage der Nation. Bonn, 1971.

Borchardt, K. *Wandlungen des Konjunkturphänomens in den letzten hundert Jahren*. Munich, 1976.

Born, K. E. *Geld und Banken im 19. und 20. Jahrhundert*. Stuttgart, 1976.

Brandt, K. *The Reconstruction of World Agriculture*. New York, 1945.

Bry, G. *Wages in Germany 1871–1945*. Princeton, N.J., 1960.

Deutsche Bundesbank. *Währung und Wirtschaft in Deutschland 1876–1975*. Frankfurt/Main, 1976.

Fischer, W. *Deutsche Wirtschaftspolitik 1918–1945*. 3rd. ed. Opladen, 1968.

Fourastié, J. *Machinisme et bien-être*. Paris, 1951.

Gerschenkron, A. *Bread and Democracy in Germany*. Berkeley and Los Angeles, 1943.

Handbuch der Finanzwissenschaft. 3rd. ed. Vol. 1. Tübingen, 1977.

Hardach, G. *Deutschland in der Weltwirtschaft 1870–1970: Eine Einführung in die Sozial- und Wirtschaftsgeschichte*. Frankfurt/Main, 1977.

Henning, F.-W. *Das industrialisierte Deutschland 1914 bis 1972*. Paderborn, 1974.

Hentschel, V. "Das System der sozialen Sicherung in historischer Sicht 1880 bis 1975." *Archiv für Sozialgeschichte* 18 (1978).

Hoffmann, W. G. *The Growth of Industrial Economies*. Manchester, 1958.

Hoffmann, W. G., and Müller, H. J. *Das deutsche Volkseinkommen 1851–1957*. Tübingen, 1959.

Hoffmann, W. G. *Das Wachstum der deutschen Wirtschaft seit der Mitte des 19. Jahrhunderts*. Berlin, 1965.

Köllmann, W. *Bevölkerung und Raum in Neuerer und Neuester Zeit*. Würzburg, 1965.

Kuczynski, J. *Allgemeine Wirtschaftsgeschichte*. East Berlin, 1951.

Kuznets, S. *Modern Economic Growth: Rate, Structure and Spread*. New Haven, 1966.

Landes, D. S. *The Unbound Prometheus: Technological Change and Industrial Development in Western Europe from 1750 to the Present*. Cambridge, 1969.

Maddison, A. *Economic Growth in the West: Comparative Experience in Europe and North America*. New York, 1964.

Mottek, H.; Becker W.; and Schröter A. *Wirtschaftsgeschichte Deutschlands*. Vol. 3. East Berlin, 1974.

Petzina, D. *Grundriss der deutschen Wirtschaftsgeschichte 1918 bis 1945.* Institut für Zeitgeschichte, ed., Deutsche Geschichte seit dem ersten Weltkrieg, vol. 2. Stuttgart, 1973.

Petzina, D.; Abelshauser, W.; and Faust, A. *Sozialgeschichtliches Arbeitsbuch III: Materialien zur Statistik des Deutschen Reiches 1914–1945.* Munich, 1978.

Rostow, W. W. *The Stages of Economic Growth.* Cambridge, 1960.

Statistische Jahrbücher des Deutschen Reiches, der Bundesrepublik Deutschland und der Deutschen Demokratischen Republik.

Statisches Bundesamt. *Bevolkerüng und Wirtschaft 1872–1972.* Stuttgart, 1972.

Stolper, G.; Häuser, K.; and Borchardt, K. *The German Economy 1870 to the Present.* New York, 1967.

Stucken, R. *Deutsche Geld- und Kreditpolitik 1914 bis 1963.* 3rd. ed. Tübingen, 1964.

Thomas, G. *Geschichte der deutschen Wehr- und Rüstungswirtschaft 1918–1943/45.* Boppard, 1966.

Veit, O. *Grundriss der Währungspolitik.* 2nd. ed. Frankfurt/Main, 1961.

Wehler, H. U. *Bibliographie zur modernen deutschen Wirtschaftsgeschichte (18.-20. Jahrhundert).* Göttingen, 1976.

Woytinsky, W. S., and Woytinsky, E. S. *World Population and Production. Trends and Outlook.* New York. 1953.

Wurm, F. F. *Wirtschaft und Gesellschaft in Deutschland 1848-1948.* Opladen, 1969.

Yeager, L. B. *International Monetary Relations: Theory, History and Policy.* New York, 1966.

Zumpe, L., ed. *Wirtschaft und Staat im Imperialismus: Beiträge zur Entwicklungsgeschichte des staatsmonopolistischen Kapitalismus in Deutschland.* East Berlin, 1976.

CHAPTER **2**

The First World War

War Financing and the Beginning of Inflation

World War I was a fairly costly affair: national income estimates for the last prewar year run at close to 50 billion marks, while the figures given for the Reich's war expenditures (in 1913 prices) were well above 100 billion marks. In current wartime prices figures close to 200 billion marks have been mentioned, which clearly reflects the loss in the purchasing power of the mark, which by the end of the war commanded only about half of its prewar value in neutral exchange markets. Such a comparison, however, does not consider the extent to which the national income was reduced as a result of the destruction and depletion of capital and the withdrawal of millions of men from the production process, losses which could not be compensated by the perhaps increased productivity of those remaining at the home front.

About 70 percent of war expenditure was financed by internal loans (mostly through 5 percent war bonds and treasury bills bought by the public), while the remainder was derived about equally from taxes and an increased money supply.[1] Taxes were raised belatedly and timidly after mid-1916; even when the initial reluctance to use this soundest of all methods of war financing was overcome, the additional revenues remained insufficient.[2] The supply of money could be

---

1. Floating German war bonds in the neutral United States in August 1914 turned out to be a complete failure. Similar efforts in other countries also showed little success.
2. The Reich and France financed about one-seventh of their war expenditures through taxation, compared to about one-fourth in Britain and the United States.

increased rather easily by various means: e.g., the Reich issued short-term interest-bearing treasury bills, which the Reichsbank— the German Central Bank—was entitled to rediscount in unlimited amounts against banknotes. Altogether the total money supply quintupled, not least through the printing of banknotes, the circulation of which multiplied by almost 13 during the war. By March 1919 the total debt of the Reich, long-term and short-run,[3] had grown to over 150 billion marks. Legal maximum and guideline prices during the war years prevented the German public from recognizing this ongoing inflation, partly because of the lack of other yardsticks. The stock market had been closed in the early days of the war and foreign exchange rates were not published, but black market prices did provide some indication, and banking circles knew, of course, how substantially the mark (as well as the currencies of the other main belligerents) had sunk in value. Thus the receivers of fixed incomes and holders of liquid assets saw themselves "taxed" for the benefit of the German war effort, which was nevertheless essentially financed through credits. Since credit financing is only a means of postponing the actual burden, in the final analysis the defeated enemy was supposed to bear the financial burden. Just as conquered Russia was required in the peace treaty of Brest-Litovsk in March 1918 to pay a considerable sum,[4] so the Western Allies would have faced similar demands in the event of a German victory.[5] Instead of being able to shift their own burden onto someone else, however, the eventually defeated Germans discovered that all victors have similar ideas, and to their disappointment found themselves confronted with staggering reparation demands.

2

War Economy and Final Collapse

To share the burden of reconstructing the war-ravaged zones of northern France and Belgium seemed only fair, and the Reich government expressed itself willing to do so, especially as Germany herself had not been a theater of war, apart from a few small areas in the east. But the Allied claim to compensation for their entire war expenditures seemed naive and was impossible to fulfill, as even without direct war damage the German economy lay in shambles. Superiority in manpower and weight of material, not superior fighting spirit or moral principle, had determined the outcome of the war, and four years of fighting had overstrained Germany's economic and military strength.

3. Approximately 40 percent of the Reich's debt was short-term.
4. Six billion rubles, or slightly over three billion dollars.
5. As late as May 1917, the Kaiser daydreamed of $30 billion each from the U.S. and the U.K., and of about $7.7 billion from France.

The withdrawal of manpower, the lack and attrition of equipment, and the preemption by the munitions industry of nitrates that would otherwise have been available as fertilizer, had bled German agriculture to such an extent that grain production after four years of war barely reached half of the prewar level. Industrial production suffered from similar strains, reaching only 42 percent of the 1913 level in 1919.

While the Allies had free access to the resources of virtually the entire world during the war, the Central Powers saw themselves encircled and cut off from overseas sources of supply. Germany, which had been solidly integrated into the worldwide division of labor, had to rely on her own limited raw materials and food supplies during the war, only occasionally slightly increased by deliveries from her mostly agricultural—at best semi-industrial—comrades-in-arms. Conquests in Eastern Europe added some Ukrainian grain and Romanian oil, while trade with the neutral Dutch and Scandinavians helped to lessen the burden of an increasingly effective naval blockade; but there were bottlenecks as far as rubber, oil, and certain metals were concerned throughout the war.

This bitter experience of an imposed, involuntary autarky was to influence future German economic policy, especially after 1933, when the geopolitical idea that the vast resources of Eastern Europe had to be secured dominated Hitler's thinking. Consideration had indeed been given in Germany to the problem of how to meet the demands of a future war long before 1914. But except for a few plans for financial mobilization lying about in drawers and some notion as to the necessary foreign trade measures to be taken immediately at the outbreak of war (essentially, freeing imports and prohibiting exports and transit shipments) no economically relevant war preparations had been made. Only four or five months after the outbreak of the war, as the real requirements of men and materiel in a technical-industrial war became apparent, did the construction and development of the German war economy begin. Thus Germany soon found herself in the position of a beleaguered fortress, where the extreme scarcity of raw materials, manpower and food demanded that she forsake the principles of a market economy and adopt economic planning. That Germany had never fully succumbed to the jungle law of extreme laissez-faire, and had always—if sometimes at a rather low pitch—maintained the regulatory and balancing functions of the state, was to the advantage of wartime planning. In addition, German industry, particularly since the late nineteenth century, had "organized" competition through a multitude of cartels under the benevolent eye of the state. Although there were precedents for state regulation of, and participation in, the economic sphere, what was needed in a fortress under siege went far beyond previous experience.

Private consumption of basic foodstuffs had to be curtailed by creating a new system of distribution which took into account the physiological needs of the various recipients according to occupation. Rationing started with bread in early 1915 and quickly encompassed other essentials like milk, meat and fats. To fill the still-remaining gaps, various substitutes appeared: coffee made out of acorns, fat made out of snails, a new kind of bread made of potato flour and cracked barley. There was also "Ersatz" wine, beer and sausage. At first communal associations consisting of several municipalities administered the rationing, but soon greater centralization became necessary. This led to the establishment of the War Food Office in May 1916.

State control in the area of raw materials corresponded largely to the organizational structure of the rationing system for foodstuffs. The civil servants lacked the necessary professional qualifications, however, and newly founded war companies, though privately owned enterprises, were thus vested with the executive power of seizure and put in charge of the allocation of scarce raw materials and industrial inputs. The "Hindenburg Program" of August 1916, often termed a turning point in German wartime economic policymaking, aimed at a reorganization of this mixed state-private system. To increase armament production and to solve the growing lack of agricultural and industrial labor, from December 1916 onward all male workers between the ages of 17 and 60 were conscripted as part of the Patriotic Emergency Service and could be assigned to essential industries, thus partly losing their freedom of movement. This "total mobilization" of labor was paralleled by a "militarization" of private industry. The War Office established in November 1916, which practically carried out the directives of the Army High Command, was granted far-reaching powers of intervention in the production process and industrial structure. Plant and equipment insufficiently used due to lack of labor or raw materials could be reassigned to industries of military importance, while low-priority industries had to shut down in whole or in part.[6] State penetration of the economy had become thorough and virtually all-encompassing. The postwar relaxation of the state's grip on the economy, though substantial, was never completely effective. That the state had started its planning role under highly adverse conditions meant that a persistent odium was attached to future planning efforts inasmuch as a state economy was understood to be a privation economy with everything shabby and in short supply.[7]

6. This state-ordered concentration reduced the number of enterprises in many branches of the consumer goods sector by one-half.

7. In the final year of the war, the daily ration for city dwellers—not always available—consisted of about 440 grams of potatoes, 200 grams of bread, 50 grams of sugar, 35 grams of meat, and 9 grams of fat (1 ounce = 28.35 grams).

Manpower shortages during the war meant, of course, increased clout for the unions—which, however, they were reluctant to use. Peace in industrial relations *(Burgfrieden)* had been agreed upon until the end of the war, a sensible thing to do in a fortress under siege. Conciliation committees for bargaining and workers' councils to safeguard their interests were created, and although both institutions only became really influential in the Weimar period, the war had nevertheless increased the unions' say immensely and placed them on an equal footing with management and the authorities of the state. On the other end of the social ladder, the aristocracy, especially the higher nobility, had continuously lost in prestige and power. When the monarchy was abolished and the republic proclaimed in November 1918, the depositing of two dozen or so royal and princely rulers on the rubbish heap of history was almost a nonevent.

But such political changes touched only the surface insofar as Germany's social and economic framework remained much the same. Neither in public administration nor in the business community nor in the armed forces was the old guard relieved. Since the progressive democratic forces, basically comprising only the Social Democrats, were backed by only about two-fifths of the electorate, their deep commitment to majority rule permitted no thorough reorganization of society and economy along socialist lines. They were forced to enter into coalitions with bourgeois parties and the traditional influence groups, and the transformation and further development of wartime regulations into state planning and nationalization programs was impossible. Instead a process of remarketization was initiated. Within a few years the insistence of the Weimar democrats upon political equality in a society characterized by economic and social inequality, and their insufficient understanding of power politics, permitted the antirepublican upper classes of the old empire to regain their previous influence with little effort.[8]

Bibliography

Bente, H. "Die deutsche Währungspolitik von 1914 bis 1924." *Weltwirtschaftliches Archiv,* 23 (1926).

Boelke, W. A. "Wandlungen der deutschen Agrarwirtschaft in der Folge des Ersten Weltkriegs." *Francia* 3 (1975).

8. Lenin, not entirely without justification, ridiculed the German Social Democrats, who before the takeover of a railroad station would duly buy platform tickets. The granting of suffrage to women, who then tended to vote according to religious criteria, thus bolstering the bourgeois parties, was at the time a serious blunder.

Büsch, O., and Feldman, G. D. eds. *Historische Prozesse der deutschen Inflation 1914 bis 1924*. Berlin, 1978.

Burchardt, L. *Friedenswirtschaft und Kriegsvorsorge: Deutschlands wirtschaftliche Rüstungsbestrebungen vor 1914*. Boppard, 1968.

Feldman, G. D., *Army, Industry and Labor in Germany 1914–1918*. Princeton, 1966.

Hardach, G. *The First World War 1914–1918*. Berkeley and Los Angeles, 1977.

Hesse, F. *Die deutsche Wirtschaftslage von 1914 bis 1923*. Jena, 1938.

Lotz, W. *Die deutsche Staatsfinanzwirtschaft im Kriege*. Stuttgart, 1927.

Ott, H. "Kriegswirtschaft und Wirtschaftskrieg 1914–1918, Verdeutlicht an Beispielen aus dem badish-elsässischen Raum." In *Festschrift C. Bauer*. Berlin, 1974.

Shotwell, J. T., ed. *Economic and Social History of the World War*. German Series. 12 vols. New Haven, 1927–37.

Skalweit, A. *Die deutsche Kriegsernährungswirtschaft*. Stuttgart, 1927.

Zunkel, F. *Industrie und Staatssozialismus: Der Kampf um die Wirtschaftsordnung in Deutschland 1914–1918*. Düsseldorf, 1974.

CHAPTER 3

The Weimar Years 1918–1933

It has become traditional to divide the economic history of the Weimar period into three phases: the immediate postwar years from November 1918 to November 1923; the interim period of relative stability up to October 1929; and the following depression years up to January 1933.

1

The Chaotic Times of Inflation and Excessive Reparation Demands

Inflation and weighty reparation demands principally accounted for the economic chaos during the first years of Weimar. The substantial though still bearable wartime loss in the mark's purchasing power turned into runaway inflation due to continuous budget deficits, unfavorable balances of payments, and increasing wage demands. Deficit spending was the main cause of German inflation. It had already been practiced during the war and increased subsequently, since the republican government did not dare, in view of widespread social unrest and revolutionary and secessionist attempts, to raise taxes further. The princely rulers had been reluctant to finance the war through taxation, in order not to undermine the industriousness and the fighting spirit of the masses. The new government not only tried in similar fashion to avoid revealing the sad truth about Germany's desperate economic situation and the need for further belt-tightening, but failed to realize fully how severe the troubles actually were.

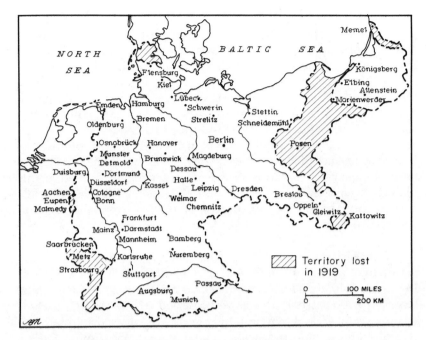

1. *The German Reich in 1920 and territories lost in 1919.*

Losses Due to Versailles and Attempts at Reconstruction

A balance sheet of the German economy at that time would include only a few credit items: her territory had not been a theater of war, her war debt was internal, and the armament restrictions of the Versailles settlement would channel energies into industrial rehabilitation instead of rearmament programs. But Versailles also meant a host of other provisions, some primarily humiliating, some of serious economic impact. The internationalization of the major German rivers, the inclusion of nonreciprocal trade advantages like duty-free exports from Alsace-Lorraine to Germany for five years or the prohibition of restrictions on imports of certain French articles, especially wine, for three years, put Germany at some economic disadvantage. Such provisions, however, were part of a general policy of provocative pin-pricking, not unlike the stipulation that all Napoleonic banners and battle-gear captured by the once victorious Germans be returned from the museums. Even though the economic historian should not overlook the importance of "psychic income," however, his prime concern lies with such robust realities as the loss of 13 percent of Germany's prewar territory, 10 percent of the population, 15 percent of the arable land, and 75 percent of the iron ore deposits, as well as a reduction of pig iron production capacity by 44 percent, of steel by 38 percent, and of coal by 26 percent. These losses—owing to the severance of Upper Silesia and Alsace-Lorraine and separation until 1935 from the Saar district—and the additional cession of all colonies meant that Germany depended to a greater extent than before on foreign foodstuffs and raw materials. They also placed an additional burden on her balance of payments, the more so as the handing over of almost the entire merchant fleet and the confiscation of her foreign investments (including patents and licenses) in the Allied countries affected the balance of services negatively.[1] Given the absence of foreign loans, a squaring of future balances of payments seemed highly unlikely even without the reparation obligations. Furthermore, the new political boundaries disrupted established economic relations and transport networks, and made costly reorganization processes necessary.

The Reich government began the general reconstruction by making attempts at putting public finances on sounder footings. As early as December 1919, the Reich Emergency Contribution called for a capital levy of up to 65 percent, payable over a period of years. In 1920 a whole set of tax reforms and reorganization measures followed, emphasizing central authority and practically changing Germany from a federal state to a centralized state, at least as far as her fiscal administration was concerned. These energetic attempts to increase tax revenues essentially failed, however, owing to the intrinsic weakness in inflationary times of a financial policy primarily based on direct taxes.[2] As taxes were still to be paid in nominal marks instead of gold marks the tax debtor had a vested interest in further inflation and tried to lengthen the already extensive span between assessment and payment of his tax debt. The low morality in matters of taxation simply reflected the natural desire to discard wartime discipline and restraints. Such a call for individualism and laissez-faire, at a time when the abnormal conditions of reconstruction demanded an exceptional degree of discipline and coordinated action, proved to be disastrous.

Sources and Extent of the Inflation

The shrinking purchasing power of the Reich's revenues contrasted with growing expenditure for reparations, service of the internal war debt, and pensions to war veterans, widows and orphans. Besides these more lasting responsibilities, there were temporary expenditures for the compensation of civilian damages, for the re-

1. The United States eventually returned a large part of the German private property originally sequestered—a notable exception to the general policy of confiscations.
2. E.g., income taxes collected in a given period were based on incomes of the previous period when nominal prices and incomes were much lower.

construction of the few devastated areas, and above all for the demobilization of the armed forces and war industry. The magnitude of the latter problem can be seen from the fact that at the time of the armistice some six million Germans were under arms, apart from vast numbers of civilians in the armaments industry. The carrying out of the detailed plans which Germany, like most of the belligerent nations, had made for this transformation was thwarted or delayed by the terms of the armistice and by the disintegration of the political system and the economy. To regain a mentality adapted to civilian needs and peaceful pursuits, to rid oneself of the virtues and vices of war, and to shake off the influence of long years of excessive propaganda, required a lot from veterans everywhere. Neither the contention that financing the liquidation of the war involved difficulties as great as the financing of the war itself nor the assertion that demobilization was primarily an industrial and social problem, and only to a minor degree a military matter, turned out to be exaggerations. The accruing budget deficits—since in the general public's view the state's credit line had long been overdrawn—had to be financed through the Reichsbank. In the four fiscal years between April 1920 and March 1924 the German government covered two-thirds of its expenditures by inflationary increase of its floating debt.

The second source of inflation was the balance-of-payments deficits, not least due to Germany's heavy reparation payments, which will be dealt with later. These deficits meant a further depreciation of the foreign exchange value of the mark, raising the cost of imports and consequently the cost of production. The described production losses due to territorial cessions and the strong need to import, typical for a war-exhausted country, resulted in higher living expenses, which in turn called for an upward adjustment of wages that the strengthened unions could muscle through, thus further raising production costs. The employers often put up only token resistance to the unions' wage demands in order to prevent social unrest and in recognition that the increased costs could be passed on by further inflation. Finally, the inflationary pressures from these three sources fed upon each other, setting a cycle of larger budget and balance-of-payments deficits and still tougher wage demands in motion, making for the greatest inflation in history to date.[3] (See table on the next page.)

Put simply one can say: it took about five and one-half years from the beginning of the war for the mark to fall to about one-tenth of its prewar value; the next decrease to one-tenth took only two and one-half years; the following one only 108 days; while in October 1923 the

---

3. It is reported that since 1946 the Hungarians have had the doubtful privilege of claiming this record.

A. *Depreciation of the Mark*

Period	Index of U.S. Dollar Rate of Exchange (1913=100)	Index of German Wholesale Prices (1913=100)
1920		
January	1,542	1,256
July	940	1,367
1921		
January	1,545	1,439
July	1,826	1,428
1922		
January	4,569	3,665
July	11,750	10,059
1923		
January	427,900	278,500
July	8,415,000	7,500,000
August	110,000,000	94,400,000
September	2,354,000,000	2,400,000,000
October	601,430,000,000	709,500,000,000
November	219,400,000,000,000	72,600,000,000,000

mark was down to ten percent of the value of the previous period every 8 to 11 days.

The Pros and Cons of an Inflation

Although the astronomic magnitude of the mark's decline was a special case, it should not be forgotten that it took place in a general environment which encouraged currency depreciation. In central, eastern, and southeastern Europe, currencies were losing heavily in value. Inflationary development is quite typical for defeated or newly established states, where the government is rather insecure and public confidence low. Since a currency without intrinsic value derives its strength from the trust of the general public in the issuing authorities, psychological factors play an important role. Neither the psychological infection that started with the Russian civil war inflation nor the frightening example of the British stabilization crisis of 1921 can be overlooked as influences. While Britain faced unemployment figures of over 20 percent, labor in Germany enjoyed virtual full employment, with rising wages which were adjusted at ever more frequent paydays to keep up with rising prices. Since production figures increased as well,[4] for a considerable time, until roughly 1922, little protest was raised against this kind of economic policy, as inflation profiteers out-numbered inflation victims considerably. Industrialists and merchants

4. German industrial production (1913=100): 1919, 42; 1920, 61; 1921, 73; 1922, 80; 1923, 52; 1924, 78. German plant food production (1909/13=100): 1920, 55; 1922, 69; 1924, 67.

benefitted from rising prices, since by comparison with the cost prices of the past the increased selling prices of the present showed huge profits.

This exaggerated profitability stimulated capital formation and thereby the producer-goods industries. The "flight into goods" increased expenditures in plant and equipment in all branches of the economy far beyond the backlog demand (due to deferred maintenance and replacement) so that resources were channelled from the consumer-goods branch to the capital-goods sector, unbalancing the production structure. To a considerable extent, it was thus a sham boom, since the apparent book profits were due to the faulty assumption that mark equals mark. Business analysts soon pointed to the need for capital preservation and suggested the use of current replacement values instead of the past cost values in cost accounting. Among experts the question was raised whether the industrial boom was not due to mere miscalculation. Indeed, it was to a considerable extent, for the mark had lost its function as an accounting unit.

Inflation not only influences the price level; it has even more impact on the price structure, since prices differ in their flexibility. Contracted incomes, like rents, pensions, insurance benefits, and salaries, either stagnated or increased slowly, while wages rose somewhat faster and residual incomes—i.e., profits—soared, which led to a more unequal distribution of incomes. But property distribution was also affected, since the holders of liquid assets lost, while investors in material assets benefitted. Debtors naturally gained at the expense of creditors; the largest borrower, the Reich, was thus able to pay off its internal war debts with ease. Foreigners were also among the winners and losers. For some time the international financial community had hoped that once peace was firmly established the depreciated currencies would return to their prewar value. Thus foreign speculators eagerly purchased marks, especially in 1920, in the hope of a future killing that was never to come. Many foreigners still profited, however, as Germany later became a cheap place in which to buy or live, in spite of astronomical prices.

As can be seen from the table, most of the time the external value of the mark fell faster than internal prices rose. Such undervaluation of the mark on the exchanges in relation to its domestic purchasing power permitted a leap over some of the highest tariff barriers and received much applause from exporting industrialists in Germany. It was caused to some extent by the reparation payments, which negatively affected the balance of payments and depressed the foreign value of the mark; but even more important was the fact that foreign financial circles, with more experience, foresaw present and future developments earlier than the general German public and anticipated additional losses in the mark's internal purchasing power. The policy of hedging against additional depreciation of the mark by buying stable foreign currencies—a measure popular among German businessmen—depressed the rate of the mark even further. The *"Ausverkauf"* ("sellout") of the German economy ended when the German businessman learned to adjust his prices in step with exchange rates, so that the gap between the internal and external values of the mark diminished and ultimately disappeared.

The learning process went still further. Internal price rises surpassed the increases in money supply as the velocity of circulation rose to a point where everyone tried to spend his money immediately, since the mark had ceased to be a means of storing value. In a further stage, prices rose faster than the sum of money supply times velocity (as in terms of Fisher's equation of exchange[5]), since the physical volume of transactions carried out with money fell because the inflation had produced so much disintegration that real business activity and employment actually declined shortly before the end of the inflation. In this final stage, as a last paradox, an acute shortage of money developed, and to have a knapsack or a baby buggy as one's purse no longer sufficed when buying a single loaf of bread or a newspaper.[6] With over 300 paper mills and some 2,000 printing presses working around the clock to produce Reichsbank notes, it was impossible to provide all the notes necessary to insure transactions at the inflated prices. The increases in the volume of money in circulation lagged so far behind the depreciation of the mark that by October 1923 German banknote circulation, expressed in dollars, amounted to only about 5 percent of the 1913 level, or about 10 percent of the level of early 1920. The mark had run its course: to pay wages firms issued their own money, often using dollars, gold or goods[7] as units of value, while the public, especially farmers with their high degree of self-sufficiency, eventually refused to accept Reichsbank notes. The slowing down and eventual stoppage of agricultural deliveries soon led to food riots in Berlin, Frankfurt and Breslau. The mark had thus lost its third function, that of a medium of exchange, and the Reichsbank had failed by its own standards, although its president seriously expressed hope that new high-speed printing presses soon to be installed would help to overcome the currency shortage. This lack of currency must have been a great disappointment for the Reichsbank, since throughout the years it had successfully supplied government and the business world with the necessary credits. With regard to the latter, the Reichsbank had fol-

5. $M \cdot V = P \cdot T$ (Money times Velocity of Circulation = Prices times Volume of Trade).
6. By November 1923 a roll cost 20 billion marks, a newspaper 50 billion marks.
7. In the provinces of Hanover and East Prussia, rye was used; in Pomerania, sugar; in Silesia, coal.

lowed the nineteenth-century Banking School holding that supplying the business world with additional money against genuine commercial bills could not have an inflationary effect. The business community could not object to such notions, for one of the rules of good management demanded the contracting of as many debts as possible and repaying them later in depreciated money.[8]

Concerning the treasury, the Reichsbank felt bound to grant one increase of the floating debt after another, when in the fiscal years 1920 to 1922 only some 40 percent of Reich expenditures were covered by revenues, and under existing political and economic conditions, no other method of financing the liquidation of the war and peacetime reconstruction was available to the German government. When the Ruhr struggle of 1923 (which in everything but name was a revival of war) necessitated additional spending, the Reich government in that year could only tax-finance 19 percent of its total budget. The ensuing rise in prices, in the understanding of the Reichsbank, was not caused by the issued money but by the unfavorable balance of payments and the consequent fall in the external value of the mark. There was some truth in this balance-of-payments argument, since at times the exchange depreciation did, indeed, run significantly ahead of the rise in internal prices, especially when large reparation payments were made. The exchange depreciation of the mark made imports more costly and domestic prices rise. Rising prices meant higher government expenditures and a greater need for freshly printed notes from the Reichsbank; consequently the mark's depreciation could be seen as a cause, not as a consequence, of increased money supply. Such reasoning, however, overlooked the fact that the government's chief method of acquiring foreign currencies for reparation payments had been to dump newly printed marks on the exchange market. Though weakness and indecision on the part of the German government were partly responsible for the complete collapse of the currency, which was reduced to one-trillionth of its prewar value, the reparation burden was primarily responsible for the catastrophic hyperinflation of 1923.

The Reparations Problem

Initially the Americans, chief spokesmen for a moderate and conciliatory peace, had proposed that no punitive payments nor any attempts to shift the cost of military operations upon the defeated nations be made, but the advocates of harsh and extreme measures won out. Thus at the Versailles conference of 1919 the appetite of the victors had reached Kaiser-like proportions and the checkered history of German

8. E.g., between July 1922 and August 1923 the Reichsbank increased the discount rate from 5 to 30 percent, while the actual depreciation in 1922 amounted to 3,000 percent.

reparations began.[9] In the Versailles treaty the total amount of the reparations obligations had been left open, because the Allies could not agree on the sum to be extracted from the Germans and its distribution. The opinion prevailed, however, that Germany was responsible for the whole cost of the war, and the Allies consequently discussed figures between 500 to 800 billion marks.[10] Allied statesmen went on building castles in the air for some time: in June 1920 they were considering 269 billion, in January 1921, 248 billion marks. In April 1921, after rejection of a German offer of 50 billion gold marks at present value, the Allies finally demanded 132 billion gold marks (roughly $32 billion) of which the French were to receive 52 percent, the British Empire 22 percent, Italy 10 percent, Belgium 8 percent and the lesser Allies 8 percent. The figure bore no relation to the claims originally presented by the victor states, but was simply the one the Allies could agree upon in view of inter-Allied debts.[11] The subsequently presented schedule of payments provided for the issue of two series of 5 percent interest-bearing bonds totalling 50 billion marks, while a third category of interest-free bonds in the amount of 82 billion marks was to be issued only when it could be shown that these obligations could be met.[12]

Of greater significance, however, was the magnitude of the stipulated annuities, which consisted of a fixed payment of 2 billion marks and a variable payment corresponding to 26 percent of the value of German exports in each twelve month period beginning 1 May 1921. As German foreign trade figures during the first six months, from May to October, showed exports of about 1.9 billion marks and imports of 2.4 billion marks—which meant a variable annuity of about 0.5 billion marks calculated on a half-yearly basis—it is difficult to see how Germany was to decrease her imports and/or increase her exports to secure the necessary foreign exchange (1.5 billion marks on a half-yearly basis) to effect her payments, the more so when one remembers that

9. In the khaki elections of December 1918, the British Prime Minister, Lloyd George, though basically disposed towards a moderate peace, had run on a platform promising full payment of the costs of the war by the defeated powers.

10. Estimates of war expenditures—not to be confused with the higher and even less precise cost of war—run at $44 billion for Great Britain, $28 billion for France and $15 billion for Italy.

11. Within the intricate system of inter-Allied debts, totalling almost $20 billion by October 1919, the U.S. had lent $4.2 billion to Great Britain, $2.75 billion to France, and $1.6 billion to Italy, while Great Britain had lent $2.54 billion to France and $2.3 billion to Italy, and France had given some $1.8 billion to the other Allies, above all to Russia. The interest rates on inter-Allied debts ranged between 0.8 and 1.6 percent.

12. It has been suggested that this third series—with its postponement of payments ad calendas graecas—was meant to be fictitious from the beginning and aimed at deceiving the public in the Allied countries. Statesmen there are said to have believed that public opinion was not sufficiently enlightened to accept a solution so short of its expectations.

foreign trade fluctuations of more than 15 percent usually involve serious economic disturbances. It is not surprising, then, that by September of that year a respite had to be granted. By March 1922, payments were officially reduced to 0.72 billion marks for the current year, and by August 1922 were suspended for six months. By that time the British were as convinced of Germany's inability to pay as the French were of her unwillingness to do so.

Matters were actually somewhat more complicated than that, however, as there were two sides to the reparation problem: raising and transfer. With regard to the financing of the reparations the German government to a considerable extent had to use a rather unsound economic method, which was, however, politically the only feasible one. Instead of wresting wealth directly from its citizens through increased taxation or by genuine noninflationary loans, the government resorted to borrowing from the Reichsbank. The additional money supply resulted in rising prices and a corresponding fall of individual real income, and thus indirectly provided the state with an enlarged share of the country's national product, which could be used for reparations.

To give the victor nations access to this share of German wealth, i.e., to effect the transfer, various ways were theoretically open. The German government could take orders from the Allies like a wholesale merchant, use its Reichsbank borrowings to acquire the desired articles on the inland market and ship them to the Allies. If the receiving nations preferred greater flexibility and desired to cut out the middleman, they could be given mark accounts to be spent at will on the German market. Furthermore, for the sake of even greater flexibility and to embed these bilateral relationships into the multilateral network of world trade, the Germans or the Allies could offer their marks on the foreign exchange market and sell them to other countries, which in turn would use them to acquire German goods and services. In short, the only true form in which a transfer of wealth could be effected was by gratis exports of German products. That, however, was the crux of the matter, as the Allies were in the paradoxical situation of insisting upon reparations while usually being utterly unwilling to receive them. Such a policy of asking for the cake and declining its acceptance was based on the fact that both the debtor and the principal creditor powers were highly industrialized states with similar production and export structures.[13] Gratuitous exports, e.g., of machinery or chemicals,

13. Harvard economist G. Haberler used somewhat stronger language: "If the very countries which insist on payment being made at the same time restrict imports by every possible device to 'improve the balance of trade' and to 'protect themselves from foreign competition,' then their policy can only be described as sadistic."
The title of "master sadist" had to go to the U.S. — "Uncle Shylock" in some contemporary circles — with its high tariff policy during the 1920s and its insistence on the repayment of inter-Allied debts.

would only create marketing problems for the respective producers in the creditor states. Since French and British industrialists and workers naturally objected to such a solution, the lion's share of many German deliveries in kind until 1923 went to agricultural Yugoslavia.

Up to 31 December 1922, that is up to a good week before the beginning of the Ruhr occupation, the Germans had made considerable deliveries, although it is difficult to establish their value. The German government claimed a total of about 42 billion gold marks, while the Allies had credited only about 10 billion gold marks. Independent unofficial estimates (one by J. M. Keynes, the other by the Institute of Economics in Washington D.C.) gave a value of about 26 billion, while explicitly accepting the justification for higher estimates. Disagreement resulted not only from ill will, but was a quite logical consequence of the fact that German prices differed from those in the receiving countries, while both differed from world market prices. In addition, almost two-thirds of the German claim derived from such items as confiscated German property abroad (28 percent), ceded German loans granted to her allies, i.e., the equivalent to the inter-Allied debts (20 percent), public property in the ceded territories and colonies (12 percent), and the coal mines of the Saar (3 percent). Whoever has studied the problems involved in establishing the value of a firm, a piece of land, or a patent, will recognize that there was sufficient ground for honest disagreement. The same held true for other German deliveries, such as over 900 oceangoing merchant ships, 5,000 locomotives, 150,000 railroad cars, 5,000 trucks and some 54 million metric tons of coal and coke (which, by the way, meant the freight capacity of about 115,000 trains with 50 cars each). Here one could honestly disagree as to whether German prices, world market prices, or prices in the receiving countries should be used; but to have credited these deliveries to the reparation account at fictitiously low prices was something else. Such deliveries, though asked for, remained deeply dissatisfying to a large segment of the business community in the receiving countries. An agreement signed in the fall of 1921, providing for direct reconstruction of the devastated areas in France with German labor and materials, was of little consequence, mainly because French industrialists and workers objected to the resulting reductions of their own markets, apart from the emotional problems involved in such a solution.

What the creditor states were really interested in were cash payments in foreign exchange. France, the main receiver, was in especially urgent need of funds to balance her budget and to recoup outlays for rebuilding her war-devastated areas. The problem was thus whether the other countries would lower their high tariff barriers to let Germany achieve the export surplus necessary for transfer, but since persistent German efforts to force goods on foreign markets would depress prices and lower the marketing chances of their foreign competitors this, too, was an unacceptable solution. In this situation the German government made frantic efforts to buy foreign currency by unloading newly printed marks on the exchange market. Up to December 1922 Germany managed to transfer a total of 1.8 billion gold marks' worth of foreign currency, bought at rapidly deteriorating exchange rates which also provided German exports with the exchange rate bonus to penetrate foreign markets to the detriment of producers in the creditor states. The situation got increasingly out of hand. Becoming impatient, the French, in cooperation with Belgium and Italy and in the face of strong opposition from the Americans and the British, declared Germany to be in default on some minor coal and timber deliveries.[14] French and Belgian troops therefore occupied the Ruhr on 11 January 1923 to extract reparations directly.[15] The Reich government was little inclined to avoid a trial of strength, hoping that the French would put themselves in the wrong and that eventually, with British and American assistance, a reasonable solution of the reparations problem could be found. Consequently in a countermove the Reich government required all officials to ignore the orders of the occupation forces, who in turn dismissed some 180,000 of them and erected their own civilian and transportation administration. Industrial workers and the local population in general, showing superb spirit and discipline under the severest privation, reacted with passive resistance and noncooperation. The struggle lasted for eight and one-half months. At first, the passive resistance campaign was rather successful, as the Reich government subsidized the families of men whom the French had dismissed, banished or shot, fueling the inflation further and bringing it to astronomical heights. Because the economy in the rest of Germany, cut off from its main source of energy and raw materials, began to disintegrate, the German government gave in on 27 September. The French had won—not without learning a lesson as to the

14. Against the perpetual inclination of the French to draw historical parallels, the British government answered succinctly: "It may be pointed out that the recovery after the short campaign of 1870–71 of an indemnity equivalent to 4 milliards [Am. billion] of gold marks is not really comparable to the enforcement of a thirty-threefold claim against a country financially exhausted by four years of strenuous warfare and blockade. The ease with which the indemnity imposed in 1871 was paid was largely the result of the credit facilities which France was able to obtain. Germany has, on the other hand, suffered from a complete inability to obtain foreign loans, arising to a large extent from the long period which elapsed before her reparation liabilities were defined and the world-wide uncertainty as to her ability to discharge them." It is usually held that by the end of 1922, Germany had fallen short in her cash payments by 1.6 percent, in her coal deliveries by 12 percent, and in her timber shipments by about 50 percent, i.e., some 100,000 telegraph poles.

15. To show their disapproval, the Americans withdrew their troops from their occupation zone on the left bank of the Rhine on 10 January 1923. Their place in this area was taken by the French.

limits of military power—and claimed a net profit of about $100 million. Foreign economists challenged this figure as too high, pointing to the fact that coal receipts for 1923 amounted to only 25 to 30 percent of those for 1922.

Diplomacy found a way out through a kind of package deal: an end of the Ruhr occupation and restoration of German rule there; stabilization of the mark to end the serious economic dislocations and do away with the German exchange rate bonus; and a new reparations arrangement that represented a compromise between Germany's ability to pay and transfer, and her obligations as imposed by the Versailles stipulations. But permanent harm had been done. The social consequences of these disastrous years—in the final analysis originating in the vindictive spirit of Versailles, which was inconsistent with a workable peace—were even more severe than the economic dislocations. The middle classes, especially holders of assets in monetary form, had suffered severe economic losses, which in many cases led to complete ruin. Profiteers, speculators, and industrial empire builders, on the other hand, had amassed huge fortunes. The general psychological effect on public opinion was enormous: the only thing one could be certain of was that nothing was certain. Contemporaries pointed out that the German term for currency, *"Währung,"* stems from the word *"währen,"* to last. It would have been surprising if such profound demoralization and total disruption of the social fabric had gone unexploited, since distress invites a deliverer. On 9 November 1923, six days before the mark breathed its last, having been reduced to the one-trillionth of its prewar value, Adolf Hitler felt encouraged to make his first bid for power.

2

The Stabilization and Prosperity Period

Mark —Rentenmark —Reichsmark

Stabilization was achieved by stopping the mechanical and psychological causes of inflation. The idea of a rehabilitation of the currency had been in the air for some time, not least as a result of the wave of successful European stabilizations, begun in Austria in October 1922.[16] The Ruhr occupation delayed German currency reform by a year, but on 15 October 1923, the Rentenbank was founded and charged with issuing the Rentenmark, whose value was set at one gold

16. The German stabilization was only partly analogous to the Austrian one: it avoided the unacceptable political price of League of Nations tutelage, and could not— owing to the absence of foreign assistance—be based upon a gold exchange standard.

or prewar mark, and at 4.20 to the dollar or at one trillion paper marks on 15 November. Rentenbank notes were not, however, redeemable in gold but in 5 percent gold mark bonds, which represented a mortgage imposed on all agricultural land and industrial property. Of course, such backing was in a sense fictitious as —in contrast to a foreign exchange or gold cover—these real estate debts could not be used abroad to regulate foreign exchange or turned into cash at home. But since this currency was apparently based on real values, it had the desired psychological effect and was eagerly received by the public, especially by the agricultural population. Consumers and producers, who had no stable money for daily use and were suffering from acute currency shortage, were prepared to accept and hold the new notes.

Although the reform was supported by all major political parties, trust in the new money would not have lasted if the main mechanical cause of inflation had not also been eliminated, i.e., the deficit-financing of state expenditures through banknote printing. Thus the absolute maximum note issue was set at 3.2 billion Rentenmarks, of which 1.2 billion were allocated to the government as a transitional credit to enable it to meet its current expenses until tax revenues started flowing in again. This meant a rigid limit to the spending powers of the government, whose budgetary deficits had been the immediate cause of inflation. As it was also necessary to limit the supply of credit to trade and industry, only 1.2 billion was employed for this purpose. Despite supplementary measures, especially in the field of foreign exchange, the stability of the Rentenmark hung in the balance for some months, but was assured by the middle of April 1924. By that time the Bank of England had provided Germany with a foreign exchange cushion, since the British government, which for quite a while had been suspicious of French policies, thought it desirable for the purpose of the European balance of power to back German monetary rehabilitation and ensuing economic recovery. The financial world in Germany and abroad became convinced that the German authorities would maintain their deflationary policy, and that with the presentation of the Dawes Plan in early April calmer times in the reparations controversy would follow. With the plan's final adoption on 1 September 1924, the basis was laid for Germany's reintroduction of the gold bullion standard, with the adoption of a new currency called the Reichsmark (RM). Equal in value to the Rentenmark, the Reichsmark, however, had to be 40 percent backed by gold or foreign exchange, and the rest covered by commerical bills of exchange. This stabilization, called the "Miracle of the Rentenmark" because it broke the vicious circle of inflation through the introduction of a new currency without gold or foreign exchange backing, would probably have been less smooth, perhaps even impossible, without thorough reappraisal of the reparations problem.[17]

The Fool's Gold of the "Golden Years"

The Dawes Plan recognized that the economic recovery of Germany was imperative and that there were, indeed, two aspects to the reparation problem: financing and transfer. Consequently a period of grace was granted, during which annuities would rise progressively from RM 1 billion (1924/25) to RM 2.5 billion (1928/29). Subsequently RM 2.5 billion (plus additional payments in accordance with an intricate prosperity index which would permit the Allies to participate in any German progress) were to be paid permanently, thus making the German people forever subject to "soccage-duty," as the nationalists and others termed it. Neither aggregate amount nor duration was laid down in the plan. It was necessary, however, to stipulate permanent payments to sidestep France's flat refusal to reduce the total bill of 132 billion gold marks. At the same time this procedure showed that the diplomats, well-versed in doubletalking and doubledealing, saw the Dawes Plan as a purely temporary measure. The funds for the reparation payments would henceforth stem from exactly defined sources, such as certain pledged taxes and duties, a transportation tax on the Reichsbahn (the national railroad system), and the interest payments on newly created mortgages of the Reichsbahn and of all large industrial enterprises. To insure that Reichsbahn and Reichsbank would live up to expectations, both were "internationalized" by placing foreign directors on their supervisory boards. The problem of transferring the annuities was entrusted to the hands of an American, who as General Agent for Reparations had to watch over the exchange stability of the Reichsmark. Since it was understood that the reparation payments were to derive from the earned surplus of the country's economic activity, this task was originally considered Herculean. It became mere child's play, however, when in the following years German foreign borrowing far exceeded the annuities: from 1924 to 1929 Germany made net borrowings of some RM 13.5 billion, while her total reparations payments in this period were only about RM 8.5 billion. But even without this fortuitous development, the system of collection and transfer,

17. A reappraisal of the reparations problem can also be found in recent literature. Revisionist writers tend in general to assess the reparations burden as much lighter than this author is inclined to do. Whether light or heavy, the reparations burden still rests like a millstone on the shoulders of economic historians of the Weimar period. The unearthing of new figures and the recalculating of old ones is without doubt a laudable endeavor, but the views of the time, representing incomputable reality, should not vanish from sight. Contemporaries like the American economist J.W. Angell held: "The reparation problem, gradually spreading its tentacles over nearly the whole of European politics and economics, at the end became the crucial problem of Western society."

under foreign supervision, if not under foreign control, would have ensured that the Dawes Plan worked as well as it actually did. Germany made her payments promptly and almost in full and was helped by the fact that between 1924 and 1929 as a whole more than half of her payments were made in kind or in Reichsmarks. During the first standard year of the Dawes Plan, 1928/29, reparations amounted to 12.4 percent of the total cost of government, represented 12.5 percent of Germany's balance of payments, and absorbed 3.3 percent of national income.

National income rose throughout the second half of the 1920s,[18] and by 1928/29 the country was at or above 1913 levels of production and general welfare.[19] By comparison with other countries, too, Germany's position at the close of the 1920s was not bad at all. The setback in relation to France and Britain as a result of the World War, and the immediate postwar difficulties, had been largely overcome in the years after the stabilization. At first, however, the stabilization brought decline instead of advance, though the impact of the deflationary policy was postponed for a while. Since real business activity and employment had actually fallen before the end of the inflation, the creation of the Rentenmark renewed confidence among businessmen, and during 1924 gave a fillip to industry and trade. But from mid-1925 to mid-1926, Germany faced a severe stabilization crisis. The capital-goods industries, which had previously expanded at the expense of the consumer-goods industries, were hardest hit, and many a recently formed combine turned out to be a colossus with feet of clay. The process of liquidating these "inflation businesses" was painful and led to considerable unemployment.[20] Inflation had artificially created jobs in such fields as commerce, banking, commodity and stock exchange activities, and many in these swollen ranks now automatically became redundant. Even more important was the fact that with a stable currency, thinking in terms of costs returned; labor, being relatively cheap, had been hoarded in all sectors of the economy during the inflation, but now it became an important cost factor again and economies were desirable. A wave of rationalization swept German industry. This was not only cost-induced, but also stemmed from technological considerations.

The war had cut German industrialists off from the scientific and

18. Between 1925 and 1929 the national income grew by 24 percent; income of employed persons by 29 percent; and income from assets and entrepreneurial activity by 17 percent, while income from agricultural pursuits sank by 3 percent.

19. Industrial production (1913=100): 1925, 92; 1928, 114; and food production (1909/13=100): 1924, 77; 1928, 90. Per capita real national income (1913=100): 1925, 86; 1928, 98; by comparison; United States: 1925, 106; 1928, 112; Great Britain: 1925, 98; 1928, 108.

20. From mid-1925 to mid-1927 over 30,000 firms went bankrupt, and the number of voluntary liquidations exceeded the establishment of new firms by almost 20,000.

technological progress achieved abroad, especially in the United States, and during the years of inflation few enterprises could afford the necessary foreign exchange to buy technical journals, to make extensive informative trips abroad, or to pay patent fees. In addition, German scientists had been ostracized, on the insistence especially of their French and Belgian colleagues, and banned from attending international conferences. The Locarno Treaty in 1925 had improved the climate, but by then many a German scientist was indulging in a "now, I won't" attitude. While a German professor in his divine right could afford such a posture, the German industrialist could not, and pilgrimages across the Atlantic became standard. Germany turned to the U.S. for technological and managerial know-how. Her war engine, with its insatiable demand for physical product, had been largely indifferent to considerations of cost. Scientific management and labor-saving machinery, mass production, assembly lines and Taylorism were some of the terms foremost in the minds of German industrialists, and the most recent technology was used in equipment, while new plants of enormous size were built to secure the fullest economies of scale. Such technical rationalization, though, was not necessarily identical with economic rationalization. The replacement of efficient, skilled and relatively cheap labor by costly modern machinery could easily turn into overmodernization, i.e., an excessive substitution of capital for labor. German industrialists had always had a tendency to emphasize technological rationality over economic efficiency, and this attitude had placed them among the forerunners of the Second Industrial Revolution in the last decades of the 19th century. The further development of German industry had proven in those days that technological rationality could be converted into profitability if technological progress was fast and markets expanding; temporary overmodernization was thus no serious problem. One can therefore not object that the German government in the 1920s, in need of an export surplus for its reparation payments, encouraged rationalization—and the accompanying import of American capital—even if it meant occasional overmodernization.[21]

Such a policy was sound and in due time Germany would have been in a position to easily earn all the foreign exchange necessary to meet her obligations. These obligations were considerable: to begin with there was the old burden of the reparations, but principal and interest on the foreign loans Germany had received since the stabilization also had to be repaid. The German balance of trade, which had been heavily passive during the second half of the twenties (except

21. American banks preferred direct loans to those German companies which introduced scientific management, since this increased the future earning potential of their debtors.

1926), was almost squared in 1929. German reparation exports had suddenly become a reality,[22] since by that time Germany had regained her former leadership, especially in the chemical industries, electrical engineering, precision instruments and optical goods production. Furthermore, Germany improved her net position in the balance of services by over two and a half times between 1924 and 1929 when she completely rebuilt and modernized her oceangoing shipping fleet, reaching over 80 percent of her prewar tonnage in 1930, and thus gaining fourth place behind Britain, the U.S. and Norway.[23] By then, however, the international economic trend had changed, and German exports of goods and services were answered with further tariffs, quotas and trade restrictions.

These German exports were not only the result of technological improvements, but of industrial reorganization as well. Rationalization also meant the elimination or restriction of competition which was felt to be troublesome and wasteful. Cartels and syndicates were considered just as cost-saving as large-scale production or integration by vertical combination, though these forms of industrial organization more frequently aimed at maintaining profits than reducing costs. Due to the existence of some 2,500 cartels by the mid-1920s, the cost reductions that did spring from technical rationalization did not in every case result in sufficient lowering of prices. Despite some legislative attempts to strengthen competition,[24] the post-inflation years were a time of vigorous and comprehensive cartelization and concentration. The most conspicuous cases were the chemical trust I. G. Farben, founded in 1925, and the steel trust Vereinigte Stahlwerke, established in 1926, two giants with 200,000 employees each. It is, therefore, not altogether surprising that the German rationalization movement has been called "the art of cutting costs while raising prices."

Prices were rising, but so was the standard of living. The *"Mietskasernen"* (rent barracks), the German version of low-income urban housing, were now replaced on a large scale by healthier and more comfortable dwellings. As rents had been frozen during the war and rent control had been maintained thereafter, public subsidies were necessary to make new construction lucrative for private builders. For this purpose the Reich allocated considerable resources, which it financed through a rent tax, i.e., by taxing those mortgagers who had

22. Volume of industrial exports (1913=100): 1925/26, 72; 1927/28, 83; 1929/30, 95.
23. The outward symbol of this recovery was the winning of the coveted "Blue Ribbon" for the fastest North Atlantic crossing by the "Bremen" in 1929 and the "Europa" in 1931.
24. The decree of November 1923 did not prohibit cartels, but tried to curb their abuse of power by securing the rights of outsiders and limiting the extent and severity of intra-industry strife.

benefitted from the inflation by having their mortgage debts revalued at only 25 percent. Besides subsidies to private residential building, public construction and public grants to nonprofit building cooperatives were the other means of improving housing and alleviating the acute shortage that had developed primarily as a result of the construction halt during the war. In addition to directing about 6 percent of all public expenditures between 1925 to 1930 into housing construction,[25] public authorities were also active in those fields that were traditionally regarded as public responsibility: besides schools and hospitals, swimming pools, playgrounds, theaters and libraries mushroomed at an amazing rate and often in accordance with architectural criteria that soon served as paradigms abroad (Bauhaus). Public authorities, which had long been the main suppliers of electricity, gas and water, not only enlarged and improved their services but also organized urban transport systems and savings banks. In addition, the states also had a foothold in the economy, especially in banking and the development of power systems. Taken together, however, the economic influence of the states and the municipalities could not compare to that of the Reich. Already the sole operator of telephone and telegraph networks, the Reich became the owner and operator of the railroads of the states, as well, thus controlling a considerable portion of the transport and communications sector. The financing of these economic activities and of housing construction, the provision of long-term agricultural credits, and of credits in foreign currencies, was exclusively, or at least predominantly, done by newly founded Reich banking institutions. Though the financing of industry and commerce remained basically the domain of private banks, government had attained a respectable position in German banking in the twenties.

Besides acting as a banker, government was an entrepreneur. The industrial undertakings of the Reich were combined in 1923 in the VIAG holding company, those of Prussia in the Preussag. Each comprised coal and ore mines, iron and salt works, and many other holdovers from the mercantilistic activities of the state in previous centuries. Though not without importance, they were small potatoes, since the original plans and promises of the revolutionary government to nationalize key industries did not materialize. The cartelization of these industries seemed to provide a solid organizational basis for nationalization, but the new government lacked the support and revolutionary spirit to push more vigorously for public ownership or management in a larger sector of the economy. Instead some joint planning

25. Public authorities built about 10 percent, nonprofit organizations 40 percent, and private investors 50 percent of all dwellings in those years.

bodies (like the Reich Coal Council and the Reich Potash Council), on which producers, traders, union representatives and independent experts were to determine output and prices in concert, were established. The Reich frequently had to use its veto on behalf of the consumer when collusion between management and labor led to price and wage arrangements ill-suited to the public interest.

In other respects the trade unions were more successful. To begin with, free and independent unions were recognized as the sole bargaining agents in industry-wide collective agreements, destroying the basis for company unions and isolated shop crews. In deadlocked negotiations a government mediator could declare his solution regarding wages, hours,[26] paid vacations and the like, which then became binding on both parties. From 1920 on, moreover, works councils were mandatory in every plant with five or more employees, to establish employment conditions at the plant level within the framework of the industry-wide collective agreement. Acting as shock absorbers, especially with regard to the introduction of labor saving equipment,[27] these works councils lessened the antagonistic feelings between management and labor and contributed to improving industrial relations. While in the period 1919–23 about 17 percent of all workers participated in strikes, in the years 1924–29 only 3 percent followed a strike call. Organized labor mediation and obligatory works councils, though much detested by conservative management, were the first solid steps towards industrial democracy.[28] German trade unionists had thus by the twenties made gains which their American brothers were to regard as pipe-dreams for a long time to come. This broadening and strengthening of the legal and factual basis of trade unionism, combined with the wider role played by the government within the cartelized market economy, distinguished the economic system of Weimar as a unique union of capitalist and socialist concepts. But a union of divergent principles does not, alas, necessarily bring forth the best of both worlds. It can easily produce less desirable results, such as, for example, the private appropriation of the profits and the nationalization of the losses of an industry.

26. Though the 48-hour week was established in 1919, by 1926 over half of the labor force worked longer, a quarter more than 54 hours.

27. This was an important function, because unemployment figures, though incomplete inasmuch as only union members were registered, averaged about 11 percent, ranging from 7 to 18 percent, between 1924 and 1928.

28. To counteract the increased union and governmental influence on the economy, management thoroughly organized itself in various *Verbände* after the war. The Reich Association of German Industry, with its 29 special branches and its almost 6,000 member associations, concerned itself with economic policy, while the Union of German Employers' Associations and its 180 member associations and some 2,800 subgroups handled matters relating to social policy.

One of the sectors in a state of severe financial embarrassment was agriculture. The postwar reconstruction attempts of German agriculture could only gradually overcome the effects of the war on crop production and livestock herds. Due to the laws of chemistry and biology, several growing seasons are necessary to regenerate an exhausted soil and five years or more to rebuild depleted cattle herds. By 1924 yields in animal and vegetable products were still about one fourth below those of 1912/13, which were not regained until 1928. As late as 1930 Germany needed annual imports of food and animal feed of some RM 4 billion, which placed a heavy burden on the balance of payments. Through patriotic appeals and a generous policy of easy farm credits the government had, therefore, encouraged the farmers to increase output. German agriculture, which during the inflation had all but wiped out its total debt of some 13 billion marks, responded by incurring new debts for rationalization purposes, which reached a similar magnitude by the late twenties. After the war, as more and more farm workers fled the land for higher wages and improved living conditions in the cities, the quantity and quality of the potential agricultural labor force declined, resulting in rising wages for farm labor. Since the employment of migrant workers, especially from Poland, as in prewar times, was no longer regarded as politically tenable, mechanization was the only possible alternative. Given the fact that interest rates had doubled and taxes quadrupled since before the war, a more capital-intensive form of agricultural production was at best capable of maintaining the level of costs but not of keeping pace with the international decline in agricultural prices. The large scale price reduction on the world agricultural market since 1925/26 was increasingly noticeable on the German market after 1927. The government tried to counteract this declining price trend by reintroducing some old protectionist tariffs when it regained freedom of action in its external trade policy with the expiration of certain Versailles stipulations in 1925. Further tariff increases were needed until 1928, but by that time German agriculture was regarded as having "not unfavorable prospects." With the onset of the depression, however, these soon turned into a mirage.

Besides the fate of German agriculture, another problem that greatly concerned contemporaries was the way in which the modernization of the German economy was partly financed. Between 1924 and 1928, gross investments amounted to about RM 70 billion for a net investment of almost 40 billion, of which two-thirds went into fixed capital and one-third into inventories. At about the same time, between 1924 and 1929, Germany had a trade deficit of RM 6.2 billion, paid RM 8.5 billion in reparations and increased her foreign exchange reserve by RM 2.2 billion; compensatory items were net capital imports of RM

13.5 billion and an unspecified residue of RM 3.4 billion. In view of this balance-of-payments situation, foreign credits were necessary to finance the imports essential for the modernization process. These expensive foreign credits, which not infrequently (about half of them in 1927/29) were short-term lendings only, running for up to six months, gave rise to heated political and economic discussions. It was pointed out that Germany was not really earning her reparation payments, which was contrary to the spirit, though not the letter, of the Dawes Plan. She did not reduce her indebtedness but replaced low-interest debts, i.e., the 5 percent interest-bearing reparation bonds, by high-interest loans, often bearing 10 percent interest or even more, which was conveniently added to the principal.[29] If someday the inflow of foreign funds ebbed, this house of cards would collapse instantly.

These sensible arguments were countered with the suggestion that the world's economic and political affairs had normalized and that in the long run everything would work out smoothly. The foreign credits would enable the modernization of German industry and agriculture to proceed much faster than if only domestic savings were used, and in due course would provide Germany with the necessary edge in productivity to increase her exports of goods and services and to consolidate and eventually to work off these debts. This view, emphasizing the long run, was correct, too; the only trouble is that in the long run—as Keynes put it—we all are dead. It is consequently as realistic as it is human to think of the present. Although it is true that most of the foreign loans were used to restore and remodel the country's productive capacity, a considerable portion went to finance housing projects. Accordingly, in the late twenties Germany was said to have the highest housing standard for its working-class population of any European country, apart from World War I neutrals like Switzerland, Sweden and Holland. Although such investments were justifiable from a social standpoint and also frequently defensible as measures to curb local unemployment—the overall unemployment rate in 1928 was still about 7 percent—purely economic considerations would have demanded allocation of these funds to more directly productive activities. Sound economics, however, are the exception rather than the rule on the national level, as well as in international relations. By 1929 repara-

29. E.g., in 1925 the German rate of interest in the capital market was 9.5 percent, as against 4.7 to 4.8 percent in the United States, the Netherlands and Switzerland, while the rates on the money market stood at 9.1 percent and 3.7 percent respectively. The rates for 1928 were quite similar. German capital imports in those years stemmed about 40 percent from the United States, close to 20 percent from the Netherlands, and 13 to 15 percent each from Britain and Switzerland.

tions were as painful a problem as at the beginning of their checkered career a decade earlier.

Admittedly the Dawes Plan had worked well—so well, in fact, that the statesmen of the creditor nations advocated a permanent and final settlement in place of this transitional arrangement. They preferred, once and for all, to have capital sums at their disposal instead of future annuities. That could be achieved by "commercializing" the German obligation, i.e., by receiving bonds which could be sold on the international market. The Germans realized that political debts would thereby become commercial debts to foreign private investors and would no longer be open to haggling and eventual reductions. It would also be necessary to abolish the various safeguards of the Dawes Plan, especially the maneuverability with regard to transfers. Against these German objections, the Young Plan came into being on 20 January 1930, and was made retroactive to 1 September 1929. Germany's debt was placed at RM 37 billion at present value and slowly rising annuities (of about RM 2 billion) were to be paid until 1988, beginning with two-thirds of the standard Dawes Plan annuity (RM 1.6 billion). Deliveries in kind, so troublesome in the past, were carefully regulated, and were to diminish and disappear altogether by 1939. The Young Plan was superior to the Dawes Plan in that it set a definite amount and time for the German reparation obligation, while doing away with the prosperity index, with foreign military occupation and with the equally mortifying supervision and control of certain aspects of German economic life, and permitted the desired commercialization. But the new plan showed little concern with making a serious attempt to establish Germany's long-term capacity to pay or to consider her contemporary economic situation. Instead, the figures established aimed at obtaining as much as possible to repay inter-Allied debts. With the total change in the world's economic situation within two years, the Young Plan was suspended (Hoover's moratorium on reparations and inter-Allied debts) in June 1931, and in effect abolished a year later.

3

The Depression Years

The Cyclical Downswing

This total change in the world's economic scenery originated in the United States. The course, causes and consequences of the Great Depression have been widely debated and are still the concern of the present-day economic historian. There cannot be any attempt here to join or even outline this debate. It is, however, worth noting that the German crisis was not only the direct consequence of the American contraction, but that Germany also sustained the international depression by having her own "crisis within the crisis."[30]

Although President Hoover had claimed in a self-serving statement that the United States had been infected by a crisis originating in Germany, this was not borne out by the facts. A giant does not topple just because a large midget falls. By 1928 American industry produced almost half (45 percent) of the total industrial production of the 24 most important industrial nations; by 1927/28 American consumption of nine principal primary products amounted to 39 percent of the total of the 15 chief importing countries. The gross national product (in 1929 prices) of this economic colossus contracted by 39 percent between 1929 and 1933, while the unemployment rate of its civilian labor force increased from 3.2 percent to 24.9 percent in this period. While American imports amounted to some $4.4 billion in 1929, the 1932 figure was a mere $1.3 billion. Besides this decline in American demand on the world market, from 1929 onward decreasing U.S. capital exports curtailed the international purchasing power of its habitual borrowers, especially of Germany, the second largest industrial nation.[31]

With some variation, similarly appalling data depicting the economic slump could be given for other major nations, though in general their figures tend to be less dismal than those for America or Germany. If international comparisons of that kind are accepted as meaningful at all, it is frequently held that in Europe the crisis was most severe in Germany. In comparison to 1928, the last depression-free year, by 1932, at the low point of the German trough, indices at current prices stood at 62 percent for the national income,[32] 30 percent for gross fixed investment, 63 percent for retail sales, 61 percent for total industrial production, 50 percent for capital-goods and 78 percent for consumer-goods production. About one-quarter of Germany's industrial production had been exported by the end of the period of postwar prosperity. Between 1928 and 1932, however, German exports declined from RM 12.3 to RM 5.7 billion, causing substantial shutdowns

30. In the whole complex of causes for the worldwide depression in 1929/30, the following are considered to be the most important: the mistaken equation of the postwar backlog demand with a long-term demand; the overestimation of the market's ability to absorb the products of the new industries (cars, photo and film equipment, synthetics); the creation of overcapacities resulting from these miscalculations; vast speculative dealings in securities; long-term investment of funds from short-term credits; international money transfers with no counterflow of goods and services; and disrupted international trade relations through restrictive measures on the part of individual states.

31. In 1928 German industrial production amounted to about 12 percent of the world's total, or 26 percent of the American level. In 1929 Germany reached 20 percent of the national income and 70 percent of the foreign trade of the United States.

32. While in the previous cyclical period the incomes of wage and salary earners, entrepreneurs and asset holders, as well as farmers, had developed quite differently, now their decline was universal and close to 40 percent.

and layoffs. In 1932 German unemployment stood at 30.8 percent; this figure compared quite unfavorably to the 7 percent unemployment of 1928, the last of the so-called "golden years," when growth began to level off. Throughout 1929 the forces of contraction were already in full operation, and the total of net fixed investments reached only 83 percent of the 1928 level. Heavy taxation and government wage policy had darkened profit expectations in the industrial sector, and brought about a decline in net fixed investments of 60 percent compared to the previous year. More important for investment decisions, however, was the fact that during 1929 the inflow of foreign capital ebbed. During 1928 the German balance of capital transactions showed a net capital inflow of about RM 3 billion, of which 44 percent was short-term,while in 1929 a mere RM 1.2 billion was registered, of which 65 percent was on short terms. The Wall Street boom, which raised the index of common stocks by about 30 percent in 1929, sucked up virtually all investable American funds, thus exerting a negative impact on the German economy, where over the last half decade economic activity had corresponded closely to the inflow of foreign capital. Here the German downward swing actually did precede the beginning of the depression in the U.S. Since a parallel to this dependence of the domestic economy on foreign capital is lacking in the other economically important countries, it should be explained briefly.

Structural Weaknesses

The financial and banking crisis that accompanied the industrial depression stemmed from the structural weakness of German banking. In the nineteenth century the main purpose of the large German banks had been the financing of the country's industrialization. They thus resembled a combination of commercial bank, investment bank and investment trust, which earned this type of banking the name Universalbank. The prime condition for their successful operation was a substantial net worth, and as a rule capital, reserves and undistributed profits amounted to a third or a fourth of their deposits and other liabilities. This firm financial basis had, however, been eroded by the inflation, and by 1929 the ratio between the banks' own funds and capital from outside deteriorated to 1:10 for all private banks and to 1:15 for the "Big Banks" of Berlin. As inflation had seriously undermined the capacity and the will to save in Germany, thus limiting domestic capital accumulation,[33] the needed funds had to come from abroad. By the end of 1930 about half of the RM 26 to RM 27 billion in German com-

33. Net capital expenditures constituted about 15 percent of real national income in 1910/13, but only approximately 10 percent in 1925/29.

mercial debts was short-term in nature,[34] and foreign funds had come to account for some 40 to 50 percent of deposits in the "Big Banks" of Berlin. Over the years, warnings had been voiced—among others by the Reichsbank—against these growing foreign debts. These emphasized their volatility, but with little response.[35] The Reichsbank had no legal means to ensure compliance with its views and many a private banker lacked a sufficient sense of responsibility. To transform short-term deposits into long-term investable funds may be regarded as the prime function of investment banking, but it requires a certain care in the selection of one's borrowers as well as considerable cash liquidity. The ratio of cash on hand and Reichsbank deposits to total liabilities amounted to a mere 3.8 percent for the German banks by 1929, compared to 7.3 percent before the war, and to the 9 to 10 percent customary for British and American banks.

This unstable German credit structure experienced its first shock when American lending began to contract after 1928, as the stock market boom detoured capital from investment abroad to domestic speculation. After Black Thursday on Wall Street on 24 October 1929, U. S. capital exports in fact renewed for a time. But they declined again in the latter half of 1930, when the slump deepened, and eventually ceased altogether due to the American banking crisis. By that time a tangle of economic and political reasons had made Germany a less attractive debtor anyway. In the Reichstag elections of September 1930, the Nazis won 107 of the 577 seats (up from 12) and the Communists 77 seats (up from 54), causing a massive recall of short-term funds by foreign creditors. Another run on the German banks resulted from the Austrian banking crisis of May 1931, when the Creditanstalt of Vienna collapsed, due in part to the actual or rumored recall of short-term lendings by French depositors to force the abandonment of the projected customs union between the Reich and Austria. At the announcement of such plans in March 1931, Germany's credit abroad suffered just as it had in 1929, when the Germans raised objections during the Young Plan negotiations. While previously Germany's dependence on foreign credit could be easily exploited for political purposes, in the spring of 1931 this lever, and with it the fragile framework of international finance, broke into pieces.

34. Of the total German commercial debt, approximately half was owed by industry, one-third by the banks, and about one-fifth each by the Reich, the states and the municipalities. German foreign assets amounted to RM 9 to 10 billion, of which 5 to 6 billion were on a short-term basis.

35. The German foreign minister, Gustav Stresemann, put it succinctly in November 1928: "If one day our difficulties become visible and the Americans withdraw their short-term loans, bankruptcy will follow."

The collapse of the Creditanstalt, one of the largest banks in Central Europe, caused great alarm in the financial world, and triggered a run of domestic and foreign creditors on the German banks as well. To prevent their breakdown due to illiquidity, which might mortally impair the entire structure of the European credit system, international assistance was rendered by a moratorium on reparations and by providing direct credit of some $150 million, mostly from Allied central banks to the Reichsbank. Although speed is of the essence in such matters to achieve the desired psychological effect and to restore confidence among the public, much time was wasted. The Hoover Moratorium, announced on 19 June 1931, did not come into effect before 7 July as time was dawdled away in tedious haggling over reparations and inter-Allied debts among the nations concerned. Thus it became too late to stem the tide, and on 13 July the Danat Bank, one of the biggest German banks, declared its insolvency, following the bankruptcy of one of its largest industrial debtors, the Nordwolle concern. Since the other large banks were in a similar predicament, due to their involvement in the financing of speculative and even outright unsound industrial undertakings through short-term deposits, the government was forced to declare two "bank holidays." In the following weeks the government had to provide the lion's share of the funds necessary for the financial reorganization of these weakened banks, as the nation's economy hinged on the continued functioning of the banking system. Unintentionally the government found itself the majority shareholder of most of the Big Banks, and thus indirectly in control of the major part of German industry.[36] One of the commanding heights of capitalism—as Lenin called such banks—had inadvertently changed hands. The grip of the state on economic life became even tighter, as the German government—in agreement with the American and British governments—issued a standstill regulation on foreign short-term debts and introduced rigid foreign exchange restrictions. The limitation on the volume of lendings which the shaken banks had to undertake reduced their credit to industry to about one-half of the predepression level by 1932. This credit squeeze, and the consequent decline in the money supply, must be seen as the most important consequence of the banking crisis, and greatly increased the deflationary tendencies in the economy.

One sector which was abnormally dependent on credit was particularly effected by the banking crisis: agriculture. In spite of all the problems this sector had to face during the late twenties, on the eve of the depression it had "not unfavorable prospects." Admittedly, farm

36. After the government intervention, 91 percent of the Dresdner Bank, 70 percent of the Commerzbank and 35 percent of the Deutsche Bank was publicly owned.

indebtedness was high. By late 1928 nearly 40 percent of all the large estates of eastern Germany were overindebted, many of them by as much as 200 to 300 percent. These debts reflected a structural problem East Elbia had been facing for decades. With rye as its main crop, the region's annual agricultural earnings fluctuated widely. In years of poor harvest, rye was sold as a high-priced bread grain; in bumper years, however, only as a cheap feed grain. In the west, farm holdings were in better shape, not least thanks to less fluctuation in the annual prices of their main products. Wages for expensive farm hands did not enter into their accounts, and their taxes had increased to a lesser extent. With their emphasis on stock-raising and dairy farming, these family businesses were, however, especially hard hit by the depression and the concomitant decline in mass incomes, since agricultural products with a relatively high income elasticity of demand experienced a steeper fall in prices. In the period 1930–32 producers received about 30 percent less for milk and eggs and about 25 percent less for meat than in the years 1925–29, while the prices for rye and plant products in general declined by only about 20 percent in the same years. The government vigorously tried to support agricultural prices and to protect the German agricultural market from the influences of the world market by such measures as enormous import duties, low import quotas and even an import monopoly, open-market purchases and stockpiling in public granaries, denaturing of bread grain and releasing it under subsidy as feed grain or for industrial purposes, compulsory quotas for the utilization of domestic grain, mandatory extraction rates, and the like. All these measures passed through successive stages of temporary success, followed by failure, as competitive processes always managed to undermine the newly contrived equilibrium. Consequently, additional governmental controls were necessary to plug up the holes in the system, finally after 1933 culminating in a completely planned agriculture aiming at autarky. Despite all these efforts of the last Weimar governments, proceeds of sales in the agricultural sector in 1932/33 were almost 40 percent lower than in 1928/29, making for declining personal incomes and an increasing number of bankruptcies of peasant farms and noble estates.

Agriculture, however, was much more than just another economic sector, it was the material basis of an important segment of the traditional German ruling class: the aristocracy. The revolution of 1918 had somewhat reduced the political and social predominance of that group, but Junker influence was still strong in the new republic. Junkers and groups politically and socially allied with them were still entrenched in the higher ranks of the Prussian civil service, of the Protestant church, and of the German army. Their powerful influence was more than symbolized from 1925 onward by the figure of Reich President von

Hindenburg. In hindsight the republicans must have viewed it as a clear political mistake that they had not destroyed the economic basis of the Junkers by breaking up their large estates.

The agrarian reform and resettlement policy of the Weimar Republic had, over the years, transferred about one-sixth of all estate lands into the hands of some 62,000 new settlers. This seemed to be doubly advantageous: the substitution of peasant farms, emphasizing the production of high-grade foodstuffs, for large estates chiefly devoted to extensive grain cultivation would solve the structural crisis of eastern agriculture and undermine the economic basis and political power of the aristocracy at the same time. Attempts by the government to speed this process by withholding further subsidies to eastern estates (the so-called *Osthilfe*) and insisting on the liquidation of those with no chance of disencumberment were answered with the charge of "agrarian bolshevism" by the aristocratic enemies of the republic. Resentment against, and rejection of, the republican state had also grown among the more humble members of the agricultural sector. The peasants and small farmers—to an increasing extent feeling the pinch of the depression—objected to the deflationary policy of the government which tended to increase their indebtedness in real terms.

The Crisis of Economic Policy

A policy of deflation was the cure the Brüning government (in office from 30 March 1930 to 30 May 1932) thought could initiate a recovery. Given the high export ratio of German industry, the government hoped that a sharp downward pressure on prices would increase the chances of German exporting industries on the world market and increase domestic employment opportunities. Several factors made this course of action preferable to a devaluation of the Reichsmark: the nervous state of the German public, which since the hyperinflation of 1923 had tended to associate exchange depreciation with impending collapse of the currency; the fear of businessmen that wages would be linked to exchange rates; the possibility that a devaluation might be interpreted as a sign of weakness and even intensify the outflow of capital; the fact that a fall in the exchange value of the mark would increase the money and possibly also the real burden of foreign claims against Germany, most of which were payable in foreign currencies; and the danger of precipitating an international devaluation race or encouraging trade reprisals by other countries. All these arguments advised against a downward adjustment of the Reichsmark. Consequently the necessary scaling down of German prices could only be effected through a policy of deflation, if the government wanted to achieve an economic recovery within the framework of the world economy and not in national isolation by means of reflationary measures. The German public, a once-burned child, had developed a mortal fear of inflation that militated against any expansion of money supply or budget deficits. Such an attitude was not unsensible and was largely shared in business and government quarters, but it was absurd to equate every policy of expanding money supply and incurring a budget deficit with inviting the horrors of another hyperinflation. A responsible policy of pump priming, nevertheless, not only faced serious psychological obstacles among the lay public but also received very little encouragement from the experts.

Professional economists regarded the depression as basically a purification crisis, cleansing the economy of the unsound enterprises created during the preceding period. Although state intervention had become an accustomed phenomenon, the opinion prevailed that the best method of shortening the crisis was to let the economy alone and allow its self-healing capacity to function, while maintaining a balanced budget. Besides this noninterventionist philosophy, lack of insight into the circulation of money and commodities was another major obstacle to a successful anticyclical policy. According to the theory of markets, a general economic crisis was unthinkable in a system of free enterprise, for in such a system product is exchanged for product, with money only serving as the medium of exchange. Localized crises of disproportionality can occur, but will only be of a temporary nature. It was not sufficiently recognized that the basic assumptions of the theorem —competitive markets and the neutral nature of money—no longer actually existed, and that a prolonged equilibrium with considerable unemployment had become a theoretical possibility—indeed, a harsh reality.

Monetary considerations were closely related to the fourth major conditioning factor of the government's deflationary policy: that old pain in the purse, the reparation payments. Faced with the virtual stoppage of long-term capital imports after 1929,[37] Germany tried to earn the necessary RM 2 billion or so for reparation payments, and another billion for interest payments, by increased exports. After years of considerable deficits, the German balance of trade, which had roughly squared in 1929, began to show huge surpluses: RM 1.6 billion in 1930 and RM 2.8 billion in 1931. The Brüning government, like its predecessors, aimed at reduction and eventual cancellation of the reparations debt, and tried to make its point by faithfully adhering to the contractual obligations. By showing Germany's willingness to pay to the utmost it was hoped to prove the impossibility of raising and transferring the stipulated sums. International experts soon acknowledged

---

37. Annual average of long-term net capital inflow: 1924/28, RM 1.4 billion; 1929/32, RM 0.29 billion.

that the "Hungerkanzler" had demanded severe sacrifices of the German population, and the indigence of the nation was established beyond doubt. But understandably this made little impression abroad. The fact that the German reparation exports aggravated the international depression and prevented a recovery of the world economy carried more weight. For this reason the final suspension of reparation payments was agreed to at the Lausanne Conference in July 1932. In return a flat payment of RM 3 billion was to be made, in 1935 at the earliest, from the proceeds of a loan. Although this final payment was never made, Germany had paid reparations amounting to about RM 55 billion, according to her own calculations, or some RM 21 billion as computed by the Allies.

The reparations burden had been quite bearable in economic terms but emotionally intolerable for the Germans. From the point of view of domestic politics the price paid for the foreign policy accomplishment of doing away with it had nonetheless been stiff. During 1930 the government had tried to raise its revenues by increasing the already existing taxes on income, turnover, sugar and beer, by introducing some new and rather curious ones, like a special rate on department store sales, or on mineral water, and a tax on bachelors. For the latter it was probably small consolation that another group had also been singled out for a special levy: the public officials. In 1931 their salaries were reduced three times, by a total of 23 percent when it became apparent that there would be a budget deficit in spite of the increased taxation and the reduction of public investments in that year to one-half of the 1929 figure. Such drastic reductions in public expenditure would not have been possible without a simultaneous increase in the mark's purchasing power.[38] Unregulated prices responded automatically to the state of the market, of course, and controlled prices were twice scaled down by 10 percent by decree. By late 1931—in the face of bitter opposition from the trade unions—standard wages as established by collective bargaining were ordered put back to their January 1927 level, while house rents were cut by 10 percent and interest rates on loans had to give way in steps to a flat 6 percent.[39] These severe cuts in money income resulted in a corresponding reduction of consumer demand and, further aggravated by falling investment expenditure,[40] led to a decline in economic activity, so that during Brüning's tenure unemployment rose from 2.3 to 6 million. His ex-

38. Expenditure of all public bodies (Reich, states and municipalities) fell from RM 21 billion in 1930 to RM 17 billion in 1931 and RM 14.5 billion in 1932.
    Wholesale prices (1913=100): 1928, 140; 1929, 137; 1930, 125; 1931, 111; 1932, 97.
    39. Wage rates (1928=100): 1929, 106; 1930, 107; 1931, 102; 1932, 87.
    40. Net investments (1928, RM 9.1 billion; 1929, 5.2; 1930, 2.5; 1931, −2.1; 1932, −0.6) amounted to about 3 percent of the national income of these years.

port-based policy of promoting employment had failed because other countries had responded increasingly with protectionist measures, and because world market prices had fallen faster than those of German export commodities. Brüning's domestic market policy for promoting employment, for which the preparations had been started in the second half of 1931, had equally little success. The planned emergency work projects (land improvements, road construction, settlements, and so on) did, however, provide a counterbalance to certain very unpopular economic measures, particularly the drastic reduction in unemployment benefits, and were supposed to show the government's good intentions from the social point of view. The employment of the jobless masses rather than a stimulation of the economy was the goal of the RM 135 million program decided on in May 1932, for which the government had succeeded in getting the tightfisted Reichsbank to provide credit. In fact, the additional expenditure of some RM 20 per jobless person was no more than an empty gesture. That was all the government intended it to be, for Brüning's cabinet neither wished to pursue a credit-financed employment policy nor considered a lasting solution of the crisis to be possible until the reparations question had been solved. A change in the economic course was thus not possible under Chancellor Brüning, who was deeply grounded in traditional economic thinking, and his claim to have been tripped "a hundred yards from the goal" bears even less relation to reality than Hoover's statement cited earlier. Success has many fathers; failure is usually an orphan.

The two short-lived governments that followed Brüning ruled Germany for the next eight months until Hitler's accession to power, and started to reverse the direction of economic policy: deflation gave way to reflation. The Papen government continued the RM 135 million employment scheme begun under Brüning and, aware that a budget deficit was unavoidable, added RM 220 million for immediate job-creating purposes. Outside the budget an outlay of RM 0.7 billion was planned, partly as expenditures of the Reichsbahn and the Reichspost (postal service). In the final analysis they were to be financed by funds from the Reichsbank. But the main emphasis of Papen's program, which it was hoped would lead to a reduction of 1.75 million in the number of unemployed by the end of 1933, was on indirect job-creating measures. To this end RM 2.2 billion was earmarked. Entrepreneurs were to be encouraged to expand production and to invest through tax credit certificates and so-called higher employment premiums.[41] These subsidies were designed to improve the cost situation

41. On payment of certain taxes, the taxpayer received certificates equal to a part of his tax liability: 50 percent in case of the turnover tax, 40 percent of the business tax, 25 percent of the land tax, and 100 percent of the transportation tax. These tax certificates

of industry, and thus lead to its rehabilitation, while at the same time positively influencing the employment situation. In view of the confused political situation, the advanced time of year, and above all the continuing uncertain sales prospects, a vigorous revival of the economy was not to be expected from these indirect pump-priming measures before the following spring. Still it was the first major step towards an anticyclical policy such as had been demanded by the trade unions and by the Nazi party for quite some time. Nevertheless, the Papen program remained a bit one-sided, as there was too little direct job creation.

The last two months of the Weimar Republic, under the Schleicher government, saw a shift in the emphasis of antidepression policy towards direct work creation. Just how endangered the republic was could be seen, for example, from the Berlin transport strike of November 1932, when Nazis and Communists closely cooperated. Following the publication of Schleicher's one-point government program—namely: "create jobs!"—the Reichsbank agreed to finance pumppriming to the amount of RM 2.7 billion. This "Luther limit" (so called after Reichsbank President Luther) included Papen's RM 2.2 billion job creation program, however, so that a mere RM 0.5 billion was left for Schleicher's emergency measures. Of that the Reich was to receive one-fifth, to be used primarily for fortifications, arms purchases and similar government defense contracts. In this the government was able to reap the benefits of the military equality granted to Germany by the Allies in December 1932. The remaining funds were to go to the states and municipalities to be used for the repair and improvement of existing installations, for road and hydraulic construction, for communal public utilities, and for land improvements and settlement. Certain conditions were attached, such as the least possible use of machines or a maximum of 40 hours' working time per week. Thus, even if other flanking measures are not considered, quite an impressive bundle of job-creation programs and devices had been assembled and tested under Papen and Schleicher which later served as the basis for the large-scale stimulation policies of the Nazis.

The Crisis of Confidence

Hitler's takeover was greeted with a considerable amount of relief, and certainly not only by the Nazis. In the November 1932 election, the latter had experienced severe setbacks: 33 percent rather than 37 per-

---

could be used within the next five years to pay taxes. In effect they represented an anticipated tax reduction, or, being eligible as collateral, could serve as security for a loan. The higher employment premiums mentioned, which were issued in form of tax certificates, were wage subsidies for employing additional workers while at the same time reducing the work week from 48 to 40 hours.

cent of the vote had returned only 196 deputies in place of the previous 230 to the Reichstag. The democratically minded public also thought in many cases that it was not a bad idea that Hitler, that incessant loudmouth and political quack, now be forced to prove his healing capacities. Surely he would fail, thus unmasking his quackery and making the Nazis the laughingstock of the nation once and for all.[42] On the other hand, the antidemocratic forces on the left, regarding fascism as an organic stage in the development of capitalism, hoped to build their society upon the ruins of Hitlerism. According to these notions, things had to get worse before they would get better.

The defenders of the republic were few, since disenchantment with the parliamentary form of government was widespread. The middle class of small and medium-sized craftsmen and shopkeepers, the self-employed, and the holders of assets in monetary form, had experienced severe losses in their economic and social position when their assets, usually held in savings accounts and government bonds, were wiped out by years of war and inflation. War and inflation profiteers, black marketeers, grafters and speculators, on the other hand, had risen to fortune and notoriety overnight. Although not numerous, the ostentatious life style of these pretentious upstarts and recently emancipated groups offended the sense of justice of the impoverished middle class and the still struggling working class. The *Ausverkauf* (sellout) of the German economy had enriched many carpetbagging foreigners and an unscrupulous minority of Germans (the "Raffkes," i.e., "the grabbers"), while the deflationary policy of the early thirties, with its concomitant salary reductions, had annoyed the public servants and undermined their loyalty to the republic. The upper layers of the bureaucracy, who had been taken over from the previous monarchical regime, had from the very start had considerable ideological reservations about the republican system, as had most academics. The armies of lesser officials, generally more interested in bread-and-butter issues, now also had good reason to be discontented. Dissatisfaction was widespread, too, among the farmers, hard pressed by the increasing real burden of their debts during the years of deflation. The Osthilfe was regarded by the ungrateful Junkers as too little, too late, while the industrial workers looked upon it as giving a free ride to the enemies of the republic. The wage earners, who during the twenties had had good reason to identify with the republic, were disappointed that the improvements in their standard of living had turned out to be ephemeral, and that prosperity had given way to mass unemployment. The improvements they had achieved fell far short of the

42. The Nazis benefitted greatly from not having been taken seriously; Charlie Chaplin's *The Great Dictator* was thus as much a disservice in the late thirties as today's unfortunate tendency to present Hitler as a funny man on American TV shows.

expectations aroused by the coming of the republic. On the other hand, the limited social advances of the employed had been sufficient to give employers the impression that Weimar was a *"Gewerkschaftsstaat,"* government of the unions, by the unions, for the unions.[43] It was high time, in their understanding, to restore the situation as it had been when they were masters in their own houses. To set up a corporate social order, in place of the organized anarchy called parliamentarism, with its three dozen parties, seemed as attractive to them as it was to a large part of the Center Party and its Catholic constituency. This crisis of confidence, affecting virtually all strata of society, was accompanied by a revolutionary atmosphere throughout the country. Political strikes, riots and resistance to legal authority, political murder and public slander were the deplorable characteristics of a chaotic society, of a fragmented economy. At the same time, the hope was awakened that national redemption and economic prosperity were just around the corner.

Bibliography

A storehouse of information on this period is the *Encyclopaedia of the Social Sciences* (New York, 1930–35), containing articles on, for instance: War Economics; War Finance; Mobilization and Demobilization; Reparations; Passive Resistance and Non-Cooperation; Rentenmark; Rationalization; etc.

Aldcroft, D. H. *From Versailles to Wall Street 1919–1929.* Berkeley and Los Angeles, 1977.
Angell, J. W. *The Recovery of Germany.* New Haven, 1932. Reprint 1972.
Baruch, B. *The Making of the Reparation and Economic Sections of the Treaty.* New York, 1920.
Blaich, F. "Die 'Fehlrationalisierung' in der deutschen Automobilindustrie 1924 bis 1929," *Tradition* 18 (1973).
Blaich, F. *Die Wirtschaftskrise 1925/26 und die Reichsregierung: Von der Erwerbslosenfürsorge zur Konjunkturpolitik.* Kallmünz, 1977.
Born, K. E. *Die deutsche Bankenkrise 1931: Finanzen und Politik.* Munich, 1967.
Brady, R. *The Rationalization Movement in German Industry.* Berkeley, 1933.
Brentano, L. "Was Deutschland gezahlt hat." *Weltwirtschaftliches Archiv* 2 (1924).
Bresciani-Turroni, C. *The Economics of Inflation, A Study of Currency Depreciation in Post-War Germany 1914–1923.* London, 1937.
Burnett, P. M. *Reparation at the Paris Peace Conference, From the Standpoint of the American Delegation.* New York, 1940.

43. The unions were rather fragmented; in 1932 the socialist unions had 4.6 million members, the Christian unions 1.3 million, the conservative unions 0.6 million, and the communist unions 36,000.

Clausing, G. *Die wirtschaftlichen Wechsellagen von 1919 bis 1932*. Jena, 1933.

Conze, W., and Raupach, H., eds. *Die Staats- und Wirtschaftskrise des Deutschen Reichs 1929/33*. Stuttgart, 1967.

Dawson, W. H. *Germany under the Treaty*. London, 1933.

Ellis, H. S. *German Monetary Theory 1905–1933*, Cambridge, Mass., 1934.

Falkus, M. E. "The German Business Cycle in the 1920's." *Economic History Review* 28 (1975).

Feis, H. *The Diplomacy of the Dollar, 1919–1932*. Baltimore, 1950.

Feldman, G. D. *Iron and Steel in the German Inflation 1916–1923*. Princeton, N.J., 1977.

Felix, D. *Walther Rathenau and the Weimar Republic: The Politics of Reparations*. Baltimore, 1971.

Felix, D. "Reparations Reconsidered with a Vengeance." *Central European History* 4 (1971).

Graham, F. D. *Exchange, Prices and Production in Hyperinflation: Germany 1920–1923*. Princeton, N.J., 1930.

Grotkopp, W. *Die große Krise: Lehren aus der Überwindung der Wirtschaftskrise 1929/32*. Düsseldorf, 1954.

Hansen, E. W. *Reichswehr und Industrie: Rüstungswirtschaftliche Zusammenarbeit und wirtschaftliche Mobilmachungsvorbereitungen 1923–1932*. Boppard, 1978.

Holtfrerich, C. L. "Amerikanischer Kapitalexport und Wiederaufbau der deutschen Wirtschaft 1919–23 im Vergleich zu 1924–29." *Vierteljahrsschrift für Sozial- und Wirtschaftsgeschichte* 64 (1977).

Holtfrerich, C. L. "Internationale Verteilungsfolgen der deutschen Inflation 1918-1923." *Kyklos* 30 (1977).

Hubatsch, W. *Entstehung und Entwicklung des Reichswirtschaftsministeriums 1880–1933*. Berlin, 1978.

Keynes, J. M. *The Economic Consequences of the Peace*. London, 1919.

Kroll, G. *Von der Weltwirtschaftskrise zur Staatskonjunktur*. Berlin, 1958.

Laursen, K., and Pedersen, J. *The German Inflation: 1918–1923*. Amsterdam, 1964.

Lewis, W. A. *Economic Survey 1919–39*. London, 1949.

Lüke, R. E. *Von der Stabilisierung zur Krise*. Zurich, 1958.

Maier, C. S. "Between Taylorism and Technocracy: European Ideologies and the Vision of Industrial Productivity in the 1920s." *Journal of Contemporary History* 5 (1970).

Maier, C. S. *Recasting Bourgeois Europe: Stabilization in France, Germany and Italy in the Decade after World War I*. Princeton, N.J., 1975.

Marcon, H. *Arbeitsbeschaffungspolitik der Regierungen Papen und Schleicher*. Frankfurt/Main, 1974.

Marks, S. "Reparations Reconsidered: A Reminder." *Central European History* 2 (1969).

Marks, S. "Reparations Reconsidered: A Rejoinder." *Central European History* 5 (1972).

Marks, S. "The Myths of Reparations." *Central European History* 11 (1978).

Mendershausen, H. *Two Postwar Recoveries in Germany*. Amsterdam, 1955.

Moulton, H. G., and McGuire C. E. *Germany's Capacity to Pay*. New York, 1923.

Néré, J. *La Crise de 1929.* Paris, 1968.

Petzina, D. "Germany and the Great Depression." *Journal of Contemporary History* 4 (1969).

Petzina, D. *Die deutsche Wirtschaft in der Zwischenkriegszeit.* Wiesbaden, 1977.

Preller, L. *Sozialpolitik in der Weimarer Republik.* Düsseldorf, 1949. Reprint 1978.

Schuker, S. A. *The End of French Predominance in Europe: The Financial Crisis of 1924 and the Adoption of the Dawes Plan.* Chapel Hill, N.C., 1976.

Skiba, R. *Das westdeutsche Lohnniveau zwischen den beiden Weltkriegen und nach der Währungsreform.* Cologne, 1974.

Temin, P. "The Beginning of the Depression in Germany." *Economic History Review* 24 (1971).

Weisbrod, B. *Schwerindustrie in der Weimarer Republik: Interessenpolitik zwischen Stabilisierung und Krise.* Wuppertal, 1978.

CHAPTER 4

The Economy of the Third Reich, 1933-1945

1

The Peace Period

Nazi Economic Doctrines

The economic plans of the National Socialist German Workers' Party—published in 1920 as part of a program of twenty-five points, of which about half dealt with economic and social questions—read like a letter to Santa Claus: the state is obligated to ensure the gainful employment and livelihood of citizens, while every citizen is obliged to work, intellectually or physically; individual activity must never clash with the interests of the community, but must be carried out within the collective framework for the good of all. A land reform policy suited to the nation's needs, confiscation of real estate without compensation for community purposes, and prevention of land speculation; a ruthless fight against usury and profiteering; wide expansion of care for the aged; the creation of a healthy middle class; these and other, similarly vague, though not unreasonable, demands climax in the old socialist slogan "public interest comes before self-interest" *("Gemeinnutz vor Eigennutz")*. Besides such generalities there were a few more specific demands: abolition of income not earned by work and toil, and "the breaking of interest-slavery"; confiscation of all war profits; national-ization of all trusts; profit-sharing in large enterprises; immediate takeover of department stores by municipalities in order to make space at low rates available for small tradespeople; the utmost consideration for small-scale enterprises in placing orders for government pur-

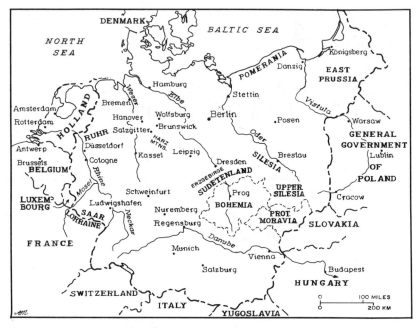

2. *Nazi Germany, including Sudetenland and Austria.*

chases; and acquisition of land (colonies) to feed the German people and to settle the surplus population.

At least on paper the party duly demonstrated its anticapitalism by proclaiming "public interest before self-interest" as a moral principle, "the breaking of interest-slavery" as a social goal, and nationalization of trusts, municipalization of department stores and land reform as economic targets. The working class—though extremely reluctant to vote Nazi—could thus not complain about insufficient programmatic regard for its interests. The strongly pro-Nazi petty bourgeoisie of tradespeople and craftsmen was also amply provided for, while its fear of proletarization and expropriation, and the more pronounced apprehensions of industrial magnates and big businessmen, were appeased by the party's distinction between "rapacious and productive capital" *(raffendes und schaffendes Kapital)*. The former was typically Jewish and employed in financial operations and commodity dealings, according to Nazi notions, the latter genuinely "Aryan" and employed in industry.

Apart from the fact that virtually all of these demands were vague and ambiguous, and could thus mean different things to different people—one of their propagandistic advantages—almost none of them would serve as major economic policy guidelines once the Nazis had come to power. There were, however, two major exceptions, which proved critical and had disastrous results: the extension of German "living space" *(Lebensraum)* and the neutralization of "rapacious capital" in the form of "Jewish parasitism" in the German economy. Both aims, with their principally political content, went far beyond mere economic motivations and led eventually to two tragedies: six years of European warfare and the extermination of six million European Jews.[1] Although the transition between economics and politics is fluid, it cannot be overlooked that Hitler gave absolute primacy to political considerations. He regarded the economy merely as one means among many in achieving his all-important political goal, the so-called self-preservation of the nation. In his view, the economy could not make its proper contribution through a strong showing within an integrated and world-wide network of industry and trade. That was something which would lead to a weakening of the agrarian part of the population, to an increasing urban-industrial proletariat, and to a general "commercialization" *(Verwirtschaftlichung)* of the nation. In spite of all his eagerness to theorize, as shown in Mein Kampf, Hitler was not at heart a party platform writer laying down high principles, but a politician proceeding in compliance with tactical considerations. Once in power, judicious maneuvering demanded that he dispense with a radical recasting of the country's economy, i.e., the abolition of interest, the expropriation of stockholders, the nationalization of large-scale enterprises, the municipalization of department stores, and the redistribution of land. What the new regime urgently needed was to win the respect and cooperation of the business community.

National Socialism was for most of the industrial magnates a perplexing and ambiguous phenomenon: anti-Marxist and fanatically nationalistic on the one hand, anti-capitalistic and revolutionary on the other. Nevertheless, it has become a deeply engraved and party-politically motivated belief that the captains of industry in general, and of some branches in particular, showed an especially pronounced liking for the Nazis. Though the final word in this matter has not yet been said, such generalizations do not stand up to unprejudiced historical scrutiny. Not very convincing, for example, is the thesis that heavy industry (coal and steel), which had allegedly suffered a great deal during the depression years and was only distantly concerned with exports, favored a Nazi takeover, and that it was eventually successful in helping Hitler to power, with Junker assistance, when the Schleicher govern-

1. This figure includes some 220,000 Jews still living in Nazi Germany in 1941. Three times this number had previously emigrated as a consequence of harassment and boycotts instigated and pursued in a casual fashion by the Nazis from April 1933 onward. After November 1938, however, a systematic policy of persecution, which had previously been forestalled by domestic and international considerations and the resistance of the ministerial bureaucracy, resulted within months in the nearly total removal of Jews from gainful activity in the professions, business and industry.

ment, reputedly backed by the exporting chemical and electrical industries and the trade unions, was toppled. Such an interpretation, frequently held by Marxist writers, does not become more persuasive when this "struggle amongst the industrial monopolies" is fused with an alleged "battle between the two financial powers" in Germany, one pan-German *(alldeutsch)*, the other American. Suggestions that there was a dividing line between anti-Nazi and pro-Nazi industrialists—depending on whether they were running an independent family concern or an anonymous company—have not been generally accepted either. Two arguments are advanced for this: that the established families lived from distributed profits, and consequently feared Hitler's anti-capitalist radicalism more than the salaried managers of anonymous joint stock companies; and that these managers, under pressure to restore the profitability of their companies, and faced with the demands of their stockholders for tangible results, were more inclined to put up with and accept Nazism than the more independent owner-industrialists. Neither has sufficient validity. The contention that certain categories of industrial magnates were more prone to National Socialism than others, and that these categories reflected distinct economic interests, is just as unconvincing as the allegation that support for National Socialism was widespread among the industrialists. There is in fact considerable evidence that the overwhelming majority of industrial magnates, with some important exceptions, regarded Hitler with disapproval and mistrust before 1933. The financial help the party received from some industrialists was frequently looked upon as an insurance premium in case of a Nazi takeover, or was supposed to strengthen the position of certain Nazi chieftains regarded as "reasonable." Furthermore, these payments to the party were quite limited, and far less than the sums given to the opponents and rivals of the National Socialists. Still, one must recognize that these sums did help the Nazi party to exist and to expand.

Revival of the Economy and Rearmament

Once the Nazis had come to power, Hitler made use of the general dislike of political and social unrest prevalent in the business community, and started an appeasement policy to ease the minds of its leaders. They soon learned that no radical remodeling of the economic and social system was intended. On the contrary, big business was asked to support the economic measures of the new regime. Hitler, who frequently showed considerable respect for business magnates, since he felt a certain affinity with daring and venturesome characters, thus assured himself of the all-important goodwill and confidence of the business community, an asset which Roosevelt—starting at about the same time and facing similar economic problems, but branded "a traitor to his class"—had to forego.[2] Consequently, though they must have known that the future of their regime depended on their success or failure in dealing with existing mass unemployment,[3] the Nazis took their time in initiating the kind of vigorous antidepression program they had demanded as an opposition party. To some extent this was making a virtue out of a necessity, as their sudden accession to power had caught them by surprise and unprepared. Hitler had to ask his cabinet ministers "to keep the public preoccupied with pure political matters as the economic decisions have still to be studied."

It was not that the party had no concept of a work-creation policy. The speaker of the party's socialist wing, and probably the most popular Nazi after Hitler, Gregor Strasser, had in May 1932 submitted a program in the Reichstag which Brüning largely agreed with, rejecting only the proposed credit financing. After being modified to a certain extent during the following months in Nazi economic publications, and by Reinhardt, the party's leading theorist on economic stimulation and later under-secretary in the Ministry of Finance, this program emphasized above all land improvement (amelioration, consolidation and flood control), construction of owner-occupied housing for workers, and transport and communication projects. The land improvement schemes were to increase agricultural production, workers' settlements were to reduce the population in urban centers, while improved transport communications would serve trade, settlement in the east, facilitate the deagglomeration of big-city areas, and, last but not least, were desirable for military reasons. Since these were productive investments, it was held that their credit financing involved no inflationary risks. The key to success did not lie in an export-oriented recovery program but could be found in a withdrawal from the world market and in economic self-sufficiency. While the petty bourgeoisie, fearing communist radicalism among workers, especially among the unemployed, approved such ideas, industrialists were quite sceptical. Anticapitalist planks in the Nazi program, such as the demand to curtail the influence of powerful concerns, reinforced their doubts about this economic policy. Although Strasser left the party at the beginning of December 1932, it was quite some time before Hitler received the kind of backing

2. The annual average number of Americans unemployed was 12.83 million in 1933, i.e., 24.9 percent of the civilian labor force; the not very effective employment policy of the New Deal had by 1938 reduced these figures to 10.39 million or 19 percent.

3. When Hitler took office in January 1933, 11.5 million Germans were gainfully employed and 6 million out of work, which meant an unemployment ratio of 34.4 percent. The maximum unemployment figure had already been reached in February 1932 with 6.1 million; when 11.9 million persons were employed, the unemployment ratio amounted to 33.9 percent.

he needed from the private sector for his own economic policy. In his coalition cabinet such key politico-economic posts as the ministries of economic affairs and agriculture were not filled by party men until June 1933. Luther, the president of the Reichsbank, had on the other hand made way as early as March for Hjalmar Schacht, who was more receptive to a broad recovery program.

By 1 June 1933, the first work-creation law, the so-called "First Reinhardt Program," earmarked one billion RM for public expenditures which by means of short-term treasury notes would return about one million unemployed to the production process. Since industrial circles still disapproved of public employment programs which were not connected with tax concessions, this plan combined indirect incentives with direct public investment expenditures. Financial assistance to the private sector of the economy took the form of subsidies or tax privileges for certain specified forms of investment, like replacement and extension of plant and equipment in industry and agriculture. Such measures essentially continued the anticyclical policies of the last two pre-Nazi governments during 1932, but were now enriched by additional allowances.

One of these incentives was the abolition of the motor-vehicle tax in April 1933, leading to an increase in private demand for cars, and creating a reserve of requisitionable vehicles for the military. After June 1933 marriage loans were granted to young couples, which also fit Nazi population policies, while the hiring of female domestics brought tax privileges, which was largely in conformity with the Nazi conception of women's occupation role.

A number of these indirect incentives aided the building industry to a considerable extent. The direct public investment expenditures for the construction of waterways, railroads, public buildings, and the superhighways *(Reichsautobahn)* which had been begun with a great deal of propaganda, almost totally assisted the building industry. The employment impact of the pump-priming policies was to be enlarged by various stipulations in the implementing statutes: e.g., that the encouraged activity had to be done by hand, unless the use of machinery was indispensible; that 80 percent of the additional workers hired had to be unemployed persons receiving relief; that the increased business activity was not to lead to longer working hours; and that the machines which had been replaced by new ones were to be scrapped so that they could not be used elsewhere. Besides these measures to create jobs without necessarily increasing output, other artificial methods were used to put the unemployed to some work somehow. Sizeable numbers were employed in an expanding state and party bureaucracy. At the same time, employers were pressed to increase their demand for labor by enlarging their personnel—though unjustified on economic grounds—or by hiring part-time workers only.[4] It is not surprising that business leaders did not think much of such a policy, because they fully believed these work-providing measures were artificial, and that a genuine recovery could result only from renewed initiative in the private sector of the economy. These objections were partly taken into account by the "Second Reinhardt Program" of September 1933, which provided subsidies of 0.5 billion RM and tax privileges of about .036 billion RM for the repair and reconstruction of residential and agricultural buildings during the winter of 1933/34. Furthermore, housing projects were more intensely promoted, investment expenditures for postal and railroad communications were increased, and relief works were expanded.

In the face of the business community's misgivings regarding direct public expenditures, and in spite of the belated start of the employment policy, the Nazi regime in its first two years nevertheless spent at least 5 billion RM, or about 4 percent of the annual GNP, to promote employment. These recovery measures, financed by budget deficits and a raising of the Reich's floating debt, could only have an effect on economic activity and employment after the usual time lag of eight to twelve months. They therefore provide no reasonable explanation for the speedy decline in unemployment in 1933. On the contrary, the immediate improvement in the labor market was more due to measures already introduced by Papen and Schleicher, which showed results in the spring and summer of 1933. The worldwide improvement in economic conditions since the summer of 1932, on the other hand, did not result in additional demand for German products. Exports in 1933 and 1934 were about 15 percent lower than in the respective preceding year. All the same, there was no decline in the index figures for the production of capital and consumer goods after August 1932, nor for the wholesale prices of industrial raw materials and semifinished goods after July of that year; in fact the index of stock prices had been moving upward as early as April 1932. To be sure, other economic indicators continued to decline: the lowest level was reached by the industrial employment index in January 1933, by the indices of all wholesale prices and of the cost of living not until April 1933. Altogether it is justifiable to regard the second half of 1932 as the trough of the economic cycle. In real terms several economic improvements could indeed be recorded, but the prevailing tone among businessmen remained pessimistic, especially in the face of the approaching slack season of the year. The final and—as far as Germany was concerned—favorable settlement of the reparations question at Lausanne

---

4. If the assumption that a pay check is more humane than a welfare check is correct, the creation of nonproductive jobs is amply justified.

proved to be just as inadequate in inducing a basic psychological change, and with it an upward economic trend, as the self-healing forces of the market system upon which many put their hopes. Hitler's accession to power improved the psychological climate considerably, exerting beneficial influences on the propensities to consume and invest.[5] Besides, as Hitler was now in a position to reap the fruits of the recovery policies of his predecessors, cleverly represented as his own, the expectations of producers and consumers were soon confirmed, thus adding further to the economic upswing. Consequently, after less than one year in office, Hitler could point to a significant achievement: by the end of 1933 unemployment was down by about one-third, and only four instead of six million were still unemployed.

In the following years the new regime was able to sustain this rapid reduction of unemployment. Contributing factors were the introduction of universal compulsory military service in March 1935, the transformation of the originally voluntary labor service, created in 1931, into the obligatory Reich Labor Service (*Reichsarbeitsdienst*, RAD) in June 1935, and intensive propaganda against the gainful employment of women.[6] By about 1936 virtually full employment had been achieved, even developing into over-employment in the last two prewar years.[7] This additional labor input contributed to the 39 percent rise of real per capita income between the years 1930/34 and 1935/39. Real wages rose, however, by only 21 percent between 1932 and 1938 and lagged behind the increase in the national income, as reflected in the declining ratio of wages and salaries to national product (down from 63.5 percent in 1932/33 to 57.5 percent in 1937/38). Though limited, these material gains were now relatively secure, since arbitrary dismissal by employers was prohibited, although it remained possible on political grounds upon request of the Nazi shop steward. Furthermore the new regime, which before 1933 had tried in vain to break the hold of the Marxist parties upon the workers, now very quickly won their allegiance, or at least their acquiescence. This was not least due to efforts to improve the social prestige of the working class through the remodeling of the employer-employee relationship. Aiming at abolishing open class an-

5. In 1933 private consumption was about 8 percent above that of the previous year, while the almost 3 billion RM of disinvestment in 1932 fell to 0.37 billion RM in the following year.

6. In the RAD young men had to perform hard work with picks and shovels for six months without payment. This relieved the labor market and served as both physical and premilitary training. Moreover, the RAD brought young people of all walks of life together and, like military service, was supposed to mitigate class consciousness and pride of place. It goes without saying that ideological indoctrination played a considerable part in the RAD system.

7. Using 30 September as the key day, the unemployment percentage amounted to 20 (1933), 12.5 (1934), 9.6 (1935), 5.7 (1936), 2.5 (1937) and 0.95 (1938).

tagonism, the Nazis forcibly liquidated the trade unions in early May 1933, and not long afterwards created the German Labor Front *(Deutsche Arbeitsfront,* DAF), an obligatory organization for some 20 million blue- and white-collar workers, henceforth called "the followers" *(Gefolgschaft)* and their employers, now named "plant leaders" *(Betriebsführer).* These leaders, however, not infrequently had to take back seats; newly established "Courts of Social Honor" *(Soziale Ehrengerichte)* could in theory, though rarely in practice, try them—in the language of the respective law—for "abuse of their position of power in the firm, having maliciously exploited the workers or insulted their honor." If found guilty, they could be cautioned, reprimanded, fined up to 10.000 RM, or even removed altogether from management of their own firm, depending on the severity of the offense. The threat of the Nazi shop steward to go to court must frequently have been sufficient to make the owner reconsider his "master-in-my-house" attitude.

In time the Arbeitsfront developed a certain sense of power. It successfully demanded improved working conditions and better housing,[8] besides providing a multitude of cheap new recreational opportunities for workers through its affiliated organization "Strength through Joy" *(Kraft durch Freude).*[9] Joy and beauty, according to Nazi propaganda, were to be the principles of a new industrial society; workers pursuing their tasks as a creative, joyous experience would be more productive, especially in a pleasant environment.[10] The price for these improvements was primarily a loss of individual liberties. As early as 1934, the immigrant to urban areas of concentration needed a permit; and after 1936/37 every worker received a Labor Book containing his individual employment record, which was necessary to obtain a new job. Between June and October 1938 partial, and in February 1939 comprehensive, labor conscription was introduced to ease the serious and growing shortages on the German labor market. To see one's economy being afflicted by over-employment was one of the worries many a foreign statesman would gladly have shouldered at the time,[11] the more so as the German recovery had been achieved at quite stable prices. The price index of private consumption rose between 1932/34

8. The annual construction of apartments (1933, 178,000; 1934, 284,000; 1935, 241,000; 1936, 310,000; 1937, 320,000; 1938, 285,000; 1939, 206,000) only in 1937 surpassed the average figure of 313,000 for the years 1928/30.

9. Already in 1934/35 the DAF prided itself on the large number of vacationing workers, 200,000 of whom participated in inexpensive cruises.

10. By 1940 the DAF proudly pointed to some 24,000 new washing and changing rooms, some 18,000 new canteens, some 17,000 gardens in industrial plants, and some 3,000 new factory sports grounds.

11. In 1938 the year-round average of unemployment as a percentage of the labor force was 1.3 for Germany, compared to 18.9 for the United States, 11.4 for Canada, 9.9 for the Netherlands, 8.7 for Belgium, and 8.1 for the United Kingdom.

and 1936/38 by a mere 4 percent, while industrial production soared by 89 percent between 1933 and 1938, reaching its predepression record level of 1928/29 as early as 1935. This extensive mobilization of the nation's resources did not suit the plans of many an economic expert outside Germany who—with the intention of discrediting Nazi economic policy—had predicted its inevitable and imminent failure.[12] It took considerable time before impartial economic studies (irrespective of whether or not the analyst liked the domestic and foreign policies of the regime) were published in the late 1930s which presented rather positive evaluations of Nazi economic policy.

The task of the contemporary analyst was complicated by the fact that almost from the beginning Nazi economic policy was made behind closed doors.[13] Secrecy was regarded as advisable since some of the countercyclical measures also benefitted the country's military potential, thus killing two birds with one stone. The Reichswehr, whose legal size had been set at Versailles at seven divisions or 100,000 men, had dreamed throughout the twenties of an army three times as large.[14] Sometime prior to November 1933, Hitler ordered the armed forces to be brought up to that level as quickly as possible without making it common knowledge that rearmament had begun in earnest. In March 1935, however, he openly renounced the Versailles limitations on German military power, reintroducing conscription and ordering the buildup of a standing army of thirty-six divisions. These two major changes in German military policy are clearly reflected in the growth of expenditures for the armed forces. While in 1933 only 1.9 billion RM were allocated for this purpose, the annual average was 5 billion RM for 1934/35, over 11 billion RM for 1936/37 and 17 billion RM in 1938. Altogether, total armament expenditures up to the outbreak of war are estimated at around 60 billion RM. In relation to the country's national income, armament expenditures amounted to 4 percent in 1933, 20 percent in 1938[15] and 14 percent on average for all prewar years. Due to the observance of secrecy regarding the Reich budget, and owing to the introduction of various new and obscure means of financing, the real dimensions of the German rearmament program remained un-

12. Nazi Germany was thus discredited in the same way as the Soviet Union, whose economic collapse had been prophesied for years by foreign critics of a different ideological creed.

13. Already the Enabling Act of March 1933 had eliminated parliamentary debate and control of the Reich budget; later on the statistical yearbooks ceased to publish budget figures, which eventually became restricted information.

14. Even such a trebling would not, however, have changed the defensive character of Germany's armed forces, as French troops stationed in Europe numbered 350,000, while Poland had some 250,000, and Czechoslovakia over 130,000 men under arms in 1929/30.

15. By comparison, in that year France spent 17 percent for this purpose, England 12 percent.

clear to contemporaries.[16] This enabled Hitler to exaggerate the actual size of his military machine and to boast in early September 1939 of having spent some 90 billions.

One method of financing the rearmament program in secret was through the issuance of Mefo-bills, which met about one-fifth of all expenditures for the armed forces in the years from 1933 until the outbreak of war.[17] Besides these Mefo-bills, worth around 12 billion RM, and some additional 1.5 billion RM in other short-term loans, the Reich incurred about 8 billion RM in long- and medium-term debts. Total Reich expenditures in the six fiscal years 1933/34 to 1938/39 were about 100 billion RM, of which only 80 percent was covered by taxes and the profits of Reich enterprises (primarily the Reichsbahn and the Reichspost). The longer-term loans were placed with institutional investors (insurance companies, savings banks) and thus financed by depositors and insured persons. Since their funds represented genuine abstention from consumption, these long-term loans meant no threat to monetary stability. So far the financial policies of the Nazi government were quite sound; the debt-financed government expenditures put unemployed factors of production to work and led to a rise in the national income, thus generating higher tax yields and accrual of savings and in turn permitting repayment or funding of government loans to a certain extent. This policy of public borrowing was fairly uncomplicated (especially regarding undesirable income-transfer effects) because the previous inflation had practically eliminated the national debt, and the increase of internal indebtedness before 1933 had been quite limited.[18] More problematic, however, were the Mefo-bills, which were either circulating—thereby taking on some of the functions of money—or increasing the money supply directly as rediscountable paper which could be used as legal cover for banknotes. They contributed quite substantially to the expansion of the money supply, which more than doubled in these six years.[19] When the Reichsbank had to

16. Today there is still room for disagreement, though in general the order of magnitude seems to be established.

17. The Mefo (Metallurgische Forschungsanstalt) was a dummy corporation founded in May 1933 by four major armaments firms, staffed by Reichsbank personnel and headed by one representative each of the Reichsbank and the Ministry of War. Armaments suppliers would draw three-month commercial bills on the Mefo and present them—duly accepted and provided with the guarantee of the Reich as debtor—for discount at their banks, which would rediscount them at the Reichsbank, or put them into circulation with their endorsement.

18. Even by 1938 the German national debt had not reached the British or French level.

19. *Reichsbank return (bill. RM)*

	31 March 1933	*31 March 1939*
Notes in circulation	3.52	8.31
Holdings of trade bills and checks	2.76	8.14
Holdings of gold and foreign currency	0.84	0.077

rediscount 2 billion RM in Mefo-bills during the politically stormy first nine months of 1938, however, something which suddenly increased the notes in circulation by 46 percent, the economy had been sufficiently remodeled—not least by the wage and price freeze decree of November 1936—to withstand any dangerous inflationary pressures.

Regulation of the Economy

That the Nazis were able to carry out their extensive rearmament program with inflation[20] or any substantial impairment of the standard of living of the masses was possible because, without following a preconceived plan, they had over the years transformed what still existed of the German market economy step by step into a thoroughly regulated economy. Though the quite complicated structure of these controls cannot be described here, basically there were three main points of departure from which to regulate the economy internally: control of consumption, control of investment and control of labor supply.

One method of managing consumption was through the regulation of money incomes by means of taxation and wage control.[21] The already extraordinarily high taxes levied during the deflation period were maintained, and even slightly increased,[22] so that while in 1932 taxes (inclusive of social insurance contributions) constituted 25.4 percent of the national income, the corresponding figure for 1938 was 29.5 percent. From 1934 on, with the increasing labor scarcity, rather rigid wage ceilings were instituted to resist any strong upward movement. Fixed wages naturally required stable retail prices, which logically made the expansion of control over all the preceding stages of the productive process necessary. While the regulation of wages took care of one important cost factor, controls of imported and home-produced raw materials were carried out either with the help of exchange control, existing cartel agreements, or the agricultural pricing policy. Trade margins, a further cost factor, were regulated through the stipulation of proportionate and later absolute profit charges.[23]

Not only consumer incomes but also capital expenditures can cause inflationary pressures if investments exceed voluntary savings. To prevent this, and to channel investable funds into desired directions

20. The index of wholesale prices rose by 16 percent in Germany between 1933 and 1938, in Britain by 30 percent, and in the United States by 34 percent.

21. From late 1936 onward the steering of consumption (*Verbrauchslenkung*) by means of propaganda was used to channel household demand, especially as regards foodstuffs, away from scarce commodities to more readily available articles, e.g., "Eat more fish."

22. The corporation tax was raised from its previous level of 20 percent to 25 percent in 1936, and 30 percent in 1937.

23. State supervision was made easier through the obligatory introduction of standard forms of accounting and uniform costing systems after 1937.

(especially armaments and the production of substitute materials), far-reaching investment controls were enacted. As early as 1933 the government had started to reserve the capital market for its own long-term borrowing by restricting the private sector of the economy to self-financing and short-term borrowing. The distribution of dividends was limited to 6 percent, which encouraged enterprises to plough back their profits and finance their expansion from their own resources. After 1934, however, when reserves of productive capacity and labor began to dwindle, and various provisions to control corporate savings no longer sufficed, additional nonfinancial measures had to be taken to guide private investments away from unnecessary projects into directions desired by the regime. Consequently, investment was carefully supervised: the establishment and expansion of companies in all major industries was generally prohibited and subject to government licensing. Entrepreneurs with an irresistible urge for company growth and little interest in their own personal fates—the regime could be rather allergic to persistent disregard of its orders—could also quite gently be brought in line through the meager allocation of imported raw materials and of workers, who were in short supply from 1936 onward.[24]

Measures to regulate supply and demand on the labor market, the third major set of devices for controlling the economy, comprised suspension of the previous work-spreading regulations as well as the increase and intensification of work. Even married women—whose proper concern was really *Küche, Kinder,* and, if it could not be avoided, *Kirche*[25]—and men above normal working age were encouraged to seek gainful employment after 1936, while a year of service for young women was made compulsory in 1935.[26] Attempts were made to overcome the growing shortage of skilled industrial workers through improved vocational training of apprentices, greater labor mobility and the like. From 1937 onward, however, the essential industries could only be provided with the necessary workers through the controlling activities of labor exchanges, which led to an almost complete abolition of freedom of domicile and freedom of employment. All these control devices developed over the years, as ineffective regulations were replaced by operative ones, while old loopholes were closed and new regulatory agencies opened. The Nazis were slowly but surely creating a governmentally guided economy where state directives instead of the laws of the market determined production and consump-

24. Orders could be enforced through the mulcting measures of the compulsory business organizations, after that by the courts, and ultimately by the Gestapo.

25. The "three K's" stand for kitchen, children and church.

26. These young girls, engaged as nurses and maids in homes and on farms, would free mothers and agricultural workers for other gainful employment.

tion, helped by the availability of well-trained and generally loyal civil servants and the existence of a dense system of industrial federations and economic associations.

During the first two years of their regime, the Nazis had subdivided the German economy into seven Reich Groups (industry, commerce, banking, insurance, power production, tourist trade, handicrafts) and combined these functional organizations with regional ones, i.e., the local chambers of commerce and industry, under the umbrella of the Reich Economic Chamber *(Reichswirtschaftskammer)* which in turn was subordinate to the minister of economics. This subordination to the state was, apart from the factor of compulsory membership, the main distinguishing feature of the new setup, while otherwise these organizations were structured along the lines of those existing previously. The same applies to the multitude of subdivisions, which in the case of the Reich Group Industry alone meant 31 Economic Groups (the former *Verbände*), subdivided into 161 Trade Groups and 137 Trade Subgroups, not counting some 332 District Groups, established for the representation of regional interests within an industry or a number of industries. In spite of the introduction of the leadership principle, such a great number of organizations tended, of course, to impede successful direction of the economy from the top, as a consequence of overlapping jurisdictions and multiple memberships. On the other hand sufficient leeway was left in the hands of the individual industrialist, as the new organizational setup was to combine so-called "responsible economic self-administration" with general direction by the public authorities.

In the long run, the Nazis aimed essentially at an economic system which would be an alternative to capitalism and communism, supporting neither a laissez faire attitude nor total planning. Consequently the state rid itself of some property, denationalizing and demunicipalizing a few undertakings,[27] and thus widening the sphere of individual ownership. Management and risk of business were to be left in the hands of private individuals to maintain personal initiative and enterprise. Excessively egoistic pursuit of private interests was, however, to be restrained by the massive machinery of "responsible economic self-administration" and an army of state officials watching over compliance with innumerable instructions and orders, together giving rise to a portentous "paper war" *(Papierkrieg)*. Though certainly not frictionless, the German economic machine worked and worked quite well, on a narrowly economic level, compared to other economic systems of the time. The organizational setup described enabled planning without

27. Without much publicity the Reich sold its share in banks with a branch system to a consortium of the "Big Three," whose reprivatization was essentially completed by 1936. Confiscated Jewish property was "aryanized" and sold to private individuals.

a fixed plan and the continued use of the price mechanism as an economic steering device, aiming at a balance between adaptability and stability. To characterize this time-consuming search for a new economic order and the necessary period of experimentation solely as senseless and unsystematic attempts to muddle through is tantamount to misunderstanding Nazi intentions and objective possibilities. Contempt for the political and social doctrines of the Nazis should not interfere with a dispassionate analysis of their economic system. The Nazis subscribed neither to central planning along Soviet lines nor to the market economy of the Western world, but selectively and without dogmatic qualms used those economic tools that seemed to serve their purposes. In one substantial sector of the economy, however, Nazi economy was significantly influenced by ideological considerations: that is, in agriculture.

Agricultural Autarky

Very soon and very quickly agriculture was reorganized in accordance with the principles of the corporate state. As early as September 1933 two laws concerning the *Reichsnährstand* (literally Reich Food Estate) and the *Erbhof* (hereditary farm)were passed, fundamentally altering German agriculture. The first law stipulated that henceforth an all-embracing national cartel would regulate food production and distribution. Farming, processing, shipping, storing, wholesaling and retailing would be controlled to ensure stable food prices and farm wages, lower taxes and fertilizer costs, as well as fair profits, through the curtailment of the middlemen's margins and the abolition of speculative dealings. A multitude of nationwide vertical commodity boards (e.g., for grain, dairy products, etc.) provided the administrative machinery, which combined direct guidance through orders and prohibitions with steering by means of administrated prices, for the realization of these goals. The core of this organizational setup was to be the *Erbhof*. This entailed estate, i.e., an agricultural production unit of between 7.5 and 125 hectares (approx. 18 to 310 acres), was declared nontransferable and indivisible. It could not be sold or mortgaged and could be bequeathed in its entirety only to a single male heir, who had to be *"bauernfähig"* ("farmer-worthy").[28] To a certain extent the *Erbhof* legislation was based on ideological considerations requiring the creation and preservation of a large farm population as the *"Blutquell der Nation"* ("blood-well of the nation"), and thus corresponding with the population theories of the Nazis. Their aim of raising the birth rate was vigorously pursued through various incentives, including extensive

28. In 1933 some 640,000 hereditary farms were established, comprising about 40 percent of the land under cultivation and housing over 5 million people.

prenatal care, tax reductions for large families, marriage loans, and the awarding of the *"Mutterkreuz"* (i.e., Mother's Medal), and through severe, even draconic legislation. After 1933 an abortion would be granted only in exceptional cases; from 1941 onward the production of contraceptive devices was largely prohibited. After 1943 the repeated practice of abortion would be punished by death.

The more economic rationale behind the *Erbhof* legislation was to stop the rural exodus and to establish a sound basis for agricultural autarky. The results were quite mixed: while the migration from agriculture to industry could not be halted (the percentage of gainfully employed persons in agriculture declined from 29 percent in 1933 to 26 percent in 1939), agricultural self-sufficiency increased somewhat. German agriculture supplied 68 percent of food calories consumed in 1928, 75 percent in 1932, 81 percent in 1936, and 83 percent in 1938/39. Given the increase in per capita consumption and the rise in population (about 400,000 annually), it was no small achievement in the crop year of 1937/38 to produce from domestic sources 89 percent of Germany's own needs in grain, 90 percent in milk and dairy products, 95 percent in meat, 74 percent in fish, and 79 percent in eggs. Regarding German fat supplies, however, the picture was less bright, as the wide "fat-gap" *(Fettlücke)* could not be closed and about half of Germany's needs still had to be imported in 1939. For years after 1933 the *"Erzeugungsschlacht"* ("battle of production") in agriculture was hampered by a series of relatively unfavorable harvests, which—together with a rising demand for income-elastic quality foodstuffs—led to temporary shortages of meat and butter in many urban areas. From 1937 on considerable quantities of fats, as well as fodder, protein and grain, were imported and stored in order to ease this pressure. Adjustments were also made on the ideological level and some pet ideas, for example the favoring of prolific smallholders, began to give way increasingly to economic practicality. The largest estate owners and big farmers in particular benefitted from a policy that encouraged the intensification and expansion of agricultural production through extensive reductions in fertilizer prices and cuts in taxes and interest rates. Altogether expenditures for fertilizers doubled between 1933/34 and 1938/39, and at the same time the amounts expended on acquiring agricultural machinery and farm equipment tripled. These improvements and others, like the reclamation of waste land and campaigns to raise the average standard of cultivation, made it generally possible to maintain the per capita consumption of foodstuffs.[29] At the outbreak of World War II German

29. Increase in per capita consumption between 1929 and 1937: flour 3 percent, potatoes 1 percent, sugar 2 percent, meat 2 percent, fish 33 percent, coffee 10 percent, cigars and cigarettes almost 20 percent; there was, however, a decrease in fats (lard, butter, margarine) of 3 percent, in milk of 5 percent, in eggs of 13.5 percent, and in tropical fruit of 25 percent.

agriculture was as fully developed as was technically and economically possible. The long-cherished hopes of Allied experts before and during the war that Germany could be starved into submission, as in World War I, remained wishful thinking. Equally erroneous reasoning and misinterpretation of facts misled many a professional observer regarding Germany's industrial development.

Industrial Independence and External Economic Relations

Achieving autarky in the industrial sector was the third main objective of Nazi economic policy, in addition to promoting employment and securing rearmament. World War I had clearly shown that protection against economic warfare was as important as powerful armed forces. To enhance German self-sufficiency and achieve coordination of the state's economic intervention as far as possible were the aims of the Four-Year Plan of 1936, which is quite frequently seen as a break in prewar Nazi economic policy. This plan was peculiar, proclaiming goals without specifying methods or presenting a timetable for their attainment, and concerning itself only with some sectors of the economy, emphasizing partial instead of total planning. Public and private sectors of the economy were to cooperate. The state would either entice private businessmen to its own ends, by granting subsidies or making sales or profit guarantees, or it would order industrialists from a particular branch of production to form compulsory partnerships (*Pflichtgemeinschaften*) to undertake a set assignment. Only as an exception, if the task was clearly beyond the means and abilities of private industry, were state firms to be founded. To strengthen Germany's industrial base, four aims were pursued: expansion of capacities; increased technical rationalization; decentralization of industrial production; and greater self-sufficiency in raw materials.

Little quantitative evidence is available as to the extent to which industrial capacities were increased—one main reason being changes in territory. The incorporation of Austria and the Sudetenland in 1938 added about 12 percent to the industrial labor force, and probably a similar amount to industrial capacity. In the Reich proper, industry on average increased its annual gross expenditures for capital purposes from 1 billion RM in 1933/34 to 4.1 billion RM in 1938/39, of which 63 percent and 80 percent respectively fell to the capital-goods industries.[30] Rationalization encompassed limitation of the number of types in order to make the most of the advantages of large-scale production, standardization of replacement parts to facilitate repairs and curb inventories, increase of labor productivity through the introduction of optimal methods, and proper selection of plant size to enhance the transparency of production planning. Though many of these attempts

30. The corresponding figures for 1928/32 are 1.5 billion RM and 65 percent.

were frustrated by private special interests, the volume of industrial production increased in the enlarged Reich by 14 percent per capita between 1936 and 1938, although the previous all-time high of industrial production in 1928/29 had already been surpassed in 1935. All in all the production of consumer goods increased by one-half between 1932 and 1939, while the capital-goods industry tripled its output, partly reflecting the greater expansion of the capital-goods sector typical during an economic upswing, as well as the greater emphasis on armaments production. To avoid enemy action against German industrial plants, a policy of dispersion was adopted so as to shift production from the highly industrialized border areas (the Ruhr, Upper Silesia, Saxony) to new locations in the center of Germany (the Hanover-Magdeburg-Halle area), which were supposedly safe from air raids and ground attacks.[31] Though in so few years no thorough reorganization of industrial location could be accomplished, various industries in central Germany showed significantly faster growth than those in the west. Since the supply of industrial raw materials could be improved only in a few isolated cases through increased agricultural production or opening up new mines, emphasis was placed on recycling and production of synthetic goods.[32] Attention focused on the manufacturing of fuel, rubber, textiles, the use of light metals instead of heavy ones and, to a lesser extent, on the production of substitutes for leather, nonferrous metals and fats. Germany, which had been regarded by foreign experts around 1930 as "especially disadvantaged" in its raw material supply, was able to overcome some of these shortages mainly through the advances of its chemical industry.[33] But it never achieved true autarky, apart from a few exceptions.[34] Substantial deficits of some strategic raw materials remained a serious weakness. Tight control of raw materials and their extensive stockpiling would at best provide temporary self-sufficiency.

Since Germany never fully succeeded in becoming self-sufficient in its industrial and agricultural necessities, economic ties with foreign countries remained important. The broad domestic recovery program of the Nazis, with its concomitant increase in income, led rapidly—given the relatively high propensity to import—to a growing demand

31. Prime show cases of this policy of dispersion were the Reichswerke at Salzgitter and the Volkswagen plants at Wolfsburg.

32. Old rubber was recycled and used oil purified; empty cans, used toothpaste tubes or any other kind of scrap metal were gathered in salvage campaigns by school children, satisfying primarily their instinct for play and treasure hunting, rather than the economy's demand for raw materials.

33. Between 1936 and 1942, production of synthetic fuel and of aluminum roughly tripled, while the output of plastics rose fivefold.

34. In 1938, home production exceeded domestic requirements for coal by 16 percent, potash by 43 percent, salt by 18 percent, cement by 7 percent, and graphite by 11 percent.

for foreign manufactured goods and raw materials essential for the extension of domestic production. At the same time Germany's export trade, which had already suffered from the devaluation of foreign currencies[35] decreased. The considerable balance-of-trade surpluses of the early thirties thus soon became a transient phenomenon, dwindling to mere 0.7 billion RM in 1933 and giving way to a small deficit of about 0.4 billion RM in 1934. A larger deficit was avoided because the loose exchange controls established during the banking crisis of 1931 had been tightened.[36] With the further speedy deterioration of Germany's foreign exchange position, the old system of percentage allocation of foreign exchange became inadequate and was superseded by the so-called New Plan designed by Reichsbank President Schacht in September 1934.[37] This scheme converted exchange regulations from a temporary stopgap measure to safeguard the Reichsmark into a permanent and unusually effective instrument in the tool kit of foreign economic policy.

The Nazi regime preferred tighter exchange controls instead of a downward adjustment of the Reichsmark as a means of alleviating the pressures on the balance of payments. A devaluation had become a distinct possibility, because there was no longer much danger of sparking off an international depreciation race—which was already well under way—or of increasing the money or nominal burden as well as the real burden of foreign claims against Germany, since the de facto nullification of reparations and the cessation of interest and redemption payments on private debts had eliminated this fear.[38] However, besides two irrational, though by no means invalid reasons—the popular fear of inflation and considerations of internal prestige—other more tangible facts argued against a policy of devaluation and for tighter exchange controls. Without exchange restrictions, i.e., by restoring the free convertibility of the Reichsmark, the German upswing would have had to proceed in cadence with the slow international recovery. Such a limitation of action in internal economic policy was regarded as undesirable, the more so as the Nazis attributed no im-

35. In April 1933 the United States suspended the gold standard and allowed the dollar to depreciate; a currency depreciation race followed. As the gold content of the Reichsmark remained unchanged, its value increased from about 24 U.S. cents to just over 40.

36. German importers initially received foreign currency amounting to 100 percent of their previous imports; this was reduced to 75 percent during 1932, and finally to 50 percent. As the decline in economic activity had considerably lowered world market prices as well as Germany's needs, these controls for quite a while presented only small obstructions to imports. Foreign creditors could still repatriate interest and redemption payments, though not the principal.

37. By spring 1934 the percentage allotments to importers were reduced from 50 to 5 percent; eventually only day-by-day allocations based on the Reichsbank's intake of foreign currency were possible.

38. In July 1933 Germany had restricted the transfer of interest and redemption payments; they were suspended altogether after June 1934.

portance to the reintegration of the German economy into the world market by means of a devaluation but on the contrary gave preference to economic isolation. Furthermore, the allocation of foreign currency had become increasingly useful as a means of influencing and controlling industries dependent on imported raw materials. Finally, as German recovery was based on an expanding domestic demand and not on an increase of exports, there was no point in deliberately worsening the country's terms of trade[39] through devaluation. This was something other nations had to put up with in trying to initiate recovery by increasing exports and reducing imports. Many trading nations shared this self-defeating idea, and the pursuit of a "beggar-my-neighbor" policy ensured not only sluggish national recoveries, but also the fact that total international trade in 1936 and 1938 still hovered around the low 1932 level of some 110 billion RM, which represented less than 40 percent of the 1929 figure.

The tight exchange controls introduced by the New Plan not only enabled Germany to square her balance of payments in the following years, but also to achieve indirectly a greater degree of national self-sufficiency through emphasis upon foreign trade with areas most likely to remain reliable import sources in times of conflict, such as Scandinavia, the Balkans and the Near East. Though the dependence of many small countries upon the German market increased considerably after 1934, and in the case of some southeast European countries even became overwhelming,[40] their share of total German foreign trade remained modest.[41] Apart from some changes in the regional structure,[42] German trade as a whole developed along rather similar lines to international trade and enabled Germany basically to maintain her share in world trade. This amounted to about 9.5 percent in 1929, 1932, and 1938, though in 1936 it fell to 8.5 percent. While the development of total German trade did not show any signs of turning away from the world market,[43] the efforts to promote national autarky became more visible in the changing structure of German imports. The Nazi aspiration to draw national food supplies "from the native soil" (*"aus eigener*

39. Terms of trade reflect the relation between export and import prices.
40. E.g., by 1939 Bulgaria received 66 percent of her imports from Germany, to which she directed 68 percent of her exports.
41. Percentage shares in German imports (1932 and 1938): Southeastern Europe 5, 9.8; Northern Europe 6.4, 11.4; Near East 2.5, 3.8. Percentage shares in German exports (1932 and 1938): Southeastern Europe 3.5, 10.3; Northern Europe 9.4, 12.9; Near East 1.3, 5.4.
42. Percentage shares in German imports (1932 and 1938): U.S. 12.7, 7.4; Great Britain 5.5, 5.2; remaining Western Europe 15.1, 11.9. Percentage shares in German exports (1932 and 1938): U.S. 4.9, 2.8; Great Britain 7.8, 6.7; remaining Western Europe 31.9, 20.8.
43. In this respect Germany held a mid-position, as between 1929 and 1938 Britain increased its share from 13.2 percent to 14.2 percent, while the American percentage fell from 14 to 10.9.

Scholle") was clearly reflected in declining food imports, the five-year averages of which dropped between 1928/32 and 1933/37 by 40 percent in volume and 60 percent in value. Regarding the import of manufactured articles—the most significant indicator for an industrialized country of its participation in the international division of labor—the decrease was even more pronounced, partly reflecting and continuing the process of disintegration of the world economy since 1929. While Germany received 2.5 billion RM worth of foreign manufactured commodities in value and 2.3 million tons in volume in the last predepression year of 1928, by 1932 this had dropped to 0.7 billion RM and 1.0 million tons, and by 1938 to a mere 0.4 billion RM and 0.5 million tons. These imports—as well as the necessary raw material supplies[44]—were paid for only with considerable difficulty, in spite of the exchange controls and the fact that the terms of trade had quite substantially turned in Germany's favor. This change was due to some extent to developments on the world market, where prices for industrial products had fallen less sharply than those for raw materials and agricultural products; but it was also partly due to the fact that Germany, with its quickly recuperating economy, could advantageously use its national bargaining strength in bilateral trade negotiations.

Bilateral clearing agreements had been introduced by those countries which had been forced to install foreign currency regulations because of the depression. These agreements were aimed at bypassing the foreign exchange market and mitigating the trade-hampering effects of these controls. Initially some multinational enterprises trading with their subsidiaries, and the few remaining foreign trade companies engaged in both import and export business, could internally arrange for their own clearing of foreign currency balances. But since regional specialization in foreign trading had long given way to product specialization, which made such internal clearing impossible, new private and semiofficial information agencies were established in 1932 with the aim of increasing contacts between importers and exporters and organizing payments in foreign commodities instead of in foreign currencies, thus widening this system of barter trade. Eventually governments themselves attempted to enlarge this barter trade and improve its organization. As early as 1932 Germany signed her first clearing agreements with some Balkan states, whose exchange controls had hindered the transfer of accumulated credit balances of German exporters. In 1934 many West European countries requested such

44. Though the total volume of German imports of raw materials and semimanufactured products had fallen between 1928 and 1938 by about 7 percent, the volume of imported iron ores increased by 60 percent and that of other processed ores by as much as 470 percent.

clearing agreements with Germany, so that the transfer of interest and redemption payments, which had been stopped a short time before, could be resumed; part of German export earnings was reserved for this purpose.[45] Consequently by the mid-1930s Germany had made clearing agreements of various types with almost all her major trading partners by opening bilateral accounts, into which importers paid in inland currency the amount owed to their foreign supplier, and from which exporters were paid in inland currency. As each clearing arrangement represented a closed system involving only two currencies, many different rates of exchange came into being. These could not, of course, be balanced out through arbitrage dealings in foreign currencies, thus making possible partial upward or downward revaluations of the Reichsmark against the currencies of certain countries. As a final refinement, while trading with one and the same country, different rates were used depending on the types of goods being traded. Though voluntary agreement had to be reached on the rates of exchange between the two negotiating countries, the one with the superior bargaining power was in a better position to achieve more favorable conditions. Hence for example the countries of southeastern Europe, which faced serious economic problems, especially in their export industries, due to their overvalued currencies, foreign trade restrictions and the worldwide depression in general, had to make concessions to the German negotiators to prevent any interruption in bilateral trade and to pacify their own exporting industries. Whether this manipulation of the German terms of trade can be expressed reasonably by the catchword "exploitation" seems to be quite doubtful, since Germany was never able to act as a monopolist, be it on the supply or demand side, nor to dictate prices or volume of trade. Trading with Germany on less favorable terms was probably more advantageous for her trading partners than not trading at all, since it provided employment for export industries and had a positive effect on their national incomes. Although German foreign economic policy clearly aimed at maximizing national interest,[46] as defined by the economic and political tenets of the regime, Nazi trade policy increased Germany's military preparedness only to a modest degree.

45. In April 1933 the Reichsbank had voluntarily transferred close to RM 0.5 billion—signaling good intentions and future impotence—by totally depleting its reserves. Between 1933 and 1939 reserves never surpassed RM 80 million, or about 4 percent of those held between 1925 and 1929. Between February 1933 and 1938 Germany decreased her foreign indebtedness from RM 19 billion to 10 billion.

46. In the 1930s the German bilateral trading system was condemned as "Schachtism" by the English-speaking world, although it was much less harmful to international trade than the generally practiced "beggar-my-neighbor" policy.

Prepared and Forced to go to War?

The allegation that the Nazis had built up a large war machine and the prophecy of a speedy collapse of the German economy ranked among the main arguments used to discredit the Nazi system abroad during the 1930s. Regarding the stability of the economy, it was contended that the Nazis had created a kind of war economy in peacetime, with full employment depending on continuous armament expenditures, which would increasingly produce inflationary pressures and thus a state of instability. Only war and conquest, which would bring additional raw materials, foodstuffs, and new additions to the labor force, could offer Hitler a narrow escape from a catastrophic economic collapse. According to other foreign observers, however, neither considerations of economic theory[47] nor the way in which the recovery policy had been handled justified such conclusions. In a country where wages were fixed, prices controlled and labor rationed, where volume and direction of production and foreign trade were strongly determined by the state, it was difficult to see how inflationary pressures could develop and threaten the economic equilibrium. Furthermore, the stabilization of economic activity did not depend upon continuous military expenditures. A certain intellectual bias along the lines of the theory of the "mature economy"[48] must have conditioned contemporary commentators to overlook or to underestimate the possibilities of directing productive powers into housing, transport, urban rebuilding, expansion of individual consumption, and the like. The established methods of economic control were indeed sufficient to carry out such rechannelling and to give Hitler ample freedom of action. His foreign policy of aggressive brinkmanship was not forced upon him by an economic system containing the germs of collapse. While the question of the permanent peacetime stability of the Nazi economic system quickly became an academic problem, interest increased in the actual size of the Nazi war machine.

In the late 1930s and during much of the war, it was assumed that for years Hitler had geared the German economy for total war, since the creation of an enormous war machine was seen as the primary purpose of Nazi economic policy. An impressive number of foreign journalists and pamphleteers, not infrequently German expatriates, had

47. It should not be forgotten that economic theory itself at the time underwent a thorough rejuvenating process.

48. Economists suggested a tendency toward secular economic stagnation as a consequence of declining investment opportunities owing to slackening population growth, the near closure of the economic "frontier," and the capital-saving function of technological progress.

maintained for years that a monolithic, militaristic, highly efficient economic machine was at the disposal of the Nazis. Naturally the latter in their turn and time had little interest to set the record straight. But even today the view is prevalent in many publications on the prewar period that by 1939 Germany had built up a military machine of enormous comparative strength, and that Hitler had long subordinated all economic considerations to the central task of thoroughly preparing for war. Studies of the Nazi economy undertaken by detached economists after the war have clearly established that by September 1939 the German economy was inadequately prepared for war, and that furthermore in the following years it fell far short of a total mobilization for the war effort. Anglo-American studies, which began with the United States Strategic Bombing Survey of 1945, emphasized Germany's high civilian consumption, her limited armaments expenditures, the small degree of self-sufficiency and the inadequate mobilization of manpower at the end of the 1930s.

Even with the rearmament program, civilian consumption rose substantially. The gross national product of 1933, amounting to 75 billion RM in 1928 prices, consisted of 59 billion in consumer expenditures, 4 billion in private gross capital formation and 12 billion in government expenditures; the gross national product of 1938—126 billion RM in 1928 prices—was composed of 74, 16 and 36 billion RM for the three categories. Though researchers face serious statistical problems, even the most cautious among them have to acknowledge that in the same period both private investment in consumer-goods industries and public expenditure for nonmilitary purposes increased substantially, in fact doubled at least. Military expenditure did rise in absolute and relative terms, as previously indicated. Nevertheless a comparison of the actual military forces at the disposal of the belligerents in September 1939 shows that Germany was only in some respects stronger than any one of her three adversaries, but was certainly substantially weaker than the combined enemy forces.

On the Continent her 105 divisions, about half of them ready for action, faced 40 Polish, 4 British and 94 French divisions, of which about two-thirds qualified for combat service. All the same, what the German army lacked in quantity it could partly make up in quality. About 3,200 German tanks confronted 2,200 French, 1,100 British and 200 Polish tanks, all of which included a larger proportion of light models, more suitable for infantry support than genuine tank attack. Besides their emphasis on tank forces, German military planners had stressed the importance of air power, and almost half of Germany's prewar military expenditures had been allocated to the Luftwaffe. Nevertheless, only some 3,600 planes (mostly of firstline category) had to face about 1,000 modern French planes and no less than 3,500 British planes, of which slightly over 40 percent were of recent vintage. Although in general the German planes were of a better quality, none of them were suitable for a strategic air offensive, but only for support of advancing ground forces in tactical action. While in the air and on land the odds were clearly on Germany's side as long as she had to face only a single one of her enemies, their combined strength was superior. The heaviest margin of superiority was enjoyed by the Western Allies at sea, where German forces were quite deficient. The Anglo-German agreement of 1935 had permitted German parity in submarine strength and the expansion of German naval tonnage to 35 percent of the British figure. While in 1939 Germany had 56 U-boats to Britain's 57 submarines, she had not undertaken any other significant naval expansion, remaining far below the agreed-upon ceiling. At the outbreak of war Germany possessed 3 pocket battleships, 2 old battleships, 2 battle cruisers, 5 light cruisers, and 17 destroyers. In almost all categories this added up to about half the size of the French navy alone or a dwarfish fraction of the Royal Navy's 12 battleships, 6 aircraft carriers, 35 cruisers, and 200 destroyers. Faced with the certainty of an unbreakable sea blockade in time of war, all-out attempts to ensure German self-sufficiency in raw materials were not at all surprising.

Though it is true that over the years substantial efforts had been made to increase self-sufficiency, Germany was still painfully dependent on essential imports in 1939, a fact Hitler and the German Staff were amply aware of. Germany still needed to import 65 percent of her iron ore and oil requirements, and only about half of the latter came from European sources. As regards copper, lead and zinc, Germany's dependence upon ore imports was even greater in 1939 than in 1933, since her refining industry had grown faster than domestic mining. Although about 80 percent of her civilian and military consumption of aluminum could be domestically processed, 90 percent of the necessary bauxite had to be imported, though almost entirely from relatively secure suppliers like Hungary and Yugoslavia. While the German chemical industry had succeeded in producing sufficient rubber, about 80 percent of all textile raw materials had to be imported in 1938. In a wide variety of foodstuffs Germany had attained a substantial degree of self-sufficiency. In bread grain, potatoes, sugar, meat, milk and coarse vegetables domestic production sufficed, but it was inadequate for fodder, fruit, eggs, and fats. Over 40 percent of the consumption of the last item was imported, reflecting the *"Fettlücke"* ("fat-gap"), the only serious food problem. Neither distribution controls nor stockpiling programs could basically overcome the scarcity in these important agricultural and industrial products. Reserves of such vital materials as bauxite, iron and copper ores were far below even half a year's requirements, while stockpiled tires and aviation gasoline would last for one month and five months respectively—at regular peace time consumption rates.

Alleged German thoroughness was also missing in the mobilization of manpower, as neither the proportion of the gainfully employed nor their working time was increased. Slightly over two-thirds of the population of working age was gainfully employed in 1939, as in 1925, and the average weekly working hours in industry increased by only 4 percent, from 46 hours in 1929 to 47.8 in 1939. Neither was this altogether quite stable labor input shifted from civilian to military-related activities. While the agricultural labor force declined, contrary to the demographic intentions of the Nazis, and public employment increased, primarily reflecting the buildup of an army of nearly 1.5 million men by 1939, the proportional size of the industrial labor force differed little in 1939 from that of 1925, and the share of consumer-goods industries in industrial employment had likewise hardly changed.

Several elements may explain the modest scale of Germany's economic and military preparedness. The lingering public fear of currency depreciation set a rather rigid limit to the deficit-financing of a larger rearmament program, especially from 1936 onward, when the economy was operating at a full employment level. Little consideration was given to an increase in taxation as an alternative to deficit spending, because the Nazis had promised "guns *and* butter." This desire not to openly impair civilian consumption—be it out of pride or in fearful anticipation of adverse public opinion inside and outside the party—showed itself clearly in the reluctance to substitute larger raw material imports for foreign food purchases from 1937 onward, and in the unwillingness to move production factors from unessential occupations into activities of strategic importance. The limited resources earmarked for such purposes were frequently misallocated, since rampant inefficiency characterized planning and execution of the armament-production program as well as the utilization of raw materials. This partly reflected the lack of leadership and the existence of strong interest groups within the Nazi party, as class antagonisms and diverging social interests were now internalized. Instead of providing dictatorial centralization and totalitarian administration, the Nazi regime has been compared by historians to "a court as negligible in its power of ruling, as incalculable in its capacity for intrigue as any oriental sultanate." Besides feuding among themselves, party chieftains and local bigwigs generally opposed cuts in private consumption and nonmilitary public expenditure (e.g., municipal improvements, party and prestige buildings), and, as a matter of ideological conviction, increased female employment. German industrialists, another influential group acting in its own interests, frequently undermined precisely those policies aiming at improved planning and greater self-sufficiency. Though Hitler would have preferred somewhat larger armed forces, in essence his political and military strategy did not call for massive preparations. He had no desire to engage in a protracted war of attrition with strategic bombing and a sea blockade. Making a realistic assessment of his country's limited economic resources, he was intent rather on a rapid campaign, a Blitzkrieg.

2

The War Years

From Blitzkrieg to Total War

The German war economy can be divided into three roughly defined stages: the Blitzkrieg phase up to the winter of 1941/42; the two and a half years of increased economic strain till summer 1944; and finally the remaining period of about ten months of all-out efforts. The first phase, often referred to as "a peacelike war economy," began on 1 September 1939 with the campaign against Poland, whose total forces of some 3 million men were completely destroyed within 36 days at a cost of fewer than 10,000 fatal German casualties owing to a new approach to conducting war. While previously military operations had aimed at physical obliteration of the enemy forces by attrition relying on one's own numerical superiority—World War I providing the last and most brutal example—the new Blitzkrieg technique aimed at paralyzing the enemy's army by disrupting or cutting the lines of supply, communication and command by means of fast tanks and tactical bombers. Though France and Britain on account of their alliance commitments had declared war on Germany on 3 September, large-scale fighting did not begin on the western front till 10 May 1940, resulting a few weeks later in French surrender on 22 June. The third and largest land war, against Russia, started in June 1941, leading to vast territorial gains and great military successes within months. These triumphs were achieved while total output of consumer goods and overall production of armaments remained rather constant, though the composition of armament production changed according to the varying military needs of the successive campaigns from 1939 to 1941. Vehicles and mobile armor were given priority before the French campaign, airplanes and naval equipment before the Battle of Britain, general army materiel before the invasion of Russia. The Russian campaign initially went so smoothly that in anticipation of an early victory armament production was reduced before the winter of 1941. Britain, whose total national product was about 70 percent of Germany's, produced only 9 percent less in armaments in 1940 than Germany. In 1941, however, the figure rose to 32 percent above the constant German output. Consequently in the years 1940/41 the British index of civil consumption (1938 = 100) averaged 84 while the German still stood at 98.5. This maintenance of peacetime levels improved the public mood, which had been badly depressed when hostilities commenced. Germany did indeed have in those years what the leading economic journal *Der deutsche Volkswirt* had promised in November 1939: "a war economy approximating as closely as possible a peacetime economy."

By January 1942, however, the very same paper had to admit that, "The winter campaign has made it quite clear that supreme military and economic efforts are required of the German people." Russia, whose economic potential had been vastly underrated, had started to counterattack by late November 1941, forcing Hitler to abandon the Blitzkrieg concept and his hopes of a Russian defeat within five months. Furthermore, in December 1941 the United States had entered the war as an open combatant after years of assistance to Britain under the "arsenal of democracy" policy.[49] In February 1942 the German armory was entrusted to Albert Speer, who as minister of armaments substantially and quickly increased the munitions output, the index of which rose in two major advances from 100 in the first quarter of 1942 to 184 in the first quarter of 1943 and, after a rather stable performance at around 208 in the remaining three quarters of 1943, to 260 in the second quarter of 1944, reaching an absolute maximum of 279 in the third quarter of that year. This brilliant performance, which greatly perplexed Allied intelligence, reflected — besides Speer's personal ability and the preparatory work of his predecessor — the amount of economic leeway still available in Germany and the increased emphasis on central control of the economy.

This achievement was not the result of a general increase in German industrial production, which throughout the war remained rather stable, but followed from shifts in the production structure and considerable changes in the employment of labor.[50] Though the size of the German army had increased from 1.4 million men (May 1939) to 7.2 million men (May 1941), this total drain of about 6 million men (about 200,000 had been lost) had decreased the civilian labor force by only 10 percent, to about 36.2 million, owing to the employment of about 3 million foreigners and prisoners of war. This non-German labor force

49. Previously, in an undeclared war, attacks by the U.S. Navy on German warships had been quite common, although Hitler had ordered his fleet to take evasive action.

50. German industrial production (1938=100): 1939, 106; 1940, 102; 1941, 105; 1942, 106; 1943, 110; 1944, 108. Shares in total industrial production in 1938 as against 1944: building industry, 25 percent, 5 percent; consumer-goods industry, 30 percent, 25 percent; capital-goods industry, 19 percent, 10 percent; basic-materials industry, 19 percent, 20 percent; armaments industry, 7 percent, 40 percent.

was raised to 4.2 million in 1942, 6.3 million in 1943 and 7.1 million in 1944, which added up to almost 20 percent of the civilian labor force in the Reich, compared to 3 percent and 8 percent during the Blitzkrieg years of 1940 and 1941. Compared to the harsh practices applied in Eastern Europe, recruitment in the West was on a more voluntary basis, though conscription occurred there as well and Vichy France was pressured into yielding her most skilled workers to Germany. This growing reliance on non-German workers was regarded as necessary because of the increasing drain by the army—by May 1944, 9.1 million men were under arms, while 3.3 million had already been killed in action—and the relatively unsuccessful drive to increase the German civilian labor force. Attempts to move home workers into factory employment, to hire older or retired men, and especially to guide women into gainful employment showed only limited success, inasmuch as the female labor force remained virtually stable between 1939 and 1944, fluctuating between 14.1 and 14.8 million. The limited increase in female employment particularly surprised postwar researchers abroad, and is normally explained by the previously noted Nazi conception of women's role in society, but also reflected the fairly generous financial support extended to servicemen's wives and their reluctance to leave their home and children at a time of intensified air raids.

While weekly working hours increased slightly to an average of 49.5 in industry, the shifting of workers, particularly from the tertiary sector to the two other sectors, was more important. Between May 1941 and May 1944, employment decreased by 16 percent in commerce, banking and insurance, and by 20 percent in crafts, while employment rose by 5 percent in agriculture, by 7 percent in transport, and by 6 percent in industry. Within industry, consumer-goods branches lost workers, while the basic materials and metal-using industries gained between 14 to 18 percent. The armaments industry increased its labor force by 28 percent between December 1941 and June 1944, while raising its output by 230 percent and using only about 50 percent more iron in 1943/44 than in 1939/40. Increased labor productivity and raw material economies resulting from rationalization and greater centralization of planning turned out to be the most important factor in this extraordinary increase in German armaments production. Standardization of munitions and simplification of the production process were not as rigorous as in the Allied countries, so that higher quality standards could be maintained. Since the quantitative superiority in arms production alone was possibly 9:2 in favor of the Allies, German policy in this phase was based on the principle "quality versus quantity."[51]

51. The development of new weapons throughout the war time and again gave the German forces a temporary armaments superiority. The machine gun 42 with its 1,500

It is no gross exaggeration to maintain that this principle was applied in the opposite sense as regards the production of consumer goods, the index of which (1938=100) still stood at 86 in 1944. However, since the armed forces took up a substantial share of such goods, expert estimates run at only 50 to 60 percent of the prewar level per civilian, which would be about one-tenth less than at the trough of the depression in mid-1932. Due to air raid damage—by late 1943 6 percent of homes had already been destroyed or heavily damaged—demand for consumer durables increased, but the situation was continuously made worse through the deterioration of product quality. Most textiles eventually were dryly referred to as made of "German wood" instead of "English wool" or "French silk." But by 1943/44, when about 40 percent of all shoes were made of leather substitutes, reducing the lifespan of a pair from the usual 33 to 4 months, humor also became a commodity in short supply. Poorer quality also became more common in food, as animal products had to be replaced by plant foodstuffs. Meat rations were cut in half in June 1943 and fat rations by a quarter in March 1944, but the per capita calorie intake remained at a reasonably high level.[52] This relatively high German food consumption was maintained through drastic rationing in the occupied territories, which also supplied a considerable portion of manufactured consumer goods. More and more orders for furniture, shoes and textiles were placed with French and Belgian firms, since such production entailed no security risk and was relatively safe against Allied air raids. Aerial attacks against German industrial sites, though inconvenient, had caused only marginal damage, so that by mid-1944 the German war economy was at the height of its capacity. Armament output was higher than ever; basic-materials industries performed at a level that would permit independence of foreign supplies for a long time, and ancillary industries were amply equipped to fulfill the current requirements of the armaments and consumer-goods industries, apart from having accumulated considerable stocks of almost all materials.

The period from mid-1944 until the capitulation in May 1945 covers the third and final phase of Germany's war economy, characterized by utmost exertion of the country's productive powers. The continuously insatiable demand of the armed forces for soldiers necessitated the lowering of the draft age from seventeen and one half to

---

shells per minute, the jet fighter Me262 with its 900 km per hour speed, the rocket V2 with its 500 km range, and the heavy tanks "Tiger" and "Panther" are some of the best-known examples.

52. While the prewar daily per capita average was about 3,000 calories, it sank to 2,500 in 1941/42, to 2,200 in 1943/44, and to 1,700 by January 1945.

sixteen, which in turn contributed to a further reduction of the male civilian labor force by 1.1 million between May and December 1944. As the raising of the age limit for female conscripts from 45 to 50 years did not provide the expected numbers, the German civilian labor force decreased in 1944 by slightly over 1.2 million, of which only some 750,000 could be replaced by foreign workers. To fill the remaining gap, the regular working week was lengthened from 48 to 60 hours, but little could be done to compensate for the qualitative decline in the labor force, as highly trained workers and specialists, who for years had been classified as "irreplaceable," were now being called up. This deteriorating situation on the labor market contributed to the decision in June 1944 to abandon the previous armament policy—i.e., to offset the enemy's large-scale production through superior quality—and to concentrate on the simplified mass-production of existing weapons. Despite the general need for more labor, temporal and regional unemployment became increasingly noticeable, as territorial losses and intensified aerial bombardments began to disrupt the proper functioning of the economic machinery.

By early 1945 about one-seventh of German industrial capacity had already been occupied by the advancing Russian army, while the Western Allies had been increasing their strategic bombardment since summer 1944. For a long time these air raids had been rather ineffective in significantly reducing German war production or preventing German armed forces from continuing their operations. For years British bombardment policy laid great emphasis on area attacks at night upon major German cities in order to undermine Germany's military power through systematic destruction of her industrial and administrative centers. In addition, this "rubbing out" of urban centers was intended to have a demoralizing effect—by bringing war to their own doorsteps it was hoped to break the will of the Germans to continue fighting—as well as economic repercussions. Under the impression that the German economy was totally and efficiently mobilized for war, it was assumed that resources for restoration in the civilian sector or for reconstruction of general manufacturing plants would have to be transferred from their previous war-related functions, and thus subtracted from the war effort. Neither the thousand bomber raid on Cologne in May 1942 (400 Germans killed) nor the series of attacks on Hamburg in July/August of 1943 (40,000 casualties) nor the bombardment of Dresden on 13/14 February 1945 (35,000 dead), to list only the best-known examples of this policy of area attack, showed the desired results. The Germans after all could give as well as take, and the fighters of the Luftwaffe combined with ground air defense took a heavy toll of British bombers. Civilians furthermore kept on working either as torpid robots or filled with hate against British terror bombing—an issue Nazi hold-out propaganda did not fail to exploit.[53] In addition, the raids on Cologne and Hamburg provided Speer with the much needed evidence that further and more thorough economic mobilization was imperative. On the other hand it must be pointed out that this British bombardment from mid-1943 onward meant the establishment of a "second front," tying up a considerable amount of men and war materiel in air defense.

More successful in impeding or even dislocating the German war effort was the American strategy of daylight precision attacks against the Achilles' heel of the German economy. Like the Blitzkrieg strategy on land, this bombing policy did not aim at attrition but at paralysis of the enemy through the destruction of power plants, oil plants, railroad junctions, dams and other crucial points in the German economy. From 1943 onward the Americans undertook, at first extremely costly, daylight precision attacks against selected key point targets, e.g., in October against the rather highly concentrated German ball-bearing industry. Since substantial inventory cushions existed and the German authorities had been relatively successful in their policy of production dispersion, and demonstrated great ability in quickly reconstructing partially damaged plants, this policy of precision attacks initially showed meager results. While losses in military output due to air raids prior to mid-1943 had been insignificant, they amounted in the second half of 1943 and the first half of 1944 to some 5 percent and 10 percent respectively. In the second half of 1944, however, air attacks were sharply increased, and total tonnage of bombs dropped on Germany in these six months equalled the amount since the outbreak of the war. The main targets were the synthetic oil industry and the transportation system,[54] and by August 1944 German production of aviation gasoline amounted to a mere 10 percent of the March 1944 output, thus grounding a substantial part of the German air force, and increasing Allied air superiority even more. Since the synthetic oil industry was highly capital intensive, immediate reconstruction attempts were very difficult and largely failed. The continued high production of armaments—the munitions output index (first quarter of 1942 = 100) reached its height with 279 in the third quarter and fell only slightly to 244 in the fourth quarter of 1944—does not therefore tell the true story.[55] Delivering new weapons[56] and ammunition to the front became increasingly diffi-

53. Bombing, like the publication in January 1943 of Allied insistence on "unconditional surrender" of the Axis Powers, to some extent drove Nazis and non-Nazis closer together.

54. Of the total of some two million tons of bombs dropped, 60 percent fell between July 1944 and April 1945, and almost a third were aimed at transport installations and the oil industry.

55. Output of tanks in 1942 and 1944: 5,600, 12,100; of airplanes: 15,500, 40,600; of ammunition: 1.29 million tons, 3.36 million tons.

56. The output of Me262's rose from 124 in December 1944 to 286 in March 1945.

cult, as the transportation system was nearly crippled. The Reichsbahn, which had till mid-1944 maintained its daily freight car loadings at the 150,000 level, provided only about 90,000 in December 1944, 40,000 in February 1945, and a mere 15,000 in March that year. The general supply situation deteriorated quickly and only quite draconian measures on the part of a watchful police force prevented early disintegration and universal economic chaos, especially the spread of black markets.

Financing of the War Effort and Finis Germaniae

For quite a while effective rationing of foodstuffs and consumer goods and controls of prices and wages had been sufficient to stabilize the Reichsmark's purchasing power, permitting an upward movement of prices of merely 12 percent until 1944 in spite of an enormous increase in currency.[57] Apart from additional taxation, loans from the public and the exploitation of occupied countries, expansion in the money supply was the main Nazi method of war financing. Taxes on income and consumption were increased only slightly, so that just about one-third of the Reich's total expenditures during the war years, an estimated 657 billion RM, of which over two-thirds were allotted to the Wehrmacht, were tax-financed or covered by other internal revenue. About one-fifth was derived from long- and medium-term loans that institutional investors (banks, savings and loan associations, private insurance companies and social insurance institutions) were required to make to the Reich. Hence, the individual saver or insurant unknowingly became a creditor of the state in an operation that has been called "noiseless war financing"; in fact he subscribed to "war bonds" but had the illusion of building up real assets. Another third of the Reich's expenditures was covered by credits from the Reichsbank in exchange for treasury bills and other short-term Reich securities. The remaining eighth stemmed from war contributions and payments of occupation costs by occupied countries. But in the long run the defeated nations were scheduled to take on a much larger burden by exporting low-priced commodities which were to be sold in Germany at higher prices thus generating customslike revenues to pay off the Reich's debts, which by 20 April 1945—Hitler's last birthday—had reached 377 billion RM, compared to some 31 billion RM at the outbreak of war.

The vastly increased total monetary capital of the country contrasted starkly with the decline of Germany's material assets, which shrank from 415 to 190 billion RM between 1938 and 1945. Experts estimated the loss in value for agricultural and industrial buildings at

57. Note circulation rose from RM 8.7 billion by mid-1939 to 24.4 billion by late 1942, and 52.8 billion by early 1945.

almost 25 percent, for movable agricultural assets and residential property at 50 percent, for private tangible wealth at over 60 percent and for movable industrial property at 75 percent. For once Joseph Goebbels, minister of propaganda and master of exaggeration and deception, had been truthful when he warned that if the Nazis left the stage in defeat, they would know how to slam the door behind them. Since Hitler was convinced that the Germans had proved themselves to be inferior in the struggle for self-preservation and that the future consequently belonged to stronger nations, he saw no point in protecting the Reich against destruction. On 19 March 1945, he ordered the demolition of all military installations, transport and communications systems, industrial plants and public utilities, as well as all material assets inside the Reich. As early as late summer 1944 Hitler had advocated such a scorched-earth policy if the enemy's advance into Germany could not be halted, while Speer had favored a mere paralysis of facilities through disassembling and hiding of certain vital parts, tempting his master with the possibility of reconquering territory and restarting industrial production. When time exposed the weakness of this argument, and Hitler gave what was later called the "Nero Order" in mid-March 1945, Speer abandoned all pretence and actively thwarted the destruction policy.[58]

Destruction resulting from fighting in the course of the Allied advance, from bombing attacks, or in consequence of last ditch battles by the retreating Wehrmacht, was substantial enough to transform vast parts of Germany into a heap of rubble. The transport system, which had previously handled 70 percent of Germany's freight by rail and 20 percent on inland waterways, was probably the hardest hit sector of the German economy. A vast number of junctions, stations, tunnels, marshalling yards and switches were no longer operable, thus almost completely crippling transport by rail, which further suffered from a severe shortage of rolling stock, since less than half of the prewar number of freight cars and only about half of the locomotives were still available. As about 70 percent of the railroad bridges across waterways were down, blocking both rail and water transport, inland navigation came to a standstill as well. Germany's main river, the Rhine, for example, was completely closed after the ruins of over half of its bridges and the wrecks of some 1,700 vessels lay sunk in its waters, while the North German seaports were filled with sunken ships. Since many of these transport facilities, like industrial installations in general, had relatively good antiaircraft defences, or had already been knocked out for good, Allied strategists had shifted a sizeable share of their aerial

58. For example, he ordered the distribution of weapons to reliable engineers and executives in charge of important industrial installations threatened with destruction, and prevented local Nazi officials from laying their hands on any explosives.

strikes toward urban centers by late 1944. While overall at least one-quarter of all dwellings was destroyed, in many of the larger cities two-thirds of the homes were demolished and millions had lost all their belongings and become "bombed-outs," living in air raid shelters, emergency camps, bunkers or cellars. Berlin, where three-quarters of the living units had been lost, had become "a city of the dead";[59] in its last concert before evacuation, its Philharmonic Orchestra had appropriately played Wagner's *Die Götterdämmerung* (The Twilight of the Gods), its majestic, funereal music announcing the destruction of Valhalla, the death of the gods, and the end of the world.

Bibliography

Adam, U. D. *Judenpolitik im Dritten Reich*. Düsseldorf, 1972.

Arndt, H. W. *The Economic Lessons of the Nineteen-Thirties*. London, 1944.

Bagel-Bohlan, A. E. *Hitlers industrielle Kriegsvorbereitung 1936–1939*. Koblenz, 1975.

Barkai, A. *Das Wirtschaftssystem des Nationalsozialismus: Der historische und ideologische Hintergrund 1933–1936*. Cologne, 1977.

Bergander, G. *Dresden im Luftkrieg*. Cologne, 1977.

Bettelheim, C. *L'économie allemande sous le nazisme*. Paris, 1946.

Boelcke, W. A. "Hitlers Befehle zur Zerstörung oder Lähmung des deutschen Industriepotentials 1944/45." *Tradition* 13 (1968).

Bonnell, A. T. *German Control over International Economic Relations: 1930 to 1940*. Urbana, Ill., 1940.

Carroll, B. A. *Design for Total War: Arms and Economics in the Third Reich*. The Hague, 1968.

Dubail, R. *Une expérience d'économie dirigée: L'Allemagne national-socialiste*. Paris, 1962.

Erbe, R. *Die nationalsozialistische Wirtschaftspolitik 1933–39 im Lichte der modernen Theorie*. Zurich, 1958.

Esenwein-Rothe, I. *Die Wirtschaftsverbände von 1933 bis 1945*. Stuttgart, 1966.

Farquharson, J. E. *The Plough and the Swastika: The NSDAP and Agriculture in Germany 1928–45*. London, 1976.

Federau, F. *Der zweite Weltkrieg; Seine Finanzierung in Deutschland*. Tübingen, 1962.

Forstmeier, F., and Volkmann, H.-E., eds. *Wirtschaft und Rüstung am Vorabend des zweiten Weltkrieges*. Düsseldorf, 1975.

Genschel, H. *Die Verdrängung der Juden aus der Wirtschaft im Dritten Reich*. Göttingen, 1966.

Gersdorff, U. von. *Frauen im Kriegsdienst, 1914–1945*. Berlin, 1969.

59. These are the words of the U.S. military governor, General Clay, on his first visit to the capital.

Guillebaud, C. W. *The Economic Recovery of Germany from 1933 to the Incorporation of Austria in March 1938.* London, 1939.

Hennig, E. *Thesen zur deutschen Sozial- und Wirtschaftsgeschichte 1933 bis 1938.* Frankfurt/Main, 1973.

Henning, F. W. *Probleme der nationalsozialistischen Wirtschaftspolitik.* Schriften des Vereins für Socialpolitik. Vol. 89 NF. Berlin, 1976.

Heyl, J. D. "Hitler's Economic Thought: A Reappraisal." *Central European History* 6 (1973).

Homze, E. L. *Foreign Labor in Nazi Germany.* Princeton, 1967.

Kindleberger, C. P. *The World in Depression 1929–1939.* Berkeley and Los Angeles, 1973.

Klein, B. H. *Germany's Economic Preparations for War.* Cambridge, Mass., 1959.

Kuczynski, J. *The Economics of Barbarism: Hitler's New Economic Order in Europe.* New York, 1942.

Kuczynski, J. *Germany: Economic and Labor Conditions under Fascism.* New York, 1945. Reprint 1968.

Lärmer, K. *Autobahnbau in Deutschland 1933 bis 1945, Zu den Hintergründen.* East Berlin, 1975.

Lütge, F. *An Explanation of the Economic Conditions which Contributed to the Victory of National-Socialism in the Third Reich.* Publ. under the Auspices of the International Council for Philosophy and Humanistic Studies and with Assistance of Unesco. London, 1955.

Lurie, S. *Private Investment in a Controlled Economy: Germany, 1933–1939.* New York, 1947.

Mason, T. W. "Labour in the Third Reich, 1933–1939." *Past and Present* 33 (1966).

Mason, T. W. *Arbeiterklasse und Volksgemeinschaft: Dokumente und Materialien zur deutschen Arbeiterpolitik 1936–1939.* Opladen, 1975.

Milward, A. S. *The German Economy at War.* London, 1965.

Milward, A. S. *War, Economy and Society 1939–1945.* Berkeley and Los Angeles, 1977.

Nathan, O. *The Nazi Economic System. Germany's Mobilization for War.* Durham, N.C., 1944. Reprint 1971.

Neumann, F. *Behemoth: The Structure and Practice of National Socialism, 1933–1944.* 2nd ed. New York, 1966.

Overy, R. J. "Transportation and Rearmament in the Third Reich." *Historical Journal* 16 (1973).

Overy, R. J. "Cars, Roads and Economic Recovery in Germany, 1932–8." *Economic History Review* 28 (1975).

Petzina, D. *Autarkiepolitik im Dritten Reich.* Stuttgart, 1968.

Schröder, H. J. *Deutschland und die Vereinigten Staaten 1933–1939: Wirtschaft und Politik in der Entwicklung des Deutsch-Amerikanischen Gegensatzes.* Weisbaden, 1970.

Schweitzer, A. *Big Business in the Third Reich.* Bloomington, 1964.

Stelzner, J. *Arbeitsbeschaffung und Wiederaufrüstung 1933–36. Nationalsozialistische Beschäftigungspolitik und der Aufbau der Wehr- und Rüstungswirtschaft.* Tübingen, 1976.

Stokes, L. D. "The German People and the Destruction of the European Jews." *Central European History* 6 (1973).

Swatek, D. *Unternehmenskonzentration als Ergebnis und Mittel nationalsozialistischer Wirtschaftspolitik.* Berlin, 1972.

Treue, W. *Deutsche Wirtschaft und Politik 1933–1945.* Stuttgart, 1962.

Turner, H. A., ed. *Nazism and the Third Reich.* New York, 1972.

Turner, H. A. "Das Verhältnis des Grossunternehmertums zur NSDAP." In *Symposium "Industrielles System und Politische Entwicklung in der Weimarer Republik."* Düsseldorf, 1974.

Wagenführer, R. *Die deutsche Industrie im Kriege 1939–1945.* 2nd. ed. Berlin, 1963.

Welter, E. *Falsch und richtig planen: Eine kritische Studie über Wirtschaftslenkung im Zweiten Weltkrieg.* Heidelberg, 1954.

de Witt, T. E. J. "The Economics and Politics of Welfare in the Third Reich." *Central European History* 11 (1978).

Woolston, M. Y. *The Structure of the Nazi Economy.* Cambridge, Mass., 1941. Reprint. New York, 1968.

CHAPTER **5**

Under Western Occupation 1945–1948/49

1

The Policies of "De-" and "Dis-"

On 8 May 1945 the Wehrmacht capitulated unconditionally, and on 5 June 1945 the four Allies formally assumed governmental power over Germany, establishing the Allied Control Council in Berlin which was to exercise supreme legislative, judicial and executive authority. At Yalta in February 1945, each of them had been allotted a sector of Berlin and a zone of occupation in which the respective supreme military commander was to have executive power and sole responsibility. Since diverging interests and different ideologies soon prevented this Four-Power government from functioning jointly and unanimously, the four parts of Germany were, in fact, governed by the zone commanders by means of existing German and newly established Allied bureaucracies. At Potsdam in July/August 1945 it was agreed not to regard Germany as a political unit any longer, but to keep her decapitated and quartered for the time being. Her eastern borders remained to be determined by a future peace treaty, though about one-quarter of her territory was placed under Polish and Soviet administration.[1] Nothing was said directly about Germany's future social and economic system. However, in the fields of finance, transportation, communication, foreign trade and industry, Germany was to be treated "as a

1. Under international law, Germany's eastern territories are at present under Polish and Russian administration pending a final peace settlement.

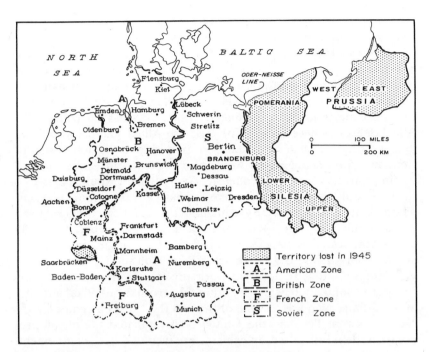

3. *Occupied Germany in 1946 and territories lost in 1945.*

whole," in order to successfully implement the agreed policies of demilitarization, denazification, administrative decentralization, economic deconcentration and industrial disarmament.

This policy of industrial-technological disarmament—of special interest to the economic historian as the only example to date of a policy of industrial retrogression—aimed in its most radical version at the complete deindustrialization and reagrarianization of Germany, as proposed by U.S. Secretary of the Treasury Morgenthau in late summer 1944. The complete destruction of the metallurgical, chemical and electrical industries, as part of a thorough conversion of Germany's economy to agriculture, would not only deprive her of the material means of waging future wars but would also be of benefit to the British in the postwar period, since they would be able to take over former German export markets.[2] Furthermore, the reparations problem would become much easier through the dismantling of German industrial plants and their delivery to the Soviet Union. This proposal, with its basic theme of "Strong Europe, Weak Germany," was officially accepted by President Roosevelt and Prime Minister Churchill at Quebec

2. Closer contact with the soil, so it was understood, would promote the moral regeneration of the savage German, tame and pacify him. Morgenthau visualized a similarly beneficial effect on the German character by a major dose of inflation and its repercussions.

in September 1944,[3] despite great misgivings on the part of the latter. The British were disquieted by an eventual political preponderance of the Soviet Union in postwar Europe, as well as by the economic drawbacks of the plan: the reagrarianization of the Ruhr and Saar industrial regions would not only render impossible a German contribution to the economic rehabilitation of Europe, since 60 percent of German exports normally originated from these areas, but could make Allied deliveries necessary, if only because Allied soldiers would not tolerate the sight of starving children. In addition, the destruction of Germany's productive power would also negatively affect her normal trading partners; and consequently, Great Britain would be able to count on only negligible exports to former German export markets. The leaking of the Quebec Agreement to the American press led to an uncommonly strong anti-Roosevelt reaction in the media. Of the 33 major American newspapers, 25 objected to the plan, not infrequently pointing out—as did U.S. Secretary of State Hull and U.S. Secretary of War Stimson—that an agrarian Germany could only sustain 60 percent of the population, while the other 40 percent would die,[4] and that Morgenthau's plan was a crime of the sort the Nazis had committed.[5] Nevertheless at Potsdam the United States initiated the major proposals on deindustrialization, which were included in the agreement, thus to a considerable extent incorporating the substance of Morgenthau's ideas on Germany into Allied policy.

The actual extent of this mass industrial destruction was established by the Allied Control Council, after considerable haggling among the victors, through the so-called Level-of-Industry Plan of March 1946. An army of Allied military and industrial experts had to determine the industrial capacity necessary to maintain in Germany "a standard of living not exceeding the average of other European countries excluding Britain and the Soviet Union," and the Control Council agreed to implement this Potsdam formula by reducing the standard of living to the level which had existed in Germany in 1932.[6] In line with this plan, German industrial capacity as a whole was to be reduced to about 50 to 55 percent of the 1938 level,[7] and consequently some 1,546 plants were to be dismantled in the Western zones alone.[8] In the

3. Roosevelt and part of the American public regarded the Germans as the devil's chosen people, from which time and again new Hitlers would spring forth. Thus Germany's power had to be broken once and for all.

4. Morgenthau considered the deportation of the excess population to North America.

5. It was generally appreciated that Morgenthau and some of his closest advisors were Jews who felt particularly strongly about Nazi atrocities and crimes.

6. Ironically, that was the year of Germany's greatest economic misery as well as of Hitler's greatest electoral successes.

7. In 1946 German industrial capacity corresponded roughly to the 1938 level.

8. The Russians advocated reductions of 60 to 70 percent, while the Western pow-

capital-goods sector—compared to the 1938 level—capacities of only one-fourth in the steel industry, about one-third in the basic chemicals and heavy engineering industries, about one-half in the cement industry, and approximately one-tenth in the machine tools industries were granted, while in the consumer-goods sector about half of the textile and shoe producing capacity and roughly one-fifth of automobile production facilities were conceded. While in almost all industries an upper limit of annual output was stipulated, e.g., 40,000 cars, 40,000 trucks, 10,000 motorcycles, 5.8 million tons of steel, some industries were banned altogether. Besides armaments, of course, the production of oceangoing ships, aircraft, synthetic gasoline and rubber, ammonia, aluminum and other light metals, electron tubes, ball bearings of all kinds and heavy machinetools was also forbidden, and all existing plants were to be destroyed. The few unrestricted industries, like furniture, glass and bicycles, were, of course, indirectly limited in their development by the reduced availability of industrial input, as Germany was denuded of much of her capital-goods industry. One heavy industry, however, was supposed to expand: the coal mining of the Ruhr, to enable the North German Coal Control Agency to organize the compulsory export of coal at below world market prices to the victor nations.[9] In addition all seagoing ships had to be turned over, as Germany was only to have coastal vessels; and German ownership of airplanes, including gliders and balloons, was henceforth illegal. Furthermore all German property abroad and, as part of "technological disarmament," all intangible assets such as patents, trademarks, licenses and firm names, were expropriated,[10] while all scientific and industrial research facilities had to close in order to end German preeminence in physics, chemistry and engineering permanently.[11] While rejecting a relatively low Soviet demand for $10 billion in reparations, the Allies at Potsdam, in recognition of the fact that the Soviet Union had as the main theater of war suffered most, agreed that the latter was to receive a share of German foreign assets as well as of the merchant fleet, the entire proceeds of dismantling in her zone and, additionally, a quarter of that of the Western zones. Of these additional deliveries from the West, 15

---

ers (the French, Americans and British—in order of increasing leniency) aimed at 30 to 40 percent. The British repeatedly insisted that they could not agree to condemn the German people to a state of perpetual misery, starvation and servitude, and that no civilized state was justified in imposing such a harsh peace on a defeated enemy.

9. Similar exports were organized for scrap and timber.

10. Altogether about 200,000 patents and some 24,000 trademarks.

11. American intelligence teams competed with their counterparts from Britain, France, and Russia in a race for "intellectual reparations." The United States acquired 650 detained German scientific experts in a program codenamed Project Paperclip, which reached its fulfillment in 1958 when Wernher von Braun and his rocket team placed the first American satellite in orbit. Thus an enforced brain-drain followed the self-inflicted one of the 1930s.

percent were, however, to be made up for in form of foodstuffs and raw materials from the Soviet zone. The ensuing Cold War not only prevented this exchange from happening—in May 1946, a mere two months after the announcement of the Level-of-Industry Plan, the Western Allies discontinued their deliveries of dismantled plants to the Soviet Union—but also initiated a change in American dismantling policy, as embodied in the revised Level-of-Industry Plan of August 1947.

The new Anglo-American plan increased the permitted level of industry in their zones by about one-third to two-fifths, bringing the statutory industrial capacity up to 70 to 75 percent of the 1938 level,[12] which meant that 687 plants were exempted from further dismantling. It was of special importance that the production limit for steel was raised from 5.8 million to 11.1 million tons, which corresponded to about 50 percent of the remaining capacity. The new directive pointed out that "an orderly and prosperous Europe requires the economic contributions of a stable and productive Germany," thus repudiating one of the basic tenets of Morgenthau's approach to postwar Germany.[13] Nevertheless, by the fall of 1947 some 859 plants remained on the dismantlement list of the three Western Allies, especially works in the steel, electrical, chemical and engineering industries. This was particularly noteworthy, since U.S. Secretary of State Marshall had on 5 June of that year presented the outline of his plan for the reconstruction of Europe. Yet in the understanding of the American government dismantling in Germany and rebuilding in Europe remained reconcilable for quite a while. In the antidismantling campaign in the United States and other Western countries, Allied economists attacked the "Strong Europe, Weak Germany" doctrine as economically fallacious, and pointed out that Germany's powerful position on the European market in the interwar period had not been an expression of economic domination, but rather a reflection of the close economic links between the European nations, for many of which Germany, in normal times, was frequently the most important customer and supplier. The artificial throttling of German industries would clearly wreak havoc on the European Recovery Program,[14] or as former President Hoover put it

12. In the consumer-goods sector all production ceilings were lifted.

13. Morgenthau's ideas had become official American policy on 14 May 1945 with the issue of the directive, known as JCS/1067, to General Clay, the U.S. military governor in Germany. He was instructed that "no steps will be taken, leading toward the economic rehabilitation of Germany or designed to maintain or strengthen the German economy." For more than two years, JCS/1067 remained the controlling directive for American occupational policies, assembled—in the words of Clay's chief advisor—"by a pack of economic idiots" who would "forbid the most skilled workers in Europe from producing as much as they can for a continent which is desperately short of everything."

14. This, or ERP for short, was the official name of the Marshall Plan.

in 1947, if Germany was to remain in economic chains, Europe would remain in rags.[15] Business and technical experts argued convincingly that dismantlement was not an efficient way of transferring reparations. While it was feasible to dismantle and ship light and relatively expensive machinery, it was generally uneconomical for heavy, bulky equipment, the type most common in the plants marked for dismantling, to be moved from its original spot. Consequently the cost of dismantling, packing and transporting frequently far exceeded the value of the equipment involved. The transfer of entire plants was considered even more wasteful since, in a given plant, size and layout of machinery were arranged and adjusted to the specific location. Removal of a plant from its original site and reerection at a new location, where conditions were likely to be different, would in most cases result in substantial losses of efficiency. Furthermore, dismantling would usually salvage no more than 10 to 15 percent of the original value of a plant.

Nevertheless, "Morgenthauism" died hard, and the Western Allies, though removing an additional 159 plants from the reparations list in April 1949, affirmed anew their intention to carry on the dismantling of 700 plants. This led the American Federation of Labor to comment that this was "a deplorable revival of the Spirit of Potsdam and the infamous Morgenthau Plan." Indeed, the race between common sense and the destructive zeal of some pressure groups and fanatics in the United States had resulted in a great speedup of dismantlement by way of the cutting-torch and explosives without regard for reutilization. Such pointless destruction increasingly led to German demonstrations, sit-in strikes and acts of nonviolent disobedience against the occupation authorities, who quickly smothered such outbursts with the threat to discontinue the vital food imports. In November 1949, when the equipment from over 600 plants had been removed and the capacity of the steel industry in the Western zones had been reduced by 6.7 million tons, the three Western Allies, in order to enhance the prestige of the government of newly established Federal Republic, exempted 17 more plants from further dismantling. For those remaining, like the Salzgitter Steel Works, dismantling was finally halted in April 1951, in the fourth year of the Marshall Plan,[16] after demonstrations by workers to save their jobs had stirred public opinion worldwide.[17]

15. It was not until 1948, the third full year of peace, that most Western countries were able to approach closely or even exceed the prewar levels of production and income.

16. At that time the Federal Republic of Germany had already received $2 billion in American aid for the reconstruction of her economy, while a total of 683 plants had been dismantled, representing approximately a value of $500–600 million.

17. Industrial disarmament lingered on in diluted form in the various restrictions imposed on the production and capacity of German steel plants and other key industries till May 1955.

While public opinion in Western countries favored the Germans during the years of the Cold War, it had played a different role in the immediate postwar period. Public opinion in the West was convinced that Germany's recent aggressive foreign policy had been concocted by her major power groups—big business, the Junkers, and the army—which had all conspired with the Nazis to wage war. To ensure future democratic and peaceful development in Germany, the victors planned to curtail the influence of these groups through demilitarization, denazification, political decentralization and economic deconcentration.

The decentralization of German administration through regional and local autonomy was, in this context, of little importance, because for quite a while German authorities had no say in economic policy matters anyway. The destruction of all military installations, and the appropriation of all matériel as spoils of war, was relatively unproblematic, too. But to "uproot the spirit of fascism and militarism" was far more complicated. Besides some reeducation measures—often of doubtful value[18]—special courts (denazification commissions) were established to screen the political past of every German. Those tainted were temporarily or permanently discharged, had to deliver part or all of their property to a relief fund for Nazi victims, or were sent to prison. In economic terms all this meant at best some altogether minor redistribution of wealth and income, as well as some redirection of human resources, not infrequently leading to a misallocation of talent, e.g., when an experienced specialist with a harmless Nazi past had to give way to an incompetent democrat.[19] By comparison, the breakup of positions of economic power, much more important in this context, consisted of land reform in agriculture and trust and cartel busting in industry. Concentration of economic power was viewed by the French as a threat to their security, by the English-speaking nations as detrimental to the proper functioning of a democratic political system, and by the Russians as unsuitable for private hands. Since only few large estates existed in the Western zones, the stipulated limitations of landed property (100 hectares in the American zone and 150 hectares per owner in the French and British zones) were of small consequence, so that little land changed hands without any compensation. The changes in the financial and industrial sphere were far more thoroughgoing. In the three Western zones an administrative body, the Liquidation Commission, was created to break up trusts and cartels,

18. Professors of history, for example, who had had too cosy a relationship with Nazism were expelled to prevent them from polluting the minds of rising generations. Forced to stay at home, they would write textbooks.

19. Reviewing denazification, the former U.S. military governor, McCloy, noted in 1950 that it would have been better "to have applied the penal aspects more promptly and effectively to the real activists while treating the great mass of lesser Nazis more leniently."

with three highly concentrated branches as the center of attention: banking, chemicals and heavy industry. The three major banks[20] were split into thirty successor institutions with geographic limits, since their previously solid grip on the German economy was regarded as harmful. As universal banks they had had considerable portfolio investments in industry and could exercise further influence by acting as proxies for their depositors at stockholders' meetings. Furthermore, their nationwide network of branches had facilitated the creation of bank money thus making them important sources of capital for industrial companies, which had to accept bank officers on their supervisory boards. The giant chemical trust, I. G. Farben, after long deliberations on how best to secure the property rights of some tens of thousands of mostly small shareholders, was finally broken up into four successor companies in 1953. While this quartering preserved the links between complementary plants to some extent, this was usually not the case in the coal and steel industries. With little regard for the established and technologically sound integration of the coal and iron branches of Germany's heavy industry, some twenty-eight independent successor companies were carved from the twelve largest coal and steel concerns, which had controlled 90 percent of Germany's steel and 50 percent of her coal capacities. The background for this decision to break the links between coal and iron was partly the desire to free coal and scrap for export.

2

An Economy of Bottlenecks

Though Germany had been a prewar raw material importing country, the immediate postwar years saw it almost completely transformed into a raw material exporter.[21] Actually, there was little else German producers had to offer foreign customers, or rather, the (Allied) Joint Export-Import Agency or its zonal predecessors, which administered all aspects of Germany's foreign trade. Consequently these bothersome and bureaucratic intermediaries had exports worth only $52 million in August-December 1945, $201 million in 1946, $315 million in 1947, and $642 million in 1948 to process. Such meager export earnings were insufficient to pay for the modest imports, which amounted to some $3.2 billion in these years, so that about two-thirds

20. Deutsche Bank, Dresdner Bank, Commerzbank.

21. In 1937 her exports consisted of 80 percent manufactured articles and only 10 percent raw materials, primarily coal. In 1946, 91 percent of all exports from the Bizone, i.e., the British and American zones, were raw materials, and a mere 4 percent manufactured goods.

of the Western zones' imports were foreign aid deliveries, chiefly financed by the American taxpayer. Apart from some very small quantities of industrial raw materials, these GARIOA[22] shipments consisted mostly of agricultural inputs, like fertilizers and seeds, and above all grain and flour. Without these official food imports, and innumerable private food parcels from magnanimous benefactors in various Western countries, many a German would have succumbed, especially during the very harsh winter of 1946/47, which brought the most severe freeze in a generation.

Despite these efforts food rations remained low. Although the Allied Control Council, in implementation of the Potsdam formula on the German standard of living, had stipulated 2,700 calories per day as the diet for a normal consumer, the official ration was set at 1,550 calories daily, or at about half of the calorie intake recommended by nutrition experts for Europeans.[23] The average daily calorie ration actually obtained during the first three postwar years amounted to about 1,300, and fluctuated between 1,080 and 1,550. It was not until December 1948 that the U.S. military governor could report that "the German people have enough to eat." Although the average German had hitherto managed to consume about 500 calories a day in nonrationed food—obtained by raising food in garden plots, from CARE parcels,[24] and by bartering or making black market purchases from members of the occupation forces or from farmers—the actual daily food intake had represented a fairly rapid starvation level. Food theft became a decriminalized crime, a *"Kavaliersdelikt,"* and everyday language adjusted to this new morality.[25] For days on end city-dwellers would not report to work and instead would roam the countryside on extensive foraging trips; industrial workers, underfed and overtired—frequently due to nightly depredation tours into nearby village gardens and fields—would provide substandard craftsmanship. Such illicit food procuring, though absolutely vital for the individual, was economically highly wasteful, for it was time-consuming and detrimental to an efficient division of labor and occupational specialization.

Decreasing specialization between industrial and agricultural activities led to a decline in agricultural output,[26] since the policy of dein-

22. Government and Relief in Occupied Areas
23. Between May 1945 and March 1948 the typical daily food ration of a German adult over 18 years of age in office or household work, a "normal consumer" in officialese, consisted (in ounces) of: bread 12.7, meat 0.7, fats 0.5, sugar 0.6, cereals 2.5, jam 0.3, cheese 0.07, potatoes 10.5, altogether 1,557 calories.
24. The Cooperative for American Remittances to Europe had been founded in the spring of 1946 on the initiative of the former President Hoover.
25. Old words like *"organisieren"* (to organize) acquired a new meaning (to get something illegally), and new terms were coined, like *"fringsen"* when the archbishop of Cologne, Cardinal Frings, justified stealing of the means of one's livelihood in a sermon.
26. Postwar food production in the bizonal area (1935/39=100): plant food 1946/

dustrialization, with its disregard for the interdependence of industry and agriculture in a modern economy, resulted in a serious shortage of capital goods used in agricultural production. Industrial disarmament aimed at curbing the output of nitrogen, basic not only to the production of ammunition but of fertilizers as well. The limitations placed on steel production also meant a smaller output of basic slag, an important source of phosphates. Aside from a lack of industrial fertilizers,[27] which was the main reason for agricultural yields reaching only two-thirds to three-fourths of the prewar level, all farm supplies made of iron, like nails, barbed wire, chains, pitchforks, spades, scythes, farm vehicles and machinery as well as spare parts were difficult to come by.[28] Consequently domestic agricultural production only sufficed for about 1,000 calories per capita per day, while the remaining third of the normal ration had to be imported.[29] In the procurement of other bare necessities of life, like clothing, household goods and shelter, the difficulties were rather similar.

Housing was especially scarce, since 18 percent of the approximately 9.3 million apartments in the Anglo-American Bizone had been destroyed, and 29 percent damaged. Only slightly more than half had survived the war intact, and of these about 10 percent had been requisitioned by the military government. As enemy bombardment had concentrated on the urban centers, so that in many large cities two-thirds of the houses lay in rubble, a "back-to-the-country movement" had spread, which could not, however, prevent general overcrowding, as shown by the increase from 3.6 persons per apartment in 1939 to 5.4 in 1948. Apart from its detrimental effects on health and the consequent absenteeism, overcrowding also affected labor performance directly, since nightshift workers frequently lacked a proper place to sleep during the day. Lack of transportation and shortage of building materials slowed down the efficient disposal of rubble and the carrying-out of repair work and reconstruction. At 1946 debris-clearing and building rates it would have taken eighty years to bring housing back to adequate levels. By February 1947 Herbert Hoover reported to President Truman in his survey of the bizonal area that the "housing situation is the worst that modern civilization has ever seen."

47, 89; 1947/48, 84; animal food 1946/47, 60; 1947/48, 50; all foods 1946/47, 67; 1947/48, 58.

27. Of the estimated nitrogen and phosphate requirements in 1946 only about one-third were available; 1947 saw slightly more, but still less than half.

28. The annual agricultural requirements for iron amounted to about 2 million tons, while in 1947 the total iron and steel production in the Bizone was less than 3 million tons.

29. During the first three postwar years the American and British governments spent almost $3 billion in unparalleled relief shipments to their former enemy to prevent disease and unrest.

That the Bizone was still some 5.3 million apartments short by 1948 was not least a consequence of the arrival of millions of Germans from the East. According to the census of October 1946, the population in the three Western zones was about 3.2 million higher than in 1939. In the Anglo-American zones some 6 million refugees and expellees were registered.[30] With the advance of the Russian armies, millions had left Germany's eastern provinces or their ancestral homes outside the Reich and taken refuge further west, while those who had stayed or returned after the fighting had ceased had been driven from their homelands, mostly during 1946. At about that time the exodus from central Germany, i.e., the Soviet Zone of Occupation, got underway. Refugees from the Soviet zone, returning non-Reich Germans and freed POW's were then the main factors responsible for the further increase of about 4 million in the West German population by 1950. To feed, clothe and shelter these additional masses presented substantial difficulties and greatly aggravated shortages in all areas; but it was accomplished with a certain degree of equity by the local German authorities. The very first distribution of these people over the two Western zones could not heed economic considerations but had to conform to the availability of housing space. The resulting accommodation in rural or semirural areas furthermore facilitated the provision of food and fuel, but offered few employment opportunities. In fact the number of expellees with an agricultural background was quite large, since many of them had had their homeland in Germany's breadbasket, but the high density of population in the West, together with the usually smaller size of the farms there, allowed no additional agricultural settling. Consequently the creation of nonagricultural jobs long remained the most pressing problem. By late 1949, 36 percent of the unemployed were still to be found among the expellees, although as a whole they only accounted for 17 percent of the total population.

The total unemployment figure on the other hand was quite low during the immediate postwar years, and only amounted to about 800,000 persons in late 1946, some 630,000 in mid-1947 and some 440,000 in mid-1948, which represented an unemployment ratio of 5.2, 3.6 and 2.5 percent respectively. These official unemployment figures were quite misleading, however, because they were greatly understated and concealed an extensive unemployment or underemployment. For the second half of 1947 it has been estimated that, under normal conditions, probably over one-third of all employed persons in the bizonal area would have been without a job. To have a job, even a fictitious one, was, however, essential, as the primary motive for working was not the need to meet living expenses but the de-

30. The French had declined to accept refugees in their zone.

sire to obtain a food ration card. Money earnings provided little incentive to work, for many people could draw on savings or easily make additional income from even the slightest black market activity.[31] Lack of clothing and shoes frequently made it much more sensible to stay at home and avoid wear and tear than to work for money that could not buy such precious items.[32] Low food rations made workers look for easy jobs and shun employment involving heavy physical work, such as in the iron and construction industries or road and railway repair work. Furthermore, since these industries could not offer partial payment in kind, it is not surprising that they provided the bulk of the half to three-quarters of a million openings that existed throughout these years, while at the same time producers of, say, cutlery, shoes, clothing, electrical goods, or cigarettes—the most treasured article of all—were inundated with job applications.[33] Absenteeism was widespread, fictitious jobs were rampant and industrial labor productivity was probably at 40 to 50 percent of the prewar level. Compared to 1936, total industrial production in the bizonal area reached a monthly average of 33 percent in 1946, 38 percent in 1947, and 47 percent in the first half of 1948. Output differed substantially among industries, and such vital branches as steel, building materials and basic chemicals reached 32 percent, 44 percent and 54 percent of the 1936 levels respectively in the first six months of 1948.

This protracted industrial revival was partly the consequence of the Allied policy of deindustrialization. Though the physical dismantling of industrial plants had in the final analysis not resulted in an enormous loss of assets—only about 8 percent of fixed industrial capital as against losses due to war damage of almost twice as much—its economic repercussions were quite substantial. The prolonged uncertainty as to which plants would actually be affected, and the temporary halts and constantly renewed starts in the dismantling program, kept the entire German business community in anxious expectation for years. Besides the closing-down of single departments and the removal of a few special-purpose machines, which led to bottlenecks and at times to losses of production of as much as 50 percent, the fragmentation of production units as part of the deconcentration program also caused considerable retardation of industrial output. The presence of Allied teams searching and snooping for drawings, patentable technologies, and all kinds of business secrets, dampened entrepre-

31. A factfinding commission of the U.S. Congress reported that a German coal miner working six days a week earned RM 60. Owning a hen that laid five eggs a week, he could make RM 200 on his weekly egg sales on the black market.

32. The supplies of textiles available in 1946/47 amounted to only one-thirtieth of the 1952 per capita consumption.

33. A worker in a cigarette factory received 800 cigarettes a month as part of his wages, worth over RM 1500 at their black market value.

neurial incentive. Businessmen who kept their enterprising spirit saw their efforts impeded by the lack of suitable factors of production, especially by the shortage of raw materials. For a while industry could live off its wartime stocks, which had still been substantial in May 1945, but scant replenishment was possible during the following years. Official raw material allocations in 1946 and 1947 not only seldom reached more than 20 percent of requirements, but were badly administered as well. The removal of centralized raw material controls in favor of a decentralized system, especially in the American zone, separated the allocation of raw materials and semifinished goods from the distribution of finished products to the consumer. This "input oriented" planning system, operating between 1945 and the second half of 1947, allocated quotas for industrial supplies to existing plants, which used them partly for production and subsequent sales, and partly to increase their inventories, i.e., they were hoarded. The following system of "output oriented" planning, making allocations only on the basis of actual sales, attempted to curb this hoarding. But what was really necessary to break this habit of the business community—a thoroughly sound policy from the standpoint of individual enterprises—was a strong hand and the will to enforce the economic controls. Simply taking over the economic regulations of the Third Reich would not suffice.

As long as that regime had existed, the regulations for the rationing of foodstuffs, consumer goods and housing, for the allocation of manpower and raw materials, for the stabilization of prices, wages, and rents, had worked fairly effectively. Genuine support for the regime and its ideology, or active patriotism in a time of war and national emergency, usually sufficed to guarantee ready compliance with those regulations; their draconian enforcement—the most flagrant violations of economic legislation were subject to capital punishment —placed a further premium on acquiescence. Voluntary or enforced, however, public cooperation eroded rapidly once political and military collapse made further sacrifices for the common good seem quite pointless to the individual. Once it was discovered that the new authorities were unable to maintain the previous ration levels, and that they were rather lax in the enforcement of the inherited wartime controls, economic misdemeanors became more frequent, as rule-breaking and evasion were not only unavoidable but also less perilous. German officials repeatedly demanded that serious "economic crimes" be made subject to capital punishment again in order to undermine the attractiveness of activity in black or gray markets. While the German business community in general was not involved in black market deals, which were considered "dishonorable" and "immoral," gray market operations were quite common. This so-called "compensation trade" resembled barter trade, since it meant the exchange of commodities as well as the payment of their fixed prices to make the transaction legal and acceptable to tax and control authorities. Though a 1942 prohibition of all compensation activity had been explicitly renewed in March 1947, firms soon had to be allowed to use part of their production in so-called "controlled compensation trading" in order to maintain a minimum of industrial operations. Experts claimed that in 1947 and in the first half of 1948 as much as 50 percent of the entire output of the bizonal economy was used for compensation deals. More or less stable barter trade terms developed, whether between individual branches or major sectors of the economy, like agriculture and industry.[34]

The wartime system of fixed and regulated prices, which had also been taken over by the occupation forces to check the existing inflationary potential, quickly became unrealistic in view of sharply increased production costs. The reduced productivity of workers due to malnutrition, lower output per machine due to obsolescence and lack of repairs, quite apart from war damage, and operation far below optimum production levels due to lack of industrial inputs, frequently raised costs far beyond the legal prices, leading to substantial pecuniary losses.[35] The consequent bankruptcies and shutdowns in the basic materials industries were welcomed by the Allies since they had the same effect as dismantling, destruction or deterioration from lack of repair and maintenance, and thus contributed to Germany's industrial disarmament. Industries with less standardized output could sidestep the disproportions in the industrial price structure and escape imminent bankruptcy through timely changes in production which were justifiable from the individual producer's standpoint but undesirable from the point of view of the country's economy, as they led to a squandering of scarce resources. By producing "new," formerly unknown goods, usually of a luxurious nature, the future prices of which were established on the basis of present production costs,[36] substantial profits could be made. Department stores, which could not supply such daily necessities as pots, dishes or cutlery,[37] offered an odd collection of expensive, low utility articles like fancy lamp shades and cigarette lighters, artistic doorstops and dolls, painted wooden plates and plastic ash trays. The general public—like the hoarding business community—

34. In 1947 a farmer near the Ruhr area had to "pay" 150 kilograms of wheat or 200 kilograms of rye or 6 kilograms of bacon for one sack of twine; for 60 shoeing-nails, half a kilogram of fat; for 100 bricks, 50 kilograms of potatoes; for 50 kilograms of fertilizer, 150 kilograms of potatoes; for one sowing machine, 4,000 kilograms of potatoes; for two grain sacks, 50 kilograms of wheat; for one electric light bulb, one kilogram of fat.

35. In some chemical plants, production costs exceeded prices by 80 percent; in various textile mills by 50 percent.

36. Up to mid-1948 over 5,000 new prices were set, mostly for "new" products.

37. Between mid-1946 and mid-1947, only every seventh person could obtain a plate; every one hundred and fiftieth a hand-basin.

was eager to buy anything, even a relatively useless article, in the hope that it would be a better store of value than paper money.[38] The Reichsmark legally bought virtually nothing any longer, apart from the highly inadequate food ration, and was only of use to pay rent, taxes, utilities, and fares. It was the cigarette, preferably of American manufacture, which, due to its relative scarcity, durability, storability and divisibility, became the newly accepted medium of exchange in a country with—as the economist Röpke termed it tongue-in-cheek—"a hair oil-ashtray-herb tea economy."

3

The Return to Reason

Since purely economic considerations carried relatively little weight in the formation of Western Allied economic policies towards early postwar Germany, a change in the political climate had to precede any major reversal in the economic field. Though the local occupation authorities cooperated quite actively with German reconstruction efforts, especially with regard to the communications system and transportation network,[39] the fundamental reconstruction decisions, essentially political in nature, had to be made in Washington. Initially American statesmen had tried very hard to shut their eyes to the ideological differences with their Russian war ally; by 1946, however, it had to be recognized that the United States was engaged in a very real competition with Communist ideology all over the world. The longstanding British apprehensions that an economically prostrate Germany would create a huge vacuum in the heart of Europe, which the Soviet Union would be only too ready to fill, slowly began to be shared by the American government as well. This led in time, as exemplified in the dismantling measures, to a change in the former fruitless and repressive policy towards Germany. The first major sign

38. Even without the benefit of economic history, the public understood the workings of inflation and subsequent stabilization quite well, not least from observing the contemporary currency reforms in neighboring France, Belgium, Holland, and Austria.

39. Internal mail service functioned normally within three months after the surrender. International postal relations were restored by April 1946, followed within another year by renewed international telephone and telegraph service. While by the summer of 1947 internal telephone traffic already greatly exceeded the prewar volume, the restoration of transportation facilities was still incomplete. Though by April 1946 the Rhine had been opened to navigation along its entire length and considerable progress had been made in repairing the ports, railroad freight service remained inadequate for some time, and had to be substituted for by inland waterborne transport. By mid-1948, however, the U.S. military governor could claim that, although still not fully back to normal, the German transport system was able to take care of the requirements of a revitalized German economy.

of a revision came with U.S. Secretary of State Byrnes's speech at Stuttgart in September 1946. Though there was hardly any change in substance in comparison to previous American policy statements, the very considerable difference in tone could not be missed. This was the first official statement since Quebec which did not endorse the "Strong Europe, Weak Germany" concept. Instead, Byrnes maintained that Germany was a part of Europe, and that recovery in Europe, particularly in the states adjoining Germany, would be very slow if Germany, with its great industrial capacity, were to be turned into a poorhouse.

Both the realization that the Soviet Union was not willing to treat Germany as an integral economic unit and the nonarrival of foodstuffs and raw materials deliveries in return for Western shipments of dismantled plants led to their stoppage in May 1946. To solve this impasse, and recognizing in general the detrimental effects of the zonal splitup into four hermetically separated areas with accompanying severe restrictions on interzonal trade and an almost complete freeze on the exchange of goods, the two English-speaking powers initiated the first major corrective step towards the renewed economic integration of Germany. As the Russians and French declined to participate, the British and the Americans merged their two zones into the Bizone on 1 January 1947, so that the British zone, with its large industrial potential but weak agricultural basis, and the more agriculturally oriented but much less industrialized American zone would compliment each other and thus gain a certain economic independence.

After the Moscow conference of the Big Four foreign ministers in March/April 1947 had revealed very considerable disagreement on the German question between the Soviet Union and the Western Allies, the former established the German Economic Commission *(Deutsche Wirtschaftskommission)* in June. In the same month the two English-speaking powers created common political institutions for the Bizone—modestly referred to as the United Economic Region—by establishing an Economic Council as its quasi-government under the supervision of an Anglo-American control authority. On 5 June, U.S. Secretary of State Marshall had called for a European Recovery Program initiated by the European states and supported by American aid, a scheme quickly rejected by the Soviet Union and her satellites in July. The revised Level-of-Industry Plan for the Bizone was announced in late August by the two English-speaking governments. On 6 February 1948—after another unsuccessful meeting of the Big Four foreign ministers in London in November/December 1947—a new charter for the Bizone was granted, which further increased German participation in its administration. As a countermove only a week later, the Soviet Union conferred extensive powers on the German Economic Commission, particularly the right to issue economic decrees for the Soviet zone and to act as a de facto government, and in March withdrew her delegates from the Allied Control Council. In the meantime France had also been won for a united Western approach to the German question. On 1 June 1948 a six-power agreement of the three Western Allies and the Benelux countries called for international control of the Ruhr, German representation in the European Recovery Program, closer integration and the drafting of a federal constitution for the three Western zones, and the creation of an Allied military security board. On 20 June 1948 the three Western powers introduced a new currency in their zones; five days later the Soviet authorities did the same in their zone, and then blockaded Berlin from 24 June 1948 to 12 May 1949 by stopping all surface traffic between the old capital and the Western zones. This move was countered by a large-scale air lift of some 277,000 flights bringing all vital supplies to the beleaguered city in "raisin bombers," as the grateful Berliners called them.

The total breakdown of the victors' alliance quickly led to the establishment of two German states, each in essence reflecting the political, economic and social concepts of its creators. In March 1949 a Soviet-sponsored People's Council called for the election of a People's Congress on 16 May. This resulted in the establishment of the German Democratic Republic on 7 October, leading without further elections to a predominantly Communist government under Soviet tutelage. On 8 April the three Western Allies agreed on an Occupation Statute which granted the Germans in their zones considerable self-government, while reserving far-reaching powers to the occupation authorities. The Parliamentary Council composed of 65 delegates chosen by the state legislatures adopted a constitution on 8 May 1949, exactly four years after Germany's unconditional surrender. With the consent of the occupation powers, the "Basic Law of the Federal Republic of Germany" came into force on 24 May 1949.[40] Elections for the Bundestag, held on 14 August, led to a conservative government under the chancellorship of Konrad Adenauer.

Before the three Western powers set the Federal Republic free, i.e., granted what came close to political sovereignty, important economic policy decisions had been made which were to influence the future development of the new state: currency reform, the end of the established system of economic controls, and admittance to the Marshall Plan.

Already in the spring of 1946 a committee of American economists had been charged with developing a plan for the financial rehabilitation of Germany. French and Soviet opposition had sub-

---

40. The term "Basic Law" was chosen to indicate that a German constitution could not be established until all Germans were free to approve it.

sequently made it impossible to reach a quadripartite agreement, and the Americans shelved their plan, realizing that the introduction of a new German currency, if not done in all four zones, would complete the breakup of Germany into separate economies. Only after the East-West split had become an accomplished fact, with the end of the Allied Control Council in March 1948, and after the repercussions of German economic paralysis upon Western Europe had become too hazardous, did the three Western powers decide on a joint currency reform for their zones. The Deutsche Mark (DM) became the new monetary unit and its ratio to the Reichsmark was scaled, according to the character of the debts, from zero (public debts), 6.5 percent (bank deposits and cash), 10 percent (mortgages and other private debts) up to 100 percent (rents, wages and prices). Initially only DM 40 per person was exchanged on a one-to-one basis for RM; two months later another DM 20 followed. In order to make it possible for shopkeepers, self-employed persons and companies to make payments, they were given an additional DM 60 for each employee. The various areas of the public sector received a percentage of their Reichsmark receipts between October 1947 and March 1948. This initial allowance amounted to about DM2.4 billion for the states and communities, about DM 300 million for the postal service and the railroad, and almost DM 800 million for the occupying powers. The initial allowance for the public sector of approximately DM 3.5 billion was more than generous when one considers that during the changeover process the private sector only received about DM 9.5 billion up to the end of 1948. To prevent a shortage of small change, the old coins at first remained in circulation at 10 percent of their former value. Furthermore, a six-day suspension of payments was declared while converted time and demand deposits were unblocked in successive stages. This devaluation of domestic currency to about one-fifteenth of its former value immediately removed the confusing and demoralizing "veil of money," and established a firm accounting basis for the formation of prices which reflected the real state of the market.

The system of official maximum prices was, however, still in operation, though it is true that the occupation authorities had tried to revise the price and wage regulations about a month earlier in order to bring the industrial price structure into line with increased production costs. Indeed, the occupation authorities wanted to maintain rationing, price controls and centralized allocations of raw materials to industry for a time, since it was assumed that decontrols would endanger the new currency through rapidly rising prices. Nevertheless, the German authorities quickly shortened the list of controlled commodities, while retaining rationing and fixed prices for some basic foods, some major industrial supplies, public utilities, and rents, thus courageously following the successful Italian decontrol policy of 1947 and providing a good example of the usefulness of historic insights. Allied anxieties were not without foundation, for prices did indeed rise quickly during the second half of 1948, when following the reduction of previously hoarded stocks production failed to respond rapidly enough to match the upsurge in demand. Since the currency reform forced rationalization, initially leading to a high level of unemployment, the economy entered a critical period. The end of the wage ceiling on 3 November led to a one-day general strike on 12 November when the unions unsuccessfully demanded renewed price controls. The effectiveness of currency reform and the decontrol measures was greatly enhanced by the promise of early and substantial American aid. Although the first allotment of ERP-funds had not yet been received, everyone knew after early June 1948 that a large supply of foreign commodities was soon to pour in. Thus by 1949 most citizens of the newly established FRG could assume that the worst was over, and that they could look with guarded optimism to the economic future of their state. In the other half of Germany things were quite different.

Bibliography

Abelshauser, W. *Wirtschaft in Westdeutschland, 1945–48: Rekonstruktion und Wachstumsbedingungen in der amerikanischen und britischen Zone.* Stuttgart, 1975.

Ambrosius, G. *Die Durchsetzung der Sozialen Marktwirtschaft in Westdeutschland 1945–1949.* Stuttgart, 1977.

Backer, J. H. *Priming the German Economy: American Occupation Policies 1945–1948.* Durham, N.C., 1971.

Balabkins, N. *Germany under Direct Controls, Economic Aspects of Industrial Disarmament 1945–1948.* New Brunswick, N.J., 1964.

Gareau, F. H. "Morgenthau's Plan for Industrial Disarmament in Germany," *Western Political Quarterly* 14 (1961).

Gelber, H.G. "Der Morgenthau-Plan," *Vierteljahreshefte für Zeitgeschichte* 13 (1965).

Gimbel, J. *The Origins of the Marshall Plan.* Stanford, 1976.

Jerchow, F. *Deutschland in der Weltwirtschaft 1944–47.* Düsseldorf, 1978.

Kuklick, B. *American Policy and the Division of Germany: The Clash with Russia over Reparations.* Ithaca, N.Y., 1972.

Lasby, C. G. *Project Paperclip: German Scientists and the Cold War.* New York, 1971.

Manz, M. *Stagnation und Aufschwung in der französischen Besatzungszone von 1945 bis 1948.* Diss. Mannheim, 1968.

Möller, H. *Zur Vorgeschichte der deutschen Mark. Die Währungsreformpläne 1945–1948.* Tübingen, 1961.

Nettl, J. P. *The Eastern Zone and Soviet Policy in Germany, 1945–1950.* New York, 1951.

Pohl, M. *Wiederaufbau: Kunst und Technik der Finanzierung 1947–53, Die ersten Jahre der Kreditanstalt für Wiederaufbau.* Frankfurt/Main, 1973.

Schmidt, E. *Die verhinderte Neuordnung 1945–1952, Zur Auseinandersetzung um die Demokratisierung der Wirtschaft in den westlichen Besatzungszonen und in der Bundesrepublik Deutschland.* Frankfurt/Main, 1970.

Stolper, G. *German Realities.* New York, 1948.

CHAPTER 6

The Making of a Satellite: Communist Germany, 1945–1970

Industrial Dismantling, Economic Disintegration, and Demographic Decline

The "de-" and "dis-" policies the victors had agreed upon at Potsdam were implemented with special vigor by the Soviet Union in her zone of occupation. This was particularly true with regard to industrial disarmament, and even before the joint Level-of-Industry Plan of March 1946 provided the legal basis for the implementation of reparations deliveries, the Soviet Union had started with the dismantling of some 1,200 plants. This and the already mentioned nonarrival of reciprocal shipments for dismantled plants from the Western zones was interpreted by the Western Powers as a violation of the agreement to treat Germany as an economic unit. Since the Soviets furthermore made withdrawals from their zone's current production—a practice not envisioned by the Potsdam agreement—and never counted them as exports, the Western Allies stopped their deliveries of dismantled plants by May 1946. Going it alone, the Soviet authorities intensified dismantling in their zone, disassembling a total of over 1,900 plants, almost 1,700 of them completely, by the spring of 1948, when dismantlement was officially ended. In the industrial sector dismantling and war damage—in a rough ratio of three to one—reduced wartime capacities by about 40 percent altogether. Since, however, fixed capital in industry had increased by over 80 percent as a result of rearmament and expansion of war production in central Germany between 1936

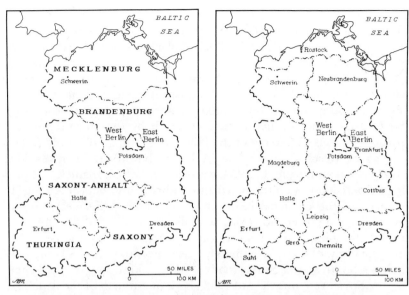

4. *Central Germany: (a) The five states of the Soviet Zone in 1948. (b) The German Democratic Republic and her administrative districts in 1970.*

and 1944, the stock of fixed industrial capital in the Soviet zone was still greater in the late 1940s than in 1936, though smaller than in 1939.[1] Production capacity, however, varied greatly from industry to industry, since the capital-goods sector had experienced losses at least twice as high as those in most consumer-goods industries. Aside from industry, the transportation sector suffered severely from dismantling; nearly all double-track railroad lines were stripped of the second track. Some one-track lines were also removed, so that in all some 13,500 kilometers of rail, representing about one-third of the track system, was dismantled. While these were substantial losses for the Soviet zone's economy, the gain for the receiving country was comparatively small. High-quality equipment from the engineering, precision-instruments and optical industries frequently reached its destination severely damaged or rusted, owing to improper disassembling or transport and storage difficulties; and, once there, the absence of the necessary blueprints created great difficulties in reassembling it. In view of this unsatisfac-

1. In the late 1940s, central Germany had a larger fixed capital stock in industry on a per capita basis than the Western zones. Although it had suffered much more from dismantling, but less from war-related damage, its fixed industrial capital amounted to 48 percent of the Western level, while migration from the Soviet zone had reduced its population to about 40 percent of the Western total.

tory situation the Soviet authorities eventually changed their reparations policy, emphasizing German deliveries from current production. In June 1946, consequently, 213 large plants were declared to be the property of the Soviet Union and transformed into Soviet corporations (*Sowjetische Aktiengesellschaft*, SAG). Since these companies represented close to a third of the zone's total industrial capacity, their speedy resumption of operation contributed greatly to the quick revival of the Soviet zone's industrial production, which by the end of 1946 approached about 42 percent of the 1936 level, compared to only 32 percent in the Western zones.[2] The SAGs, which were gradually resold to the German authorities by 1954, were mostly key companies, comprising 80 percent of both the petroleum industry and potash mining, 50 percent of the chemical industry, 40 percent of the electrical, automobile, and power industries, and about one-third of the engineering, coal-mining, and metallurgical industries. During the late 1940s and the early 1950s approximately every seventh industrial employee held a job with a SAG, thus actually working within, and for the benefit of, the Soviet economy. Up to 1953 about one-fourth of the zone's national product had on the average to be spent on occupation costs and reparations payment,[3] which were gradually reduced and finally discontinued in August 1953. It is generally estimated that levies on current production by means of the SAGs or other methods brought higher reparations than dismantlement, possibly twice as high. Not only commodities but also people had to be exported; apart from the Soviet share in "intellectual reparations," in 1946 the entire personnel of dismantled plants were frequently deported to the Soviet Union.[4] There they met millions of German POWs and civilians doing forced labor. Some remained till the late 1950s, the last not returning until 1961. Not counting the contribution of these forced laborers to the reconstruction of the Soviet economy, some estimates place the total value of goods and services taken by the Soviet occupation authorities between 1945 and 1955 at $30 billion, a sum about three times the size of the original Soviet reparations demand, and nearly twice the $14 billion spent under the auspices of the Marshall Plan in Europe up to mid-1952.

As a Soviet satellite, the German Democratic Republic not only had to forego the grants and loans of the European Recovery Program but

2. Soviet military authorities were not hampered by any directive similar to JCS 1067, i.e., to take no measures conducive to resumption of production, but on the contrary even went against the Potsdam agreement, emphasizing rapid reconstruction of plants producing synthetic rubber and gasoline. Compared to 1944 industrial output, the end of 1946 saw a level of about 30 percent reached in the Soviet zone and about 25 percent in the Western zones.

3. Estimates for the Western zones run at 11 to 15 percent between 1946 and 1949.

4. Soviet authorities claimed that the workers' contracts did not end with dismantlement and had to be honored wherever the plant might be reconstructed.

was also hindered from participating in the coordinated European-wide reconstruction program and the rebuilding of the traditional intra-European trade links.[5] For a region situated in the middle of central Europe, and forming the heart of the former German Reich, this was an especially severe handicap, since geographic situation and relative scarcity of industrial raw materials had long ago led to close economic ties with the other German regions and adjacent foreign countries.[6] In the late 1930s central Germany had not only been the most intensively industrialized area in Germany[7] but also the one most dependent on interregional economic exchange.[8] Division of labor and exchange of output had been especially pronounced in the area of industrial production,[9] of which central Germany manufactured about 30 percent by the mid-forties. With about 28 percent of the German population in 1946, this indeed looked like an adequate share, had it not been for substantial disproportionalities in the industrial structure. Though the central German share in the Reich's consumer-goods and capital-goods sectors amounted to 31 and 32 percent respectively, intrasectoral imbalances were substantial.[10] The basic-materials sector, however, was the real Achilles' heel of the central German economy, since it produced only about 2 percent of the Reich's hard coal and pig

5. While only about a quarter of central German foreign trade went to the countries of Eastern Europe in 1947, the following year and the fifties and sixties saw this raised to three-fourths. Of the remaining quarter, two-thirds consisted of trade with the FRG in 1950, one-third in 1970.

6. Essentially nature had well endowed central Germany only with rock and potassium salt, lignite, and copper, of which it had produced 60, 65 and over 90 percent respectively of the Reich's totals in 1936.

7. Net industrial output per capita, in 1939, in RM: Berlin 855, central Germany without Berlin 725, western Germany 609, eastern Germany 249, Reich as a whole 600.

8. 1936 deliveries to other German regions (and to foreign countries) in percent of total production: central Germany 43 percent (11 percent); eastern Germany 43 percent (5 percent); western Germany 18 percent (13 percent). Supplies from other German regions (and from foreign countries) in percent of total consumption: central Germany 45 percent (8 percent); eastern Germany 39 percent (10 percent); western Germany 18 percent (12 percent).

9. In 1936 central Germany shipped almost two-thirds of its industrial output to other areas—15 percent to foreign countries, 9 percent to Berlin, and 40 percent to other German regions—and received, in return, a similar share (6 percent, 9 percent and 46 percent) of its industrial consumption. Western Germany by comparison sold only two-fifths of its industrial output (18 percent abroad and 22 percent to other German regions), and received merely a third (12 percent and 21 percent) of its industrial consumption from other areas.

10. For instance the consumer-goods sector in central Germany accounted for 25 percent of the food processing industry, 43 percent of the textile manufacturing, and 80 percent of the hosiery production of the Reich. The capital-goods sector comprised 29 percent of the chemical industry (but few plants for plastics, coal tar dyes and pharmaceuticals); 36 percent of the engineering and automobile industries (including 20 percent of agricultural machinery production, 24 percent of locomotive construction, 39 percent of the machine-tools branch and 73 percent of the output in textile machinery); and 34 percent of electrical engineering (but primarily the production of light electrical equipment).

iron and some 7 percent of its steel output by the end of the war. Imports of industrial materials from both the Ruhr and Upper Silesia, the latter of which produced 18 percent of the Reich's hard coal, 16 to 20 percent of its nonferrous metals (especially copper, nickel and tin) and 9 percent of its semifinished rolled steel, were thus of vital importance.

The historically inappropriate labeling of central Germany as "East Germany" has increased the tendency to overlook the fact that after 1945 central Germany's trade ties were severed in two directions, i.e., not only with the West but also with the territories east of the Oder-Neisse line. A few words about these Prussian provinces of Silesia, Pomerania, East and West Prussia and parts of Brandenburg are called for. These provinces comprised 24 percent of the Reich's territory and 14 percent of its population, and they contributed 10 to 11 percent of Germany's national income in 1939. The economy there had its unique features, owing to the relatively high share of agriculture in total production, the great importance of Silesian coal as a regional source of energy, and the wide distribution of mostly small and medium-sized industries. As 23 percent of Germany's prewar agricultural production originated there, these areas rightly deserved to be called "the breadbasket." Industrial production, however, was less important, amounting to only 6 percent of the Reich's total, though 8 percent of the hard-coal deposits, 17 percent of the lignite deposits, 39 percent of lead ore and 64 percent of zinc ore deposits known by the late 1930s were located there and formed the basis of a mining industry that produced one-eighth of the Reich's total. Despite being in an industrial deficit area housing only 8 percent of the Reich's consumer-goods industries and 15 percent of handicraft production, and thus achieving a statistical self-sufficiency of 78 percent, local industry sold about two-thirds of its production in other parts of Germany or abroad. Eastern Germany therefore not only functioned as an agricultural complement within the German economy but also participated effectively in the industrial division of labor. The severance of the eastern provinces consequently created imbalances within the German economic structure. As trade links were especially close with central Germany, that region was severely affected.[11]

While the partitioning of the integrated German economy and the dismantling of industry above all affected the material means of production in the Soviet occupied zone, the availability of labor was determined by the structure and development of the population. At the outbreak of war, central Germany had 16.7 million inhabitants; due to

11. In intra-German trade, eastern Germany shipped 50 percent of its industrial deliveries to central Germany, 20 percent to Berlin and 30 percent to western Germany, and received its industrial supplies at the rate of 33 percent from central Germany, 20 percent from Berlin and 47 percent from western Germany.

the influx of expellees from the East this figure rose to 18.6 million in 1946, but fell back to the prewar level in subsequent years as a result of a new flight westward till the erection of the Berlin Wall in August 1961. This quantitative decline was accompanied by qualitative losses, since the East-West migration included a more than proportionate percentage of young adults and males, thus having short-run as well as lasting effects—through a lower birth rate—on the central German age and sex structure. Furthermore, of the 3 million[12] who left between 1950 and 1961, 60 percent were gainfully employed, including a high degree of skilled workers and self-employed persons.[13] While this "voting with their feet"—as the Free World termed it, ironically in Lenin's words—was a source of continuous political embarrassment for the Communist regime, it remained, for quite a while, a matter of little economic concern. Experts have argued that this steady demographic loss was actually an economic advantage to the GDR economy. There were fewer mouths to feed, fewer bodies to house, and fewer minds to school, while employment in both industry and agriculture was substantially larger than necessary for production until the late 1950s. However, underemployment—"hidden reserves" in planners' parlance—eventually gave way to increasing labor shortages, so that *"Republikflucht"* (flight from the republic) became a serious economic problem. The quantitative losses were compensated for by an increase of women and old people in gainful employment, thus achieving one of the highest employment ratios in the world.[14] In the eyes of the Communist rulers, there was also a qualitative improvement of the population, since many of the refugees either belonged to undesirable strata (big landowners, industrialists, officers), were members of an independent-minded intelligentsia (teachers, professors, jurists, engineers), or represented a reactionary middle class (small and medium-sized traders, craftsmen and farmers) or other politically unreliable elements not prepared to go along with the Sovietization of the economy.

2

The Sovietization of the Central German Economy

A Soviet-type economy is characterized by the predominance of state ownership of the means of production and the allocation of re-

12. This was the net migration, as 3.5 million left for the FRG and about 0.5 million moved to the GDR.

13. From 1954 to 1961 close to 6,000 physicians and pharmacists, 8,000 lawyers, 750 professors, and about 17,000 each of teachers and engineers left the GDR for the FRG.

14. Although the working-age population declined by almost 15 percent, to 10.4 million, between 1950 and 1968, the number of gainfully employed persons declined by less than one-half of one percent, to 8.4 million, in the same period.

sources by administrative decision rather than by a market mechanism. On the ideological plane, communists argue that private possession of the means of production is the cause of the division of society into two classes, capitalists and proletarians, exploiters and exploited. The basic contradiction of the capitalist society, i.e., collective production and individual appropriation of the manufactured commodities, can only be redressed by abolishing private ownership of the means of production. The political argument of communism emphasizes that the political power of the ruling classes is based upon their economic power, i.e., their ownership of the means of production, and that a transfer of title is necessary to assure the lasting political predominance of the working classes. Since some branches exert a dominating influence upon the rest of the economy, it is imperative to place these "commanding heights of the economy" (banks, insurance companies, large industrial concerns, foreign trade and the transport and communications systems) under state control. In economic terms, communists finally explain the need for public ownership of the means of production as being a logical consequence of the superiority of governmental planning of production and consumption, as compared to the market mechanism. The greater rationality and higher efficiency of planned economic processes should be achieved by smooth cooperation between the planning authorities and the individual production unit; and it should not be endangered by the personal interests of a private, and possibly antagonistic, owner. These arguments, however, played only a minor role in the nationalization debate in the Soviet zone, since the communist demand to punish and dispossess so-called "warmongers," "Nazi activists," and "industrial monopolists" stood in the foreground of discussions. Accordingly, expropriations were, at first, an integral part of demilitarization, denazification, and deconcentration, while they later became the penalty for persons who had allegedly violated governmental controls or become outright "enemies of the state."

As early as July 1945 the speedy transformation of the previous mixed system of private, semiprivate and public banking into centralized state banking began.[15] In a similar fashion the other exponent of "finance capitalism," private activity in the insurance field, was eliminated, and all existing companies were ordered to merge into five public insurance corporations, one for each state. Thuringia started to transfer all mineral deposits and mining enterprises to state ownership in September 1945. It was followed by the other states within the next two years. This was the period when the first phase of nationalization in industry took place. In October 1945 the occupation authorities or-

15. This move was coupled with the blocking of a large proportion of bank deposits, thus sharply reducing the inflationary potential.

dered the sequestration of some 10,000 industrial enterprises owned by alleged "war criminals" or "Nazi activists,"[16] the Reich, or the Prussian State; and in June 1946 the subsequent transformation of about 200 of the largest and most important industrial enterprises into 25 SAGs was ordered. While a few hundred enterprises were returned to their owners, the fate of some 9,300 industrial enterprises, among them 3,800 factories, was to be decided on the basis of a plebiscite on expropriations, held in June 1946 in Saxony, the state where more than half of all the enterprises in question were located. Since the overwhelming majority there voted for expropriation, the result was taken as indicative of public opinion in general and served as the basis for expropriation in the other states as well. The status of ownership of expropriated enterprises remained unclear for almost two years, since the five states were only entrusted with the utilization of the plants. This reflected the official policy of the occupation authorities not to undertake a remodelling of the German society along Soviet lines but to create a bourgeois-democratic system along the lines of the ideals of the revolution of 1848. It is difficult to say to what extent it was regarded as unwise "to nationalize a heap of debris," or whether it was feared that a too hasty nationalization would bring further disorganization of the economy and then have to give way to a new economic policy along bourgeois-market lines as had occurred in the Soviet Union in the early 1920s. Any possible hopes among the Soviets that communism would make further advances in the West were thwarted by the change in American foreign policy. The announcement of the Truman Doctrine in March 1947 ended the need for Soviet windowdressing for the benefit of the suspicious Germans in the Western zones.

From 1947/48 onward the Soviet Union added a new dimension to her relations with the satellites, as well as her occupation policy towards Germany. While previously many roads had been conceded to lead nations to socialism, the Stalinist approach was now declared to be "the only possible way to socialism." By mid-1947 the suspended expropriations started anew, and by April 1948 the expropriated enterprises received their final legal status as People's Works (*Volkseigene Betriebe*, VEB). Together with the SAGs, these produced about 60 percent of the zone's industrial output at that time. The remaining private enterprises, still accounting for 40 percent of industry's gross product, saw themselves confronted with a host of detrimental measures in the fields of taxation, prices, and planning during the second phase of nationalization from 1949 to 1955. Instead of outright dispossession, various

16. Almost every businessman could fit the definition, since virtually all had eventually become party members (if they intended to outlive Hitler), or employed foreign workers, or produced some sort of material useful for the armed forces.

means were used to achieve "functional expropriation,"[17] reducing the private entrepreneurs' share of industrial production to 15 percent by 1955. A third phase of deprivatization between 1955 and 1970 saw the percentage of the private sector reduced to about 2 percent, mostly as a consequence of the transformation of private enterprises into semipublic companies. In order to assure a better and more regular supply of machines, raw materials and labor, and to broaden their capital basis, entrepreneurs transformed their enterprises into limited partnerships; the state, represented by a VEB or a bank, became the limited partner, while the previous owner-manager would henceforth function as managing director and general partner with unlimited liability.

Part ownership and joint management was expecially advocated for craftsmen, since the Communist leadership had to tolerate private activity in crafts as a result of the great need for consumer goods and services. Though the first handicrafts cooperative (*Produktionsgenossenschaft des Handwerks*, PGH) was founded as early as 1953, less than 300 existed in 1957, producing about 5 percent of the sector's gross output. After 1958, however, cooperatives rose in number due to increased discrimination, especially in taxation, against private operators, whose share in gross production declined to about 50 percent in 1970. Another sector in which small businesses traditionally played an important role, the retail and wholesale trade, experienced an even quicker decline of individual ownership and management. The occupation authorities encouraged the founding of consumers' cooperatives, which by the end of 1946 had increased their retail outlets from about 2,000 to 6,000, handling roughly 14 percent of the total retail trade. Even more important for the rapid deprivatization of the retail trade was the state-owned trading organization (*Handelsorganisation*, HO) founded in November 1948. Its initial purpose had been to sell food and consumer goods without rationing, but at exorbitant prices, in order to skim off surplus purchasing power and to counteract blackmarketeering. Soon the HO branched out into the retailing of rationed articles as well; by 1950 it was already handling about 30 percent of the retail trade's turnover, compared to the 17 percent of the consumer's cooperatives and the 53 percent of private stores. From the early 1950s onward, the private sector quickly declined under increased economic pressure, especially through discrimination in the delivery of goods, handling 32 percent in 1955, 16 percent in 1960 and about 10 percent in 1970, while the HO increased its share to about 45 percent and that of the consumer's cooperatives rose to about 35 percent in 1970. The remaining 10 percent was handled by the so-called commission trade, i.e.,

17. For example, just as the price freeze in the immediate postwar years assisted deindustrialization in the Western zones, it could foster deprivatization in the East.

semiprivate enterprises with state partnership, quite similar to those in industry. The deprivatization at the retailing level had been preceded by the establishment of state agencies for foreign and interzonal trade and a quick absorption of private wholesale trading. After 1948 public agencies, which had been founded in 1946, functioned as holding organizations for the entire wholesale trade, whose private sector declined from 38 percent of sales in 1950 to 10 percent in 1955 and 2 percent in 1970.

While the deprivatization in the secondary and tertiary sectors was pursued with relative continuity, this was not—at least not at first sight—the case in agriculture. In accordance with the Potsdam agreement in September 1945, the Soviet occupation authorities ordered the expropriation without compensation of all landed estates of more than 100 hectares (some 7,000 estates altogether) as well as all the farms, regardless of size, of "war criminals" and "Nazi activists." The expropriated lands, comprising about 30 percent of the agriculturally used area, were mostly turned over in lots of 5 to 8.5 hectares for a rye equivalent of 1 to 1.5 tons per hectare to some 210,000 so-called new settlers, i.e., primarily farmers and farm workers expelled from the East. Some land was distributed to enlarge the acreage of some 120,000 smallholders, while about one-third remained under large-scale cultivation as People's Farms (*Volkseigene Güter*, VEG). This phase of agrarian reform, with its emphasis on smallholdings, was followed by a period of protracted collectivization beginning in 1952 and ending in 1959.[18] The means of initiating the creation of collective farms (*Landwirtschaftliche Produktionsgenossenschaft*, LPG) among the new settlers, with their small and inefficient holdings representing about 10 percent of the agricultural land, were provided by the machine- and tractor-lending stations, which served as collection and distribution agencies for the farm equipment and agricultural machinery expropriated from the large estates. During 1952 and 1953, so-called Type I cooperatives, those with the lowest degree of collectivization, in which only the fields were tilled together, made some headway, accounting for almost 12 percent of the land under cultivation. After a short halt, and even some regression as a result of the workers' uprising of 17 June 1953, when only the intervention of Soviet military force saved the regime of the German communists, collectivization quickened, increasing the share of the LPGs to 45 percent in 1959. Most of the newly founded cooperatives belonged to Type III, which required total collectivization, including livestock, implements and machinery, and permitted

18. The similarities with the agricultural policy in the Soviet Union between 1917 and 1928 are obvious, reflecting in both cases the ideological aim of forging an alliance between the industrial proletariat and a land-hungry peasantry.

only a very small amount of individual farming.[19] Despite severe discrimination in tax rates, prices, supplies of agricultural inputs, delivery quotas, debt liquidation and the use of other governmental weapons in "the class struggle in the countryside," the old established peasantry, owning as it did about two-thirds of the agricultural land at the time of the land reform, and possessing large enough holdings as well as the skill and determination to hang on, only very slowly joined cooperatives. Thus in 1959 slightly more than half of the agricultural land still remained under private cultivation. The spring of 1960 brought a very short but extremely intensive drive for collectivization, completing "the liberation of the peasants in the GDR," as the communist leadership called it. Within slightly more than three months, a quarter of a million individual peasants were made to join LPGs, whose share of agricultural land consequently jumped from about 45 percent to 85 percent in 1960. Throughout the 1960s the LPGs kept this share, while the general trend towards the most collectivized type of agriculture continued.[20]

While deprivatization of the means of production was undertaken more or less slowly and in fits and starts in the various sectors and industrial branches of the economy of the Soviet occupation zone and the later GDR, the introduction and extension of a system of state planning came much more rapidly. Right after the war no explanation was needed to justify those further controls which were imperative in an economy characterized by a severe scarcity of all the bare necessities of life.[21] The existing economic system already contained strong elements of governmental guidance of production and consumption, so that intensification of the economic controls of the Nazis was all that was necessary to meet the pressing requirements of the day. Once large-scale deprivatization had been embarked upon for political reasons, it followed that state planning had to be the consequence of state ownership of the means of production. Although only part of the means of production was as yet in government hands, the managers of state-owned enterprises needed some guidelines as to what, when and how to produce. Communists stress that the uncoordinated production both of individual enterprises and of whole branches results in the continuous recurrence of serious economic crises. It follows that it was very important to them to replace the "anarchy of the market" by the planning of the entire economy's production of goods and services as soon as politically possible, in order to achieve fast, balanced growth.

19. That is, half a hectare of arable land and the keeping of two cows, two pigs, five sheep, plus other small livestock, per family.

20. Share in agricultural land 1960 and 1969: LPGs Type I and II, 32 percent, 14 percent; LPGs Type III, 53 percent, 72 percent.

21. There is no need to offer a description here of the situation as regards the provision of shelter, food, clothing, etc., which was essentially not unlike that in the Western zones.

3

The Economic Development of the German Democratic Republic

Right after the war the Soviet Union not only permitted but required the full utilization of the remaining industrial capacities in her zone,[22] which brought the index of industrial output (1936=100) to 42 by the end of 1946 in an almost feverish reconstruction phase. Basic-materials industries, less affected by dismantling, even reached 52 percent of the 1936 level. On the other hand the consumer-goods industries and the thoroughly dismantled metal-working industries reached only 39 and 29 percent respectively. The first institutionalized planning attempts started with the so-called Half-Year Plan for the last six months of 1948, immediately following the currency reform.[23] Until the end of 1948 planning activity was confined to industry, emphasizing rapid reconstruction and reparations deliveries. Probably more important was the organizational preparation for the Two-Year Plan of 1949/50. While this first comprehensive economic plan projected the restoration of war-damaged and dismantled productive facilities to the prewar level, it has been estimated that by the end of 1950 the GNP had only reached 77 percent of that for 1936,[24] although the planning authorities claimed they had indeed attained, and even surpassed, the set goal.

This touches on the thorny problem of comparing the official national income statistics of any communist country with GNP figures calculating a country's annual total production of goods and services as recommended by the United Nations. Granted that the GNP concept does not cover some borderline activities because they do not find a visible market expression, it is still a relatively well-defined, more comprehensive analytical tool than the gross or net material product version of national income accounting used by the Comecon countries, which excludes as nonmaterial or nonproductive various activities such as governmental, professional, personal and domestic services, banking, insurance, and housing; in short, a sizable part of the tertiary sector is left out. In spite of the well-known set of problems stemming from differences in purchasing power, price and production structures, convention recommends the use of the GNP concept for inter-

22. In the Allied Control Council, the Soviet Union advocated low capacity ceilings for the Western zones since she was to partake in the dismantling proceeds.

23. Since a planned economy depends less on the proper functioning of the monetary mechanism than does a market economy, and since the blocking of deposits in 1945 had already substantially reduced the volume of money, the devaluation of the Reichsmark was rendered less drastic than in the Western zones. The conversion ratio to the new domestic currency was able to stand at somewhat better than 10 to 1.

24. The corresponding sectoral indices are 70 for industry and handicrafts, 73 for agriculture, 60 for construction, 89 for transportation and communication, 56 for trade, and 99 for other services.

national comparisons. It has its weaknesses but among the blind the one-eyed is king.[25]

Little insight can be gained by yielding to the predilection communist economists have for material production (goods and productive services), of which industrial output is the most important item. For 1950 the Statistical Office of the GDR claimed an 11 percent increase of total industrial production over 1936, i.e., the very same rise as reported by its Western counterpart for industry in the FRG. For the next two decades increases of 434 percent in the GDR and 324 percent in the FRG were officially claimed, paralleled by reported expansions of some 40 and some 70 percent respectively in the industrial labor force. Neither significantly longer working hours (which were actually close to the FRG level) nor greater labor productivity (which in fact was at least 20 percent below the FRG level[26]) can account for the allegedly faster growth of the GDR industry between 1950 and 1970. Different statistical methods, especially the use of the gross principle (i.e., including all previously counted values) in determining production figures, do, however, explain the higher percentage growth of GDR industry. Growth was indeed faster in the Soviet zone right after the war,[27] but this was also the time when—mostly due to dismantling—the previous lead in industrial labor productivity turned into a permanent lag. Western economists assume that the 1936 level of industrial output was regained not, as claimed, in 1950 but a year or two later, while the former peak level of 1944 was attained around the mid-fifties. Estimates of total gross national product (1936=100) come to 108 for 1955,[28] as compared to 77 in 1950, which signified considerable achievements in anybody's arithmetic,[29] reflecting a decade of im-

25. The author has no qualms about admitting that time and again he has valiantly ventured into the "growth figures jungle" in Western and communist publications. He has always returned slightly dizzy, hoping to have the numerical proportions and orders of magnitude right. Since the GDR uses the Comecon concept (System of National Accounts), the "numbers game" is anything but an intellectual pastime.

26. While central Germany had a higher per capita industrial production (some 7 percent in 1936 and some 11 to 12 percent in 1939 and 1944) than the western half, between 1950 and 1962 it was 20 to 21 percent lower; and estimates for the late sixties indicate a widening gap of about 30 percent. Though this author is inclined to insist on a much wider gap insofar as the credibility of economic statements made by communist chieftains is concerned, it may be added that in the spring of 1963 party leader Ulbricht admitted approximately 25 percent lower labor productivity for his state.

27. Some credence can be given to the respective index figures on industrial production (1936=100) in the Soviet and the Western zones: 1946, 42 and 33; 1947, 54 and 38; 1948, 71 and 60 (first six months, 47).

28. The corresponding sectoral indices for 1955 are 120 for industry and handicrafts, 92 for agriculture, 90 for construction, 124 for transportation and communication, 95 for trade, and 98 for other services.

29. Official GDR statistics claim average annual rates of 18 percent for industrial production and of 14.6 percent for national income, while Western calculations concede 14 percent for industrial output and 8 percent for GNP.

mensely hard work and abstention from consumption, the more so as they were accompanied by important structural changes laid down by the first Five-Year Plan of 1951/55.

Besides the faithful fulfillment of the reparations commitments to the Soviet Union, to which this plan accorded absolute priority, as well as the reorientation of the GDR's trade by reason of her membership in Comecon from 1950 on, the plan stipulated the expansion of the public and cooperative sectors at the expense of the private sector since—as GDR President Pieck put it—"economic planning is class struggle." To improve the lopsided structure of the economy, the creation of heavy industrial underpinnings was actively pursued. Basic-materials industries (coking plants, smelting works, foundries and rolling mills) and capital-goods branches (heavy mechanical and electrical engineering, metallurgical equipment) were founded, while already existing capital-goods branches (such as machine tools, light and electrical engineering) were enlarged for export purposes, primarily to relieve Soviet bottlenecks in these fields. Considerable investment was also made in the buildup of an oceangoing fleet and increased energy production on the basis of domestic lignite deposits, while only limited resources were allocated to agriculture, the consumer-goods industries, housing, the infrastructure in general, and the replacement and modernization of existing plants and equipment.

This investment policy not only reflected the priorities of the German communist regime but also demonstrated close adherence to the Stalinist doctrine of "planned and proportionate economic development," requiring the buildup of all industrial activities. While such a development concept may have its merits for an industrializing country, for an advanced economy it means considerable nonspecialization, small-scale economies, and withdrawal from participation in the international division of labor. The resulting growth losses tended to aggravate the disadvantages which derived from the adoption of Soviet-type institutions, e.g., collectivized agriculture, physical output planning and coercive labor-management controls. In the absence of positive incentives (an attractive assortment of consumer goods), the negative inducements to insure labor productivity were connected with the introduction of a Stalinist-type work and performance control system.[30] The government's attempts to make this system more stringent, as well as the general dissatisfaction with the slow improvement of the

30. Like Stakhanov in the Soviet Union, the miner Adolf Hennecke became the zone's symbol for the "Activist Movement" in 1948, when under optimal (better to say: rigged) working conditions he was able to overfulfill his norm. The result of such "communist competition" was held up as a model worthy of imitation, and provided planners with some information about working capability in various activities. It is worth thinking about the fact that such a system was introduced into a country whose working class had for decades propagated the slogan *"Akkord ist Mord"* (piecework is murder).

standard of living, resulted on 17 June 1953 in numerous strikes and demonstrations by the industrial workers of Berlin and other major cities.[31] Though this uprising did for a time badly shake the regime of the German communists, who saw themselves forced to sound certain tactical retreats in their economic policy, the decisive cause for the temporary change rested in the Soviet Union.

After Stalin's death in March 1953, his successors entered upon a "New Course" which had its emphasis on the economic sphere. The one-sided orientation of economic planning towards the development of capital-goods industries was to be ended in favor of more growth in the consumer-goods industries. The resulting measures by the Malenkov government were hurried and improvised, and within a short time had actually increased the difficulties of the Soviet economy. By the end of 1954 they had caused not only Malenkov's ouster but also a revision of economic policy, i.e., a return to the previous priority of the capital-goods industries. However, this revision came with the important qualification that, henceforth, consumer-goods industries and agriculture should be given preferential treatment. Such a multigoal policy called for better use of available domestic resources and greater regard for the natural difference in industrial location through the reactivation of Comecon,[32] i.e., extended economic integration and specialization within the communist bloc and coordination of national planning. In each case the German communists accommodated themselves quite quickly to the changes in Soviet economic policy. During the Malenkov phase, for instance, concessions were made to the peasantry, and some decollectivization was permitted in order to lessen political friction and rapidly increase agricultural output.[33] Furthermore, reparations deliveries to the Soviet Union were lowered and eventually discontinued by August 1953. Investable funds were channeled from the capital-goods industries to industries closer to the consumer, involving respective changes in the first Five-Year Plan.[34]

The second Five-Year Plan, announced in March 1956 and projected to 1960, took full account of the double-line economic policy under Khrushchev. It continued to pursue certain aims of the first

31. This first challenge to the Soviet Union's control system in Eastern Europe—"a fascist provocation" in communist parlance—ironically came from the class the communists purported to represent.

32. Previously Comecon had lived in the shadow of the doctrine of "proportionate economic development," which for the East European satellites had meant a repetition of the prewar industrialization experience of the Soviet Union and increased economic autarky rather than an intrabloc division of labor.

33. The number of LPGs declined from 5,389 in June 1953 to 4,958 by early 1954.

34. Altogether the plan underwent four major changes during its five-year term. Since planners decide on the basis of their last revision whether their plan has been fulfilled, timely adjustments regularly result in later "plan fulfillment."

Five-Year Plan, such as further development of capital-goods and to a lesser extent basic-materials industries, and increased nationalization in industry and collectivization in agriculture. At the same time it promised changes in the field of consumption, e.g., an early end to food rationing,[35] a better supply of durable consumer goods, the introduction of the seven-hour day and the forty-hour week in some industries, and higher investments in housing. The called-for average annual growth of the economy of 8 percent was to be achieved through increased productivity of labor, which was to result from nationalization and collectivization and through "socialist division of labor" within the Comecon bloc, featuring the coordination of planning, intensified trade, particularly of raw materials imports, and product specialization, especially within the engineering branch.[36] Since this plan was born under an unlucky (Soviet) star, the crises in Poland, Hungary and at the Suez Canal in the fall of 1956 delayed its implementation till early 1958. The breakdown of Polish coal and coke deliveries forced the GDR authorities to make do with reduced yearly plans (aiming at 5 percent annual growth after October 1957) and certain priority programs. Nevertheless, though 1956 brought the planners in the GDR considerable disappointment, the following two years showed remarkable growth.[37]

Under these bright auspices the German communists, probably deceived by their own statistics and by a stretch of reduced growth in the FRG,[38] in July 1958 proclaimed the "principal economic task" *(ökonomische Hauptaufgabe)* for the coming years in the presence of all the Moscow bigwigs. As the Soviet leaders had recently called upon the Russian people to catch up with and overtake the United States in the most important branches of agriculture and industrial production by 1970—"but possibly even earlier"—the German communists did not want to look inferior, and announced similar intentions with regard to their ideological archenemy, the FRG. They tacitly discarded their second Five-Year Plan and instead adopted a Seven-Year Plan for 1959/65, synchronizing it with the first Seven-Year Plan of the Soviet Union.

35. The premature halt of food rationing in May 1958 resulted in a rapid rise of meat and butter sales and consequent shortages. Informal rationing through customers' registration at the local meat and dairy markets lasted, at least in some areas, until 1966.

36. Though the discarding of the Stalinist industrialization doctrine meant some improvement, the GDR, as an advanced country, could not expect much gain from division of labor with countries mostly in an early stage of industrialization, and consequently lacking a highly differentiated production structure and sufficient consumption capacity.

37. Official sources claimed growth rates for national income and industrial production of 4.4 percent and 7.4 percent in 1956, 6.9 percent and 11.1 percent in 1957, and 10.9 percent and 12.4 percent in 1958.

38. GNP growth rates in the FRG averaged 4.7 percent for 1957/58 compared to 9.6 percent in 1955/56.

The relevant law of October 1959 stipulated the principal economic task: "to increase production and the productivity of labor in order to catch up with and surpass the per capita consumption of West Germany in most of the industrial consumer goods and foodstuffs by the end of 1961, thereby demonstrating the superiority of the socialist over the capitalist social system."

These ambitious aims at attaining an annual growth rate of about 7 percent were to be reached through increased industrial labor productivity as a result of collectivization of the crafts and "new forms of socialist team-work," especially by "brigades of socialist working and research groups." Further nationalization in industry and collectivization in agriculture, extended foreign trade with Comecon as well as capitalist countries, and continued emphasis upon the capital-goods industries, especially the chemical, electrical and engineering branches, and power production, were to assure the realization of the "principal economic task." The Seven-Year Plan, however, conceived from the beginning as the decisive battle between communism and the West, experienced the same fate as its predecessors, and soon ran into trouble as growth rates took a steep plunge.[39] The growth crisis of the early 1960s compelled the GDR leadership to silently drop its Seven-Year Plan by summer 1962,[40] after it had earlier ceased to mention the achievement of the "principal economic task" by the end of 1961. Most of all, their own boasting had been a cause of their embarrassment, since even according to Western estimates, growth of GNP in the GDR during the second half of the 1950s had been quite impressive, amounting to 5.8 percent annually.[41] Truly this was an achievement the planners could proudly present;[42] but since the FRG had not rested on its laurels, the GDR gained little ground and still remained substantially behind in per capita consumption.[43] What had been gained was quickly lost again; and 1961, the target year of the "principal economic task," found the planners empty-handed when temporary rationing of certain foodstuffs like butter, milk and potatoes had to be reintroduced, supplies of meat and occasionally even bread became irregular, and

39. Official sources claimed annual growth rates for national income and industrial production of 8.5 percent and 7.6 percent in 1959, 4.6 percent and 5.8 percent in 1960, 1.6 percent and 6.7 percent in 1961, and 2.7 percent and 4.6 percent in 1962.

40. At that time, plan arrears amounted to 25 percent in investments and 35 percent in industrial output.

41. By 1960 indices (1936=100) reached 167 for industry and handicrafts, 107 for agriculture, 146 for construction, 147 for transport and communication, 125 for trade, 101 for other services, and 137 for GNP.

42. Annual percentage growth of GNP, 1956/60: United States 2.3, Great Britain 2.4, France 4.4, Italy 5.9, FRG 6.6.

43. Percentage estimates of per capita consumption in the GDR compared to the FRG: 1957, 66; 1958, 71; 1959, 72; 1960, 72; 1961, 69; 1962, 65; 1963, 65.

industrial consumer goods began to fall off seriously in quantity and quality. Official blame for this poor performance fell on poor work discipline, and increasing "consumerism" *(Konsumentenideologie),* the need to make the economy "trouble free" *(störfrei),*[44] and "flight from the republic." The latter—not least due to the incapacity of the GDR's Soviet-style economic system to accommodate consumers' wishes— had to serve as the simpleminded excuse for the erection of the Berlin Wall, which the Free World at once regarded as the stony memorial of the political bankruptcy of the German communist regime.

In October 1962, new and more modest targets (4.4 percent annual growth of national income) for another seven-year period till 1970 were announced. This "second" Seven-Year Plan was never formally enacted, however, because of the uncertainty about the effects of the reforms in the planning setup started at the same time. Till 1966 single year plans directed economic development, while a new Five-Year Plan for 1966/70 merely indicated the spread of the growth rates (5.6 to 6.4 percent per year), which on account of the quite positive results between 1964 and 1966,[45] were slightly higher than the projection of 1963. On average the lower planning ceiling was approximately reached in the second half of the 1960s, indicating that the phase of sluggish performance during the early sixties had been permanently overcome.[46] Viewed over longer periods, Western economists ranked the growth performance of the GDR as comparable to that of the FRG. For the sixties an annual growth rate of real national income of 4.5 percent for the GDR and 4.8 percent for the FRG has frequently been mentioned, while for the period 1950 to 1967 compound annual rates of gross national product per unit of labor of 4 percent for the GDR and 4.4 percent for the FRG have been given. This assured both economies of a good middle position in the international growth league, be it of planning or market provenance.[47] The actual organiza-

44. During 1961 and 1962 the communist leadership tried to lessen economic ties with the FRG and to replace them by increased trade with other western countries. An unwise, though legally correct termination of the intra-German trade agreement by the FRG in September 1960, so as to counter the permanent harassment of Berlin by the GDR authorities, had triggered this move. During 1961/62 intra-German trade was indeed about 10 percent below the 1960 figure, which was almost reached again in 1963 and quickly surpassed thereafter. In the mid-sixties less than 1 percent of the FRG's net product was sent to the GDR, which returned less than 2 percent of her net output.

45. Official data claimed annual growth rates for national income and industrial production of 3.4 percent and 6.6 percent in 1963, 4.9 percent and 6.2 percent in 1964, 4.6 percent and 6.6 percent in 1965, 4.9 percent and 6.7 percent in 1966.

46. Average annual growth rates of national income, officially stated, were 3.7 percent for 1961/65 and 5.8 percent for 1966/70.

47. GNP growth rate per unit of labor among the leaders for 1950/67: Yugoslavia 5.4, Romania 5, Italy 5.2, Japan 6.6.

tion of planning, however, changed frequently in the GDR, as the discarding of a plan usually also called for reorganization of the planning setup.

4

Centralized Planning—Problems and Reforms

Right after the war the existing regulations of the Reich served as the administrative basis for the economic controls and planning attempts of the five newly created states and later of the German Economic Council, both under the general guidance of the Soviet occupation authorities. Until well into the 1950s Soviet economic experts remained the dominant influence on the GDR economy and provided valuable assistance to the inexperienced German regime in showing how to establish a planning system along Soviet lines, i.e., centralized and comprehensive direction of the economy. A whole hierarchy of planning authorities was created, headed by a ministry of planning, renamed the State Planning Commission in November 1950.[48] Be it for whole branches or entire districts,[49] the planning bodies at the intermediate level were to guide and control the individual production unit, e.g., VEB, VEG, LPG or PGH.

As a kind of economic general staff, the State Planning Commission received its principal economic policy directives from the leaders of the Communist Party (who in turn followed the Moscow line[50]), and was charged with establishing the general perspective by developing a multi-year plan, quantitatively defining the basic macroeconomic proportions and their development. Furthermore, it had to draw up corresponding annual plans, the more detailed criteria of which would be filled in by the subordinate planning bodies on the intermediate level. These agencies were to break down the total figures for their particular branch or region and present the individual production unit with a detailed plan directive drawn up in two interrelated versions, i.e., in physical and value terms. The production unit would then establish what input it needed to turn out the required quantities and return this information, plus appropriate counterproposals, to the higher authority. Each of the successive stages of the planning hierarchy would then attempt to bridge the gap between plan directives handed down and plan proposals returned. Based on these plan proposals, the State

48. It corresponds to the Gosplan in the Soviet Union.
49. In 1952 the five states had been divided into 14 (with East Berlin 15) new administrative districts.
50. This was regarded as good thinking, since a communist slogan insisted, "To learn from the Soviet Union means to learn how to win."

Planning Commission would finally establish a compatible pattern of the subplans by ironing out internal inconsistencies in the material balances.[51] Since discrepancies from the original party directive could be considerable, the final fiat of the party leadership would be needed for any necessary adjustments. Passed into law, the mandatory plan figures were conveyed down the administrative ladder, with the advice to keep a careful watch on the "plan discipline" of one's subordinates, as plan infractions were open to prosecution. Though the bureaucratic structure has undergone continuous change since 1948—always faithfully copying the latest Soviet innovation—for about one and a half decades the organizational setup of planning in the GDR reflected this scheme of arrangement, and actual planning remained based on central direction, material balances, long-term price fixing and strict plan adherence of the individual production unit.[52]

Management of an economy along such principles had a host of consequences, of which only those relating to planning technique and those stemming from the reactions of the individual production unit will be briefly sketched here. Regarding planning it can be said that the more centralized and detailed it is, the longer plan preparations will take and the more dated the planning data will be when the plan is implemented.[53] Aside from this time problem, which makes for delays in plan implementation and necessitates early plan revisions, there is the question of planning along territorial and functional lines, i.e., the need to coordinate the plans for single branches with those for entire regions. Furthermore, the great variety of products in an advanced industrial economy tends to increase faster than the ability of the planners to establish consistent material balances for them. The consequent need to group similar and related products together in order to reduce the number of individually planned products—an aggregation only feasible through realistic prices —creates difficult planning problems with regard to price structure and price level for the leading control agencies, easily resulting in inconsistencies in the material balances. Pronounced disproportionalities within the GDR economy sharpened the awareness among its economists of the defects in the comprehensive central planning system, and led to the discussion of alternative steering mechanisms. With proper ideological protection, some GDR economists argued in the mid-fifties that, once the dictatorship of the proletariat had been firmly established, a conscious shift from state

51. A material balance juxtaposes physical requirements of a commodity against expected availabilities from production and stocks making due allowance for foreign trade.

52. Up to the mid-fifties, value-term planning was increasingly of only subordinate importance, but made a certain comeback afterwards.

53. The high hopes of planners in the use of mathematical models and electronic computers to rid planning of its slowness, crudity and inaccuracy remain to be fulfilled.

planning towards a market guided by a system of economic levers belonged to the logical dialectics of development. They argued further that it would form part and parcel of the withering-away of the state postulated by Marxian teaching, and that failure to comply with these inexorable dialectics accounted for observable, dangerous contradictions and tensions.[54]

Contradictions were particularly flagrant on the lowest planning level, where the individual production unit reacted to the mandatory plan figures in a rational manner by taking various measures which, in effect, partially thwarted the intentions of the central planning authorities. Since emphasis was placed on plan fulfillment in each year, the limited time horizon of management resulted in attempts to do just that, even if it militated against plan fulfillment in, say, four years, by, for example, overloading of plant and machinery or providing insufficient maintenance of capital equipment. Neither the improvement of the productive apparatus by adopting a new process nor the introduction of a new product looked attractive to the production department, which was afraid to switch from one form of production to another and possibly to jeopardize plan fulfillment; nor could it be of interest to the procurement department, which then had to provide new or additional inputs. Since these legitimate concerns were not confronted, as in a market economy, by the interest of a nagging sales department pressing for new or better products, spontaneous innovations remained rare.[55] This tendency was enforced by the plan's emphasis upon physical output instead of sales. To sacrifice quality for quantity, limit the product line to a few articles which were easy to plan for and produce, disregard the service dimension and care solely about the material dimension of production, was justifiable from the producers' standpoint but detrimental to the consumers' welfare. Management should also, from the overall economic point of view, be criticized for being more concerned about underproduction than overspending, since physical plan fulfillment ranked supreme; for showing little interest in avoiding waste, as plan allocations were made on the basis of last year's input; and for misinforming superior planning authorities about productive capacity, or about the true costs of a new product or process, in order to assure a "soft" plan, leading to lower utilization of capacity, hoarding of supplies and labor, and "empire building."[56]

54. Such reasoning was politically unacceptable to the communist leaders of the GDR and was quickly discouraged.

55. In the mid-fifties the Polish economist and planning theorist Oskar Lange stressed the adverse psychological impact of excessively centralized planning with its strong grip on details down to the lowest level giving rise to apathy and nihilistic attitudes.

56. As physical allocation provided the procurement department with only a hunting license and not with a guarantee of timely deliveries, the individual production unit would try to set up its own sources of supply, resulting in corresponding excess capacities and a reduced division of labor.

It is not surprising that all this contributed to the high production costs of GDR industry in the late 1950s and early 1960s. Obsolescence of plant and equipment contributed to high specific consumption of industrial inputs like raw materials or fuel.[57] An undercapitalized and fragmented building industry led to long construction periods.[58] Low quality and almost immediate obsolescence of newly installed industrial plant and equipment were frequently criticized by party leaders.[59] Rapid growth of stocks after the mid-1950s, either of unsalable goods mainly reflecting the desire to increase output, or of scarce materials hoarded by production units weary of irregular supplies, was another highly visible piece of evidence of economic malfunctioning in national accounting figures. Probably the most critical of all inefficiencies, however, was caused by the substantial wastage of labor,[60] an extravagance an economy with a stagnant work force could ill afford.

Though these and similar economic malfunctionings, which reflected the crudity of Soviet-type planning and control devices, could also be found in the other Comecon countries in the late 1950s and early 1960s, explaining their desire for economic reform, the economy of the GDR evidenced a number of peculiar characteristics which provided the motive for the early search by her economists for more efficient management methods.[61] As the most industrialized country within the Soviet bloc, the GDR was the first to face the unsuitableness of central comprehensive planning for an advanced economy,[62] as was clearly reflected in her sharply declining rates of economic growth, especially in the early 1960s. The growing shortage of labor, as a consequence of persistent "flight from the republic," had early on given rise to the economists' concern with labor efficiency and technological improvements, the more so since the GDR, the only debtor of reparations deliveries (mostly consisting of not very sophisticated capital goods) was for quite a while provided with secure outlets. These permitted its industry not only to pay little attention to quality and variety in commodity production, but also to live on the technological and scientific inheritance of the past. By international comparison, the declining

57. Compared to international standards, power plants consumed over one-third more fuel per kilowatt-hour in the early sixties, while steel consumption in relation to the value of machinery produced was almost three times as high.

58. Construction in the 1950s usually took twice as long as in the FRG.

59. Around 1960 critical comments were made about the design of textile machinery, a leading export article in the prewar period, and therefore perhaps indicative of the general state of machine technology in the GDR.

60. The high and rising percentage of industrial workers making repairs in the early sixties, for example, is symptomatic of this situation.

61. For quite a while the Party frowned on such theoretical or, even worse, practical attempts, as "managerism."

62. Not surprisingly Czechoslovakia, the industrial runner-up, soon followed and tried to develop a conceptual framework which fused the market system with communism.

productivity of the GDR was continuously demonstrated by the economic accomplishments on the other side of the German-German border. Exposure to Western markets was a result of geographic proximity and the GDR's high degree of dependence on foreign trade (as a heavy importer of raw materials and agricultural products and exporter of finished goods), and it was conducive to discussions of economic management. The coexistence of nationalized, semi-public and privately owned production units in industry and agriculture—unparalleled in the Soviet block—made the search for new economic steering devices necessary and encouraged discussions on planning and management systems. Equally unique within the Comecon block was, and is, the traditionally conscientious German attitude towards work, the high regard for skill, and the sensitivity to problems of efficiency, fostering interest in well-run, well-organized production units. Nevertheless, the decisive impulse had to come from the Soviet Union.

It did not materialize before the fall of 1962, when ideas on economic decentralization and a greater role for value categories in planning, already debated in the Soviet specialist press for years, were outlined in a Pravda article, thus acquiring political respectability.[63] The consequent liberalization of the discussion in the stagnation stricken GDR resulted, after practical testing, in the general introduction in July 1963 of a New Economic System (*Neues ökonomisches System der Planung und Leitung der Volkswirtschaft,* NÖS) in order to widen the scope of both decision making by the lower echelons and industrial guidance through value parameters (such as prices, rates of interest, rents and profits).

To reduce centralized control, new centers of economic power had to be created as a first reform measure. The largest and most important of the VEBs had already been grouped according to industry into some 90 Associations of State-owned Enterprises (*Vereinigung Volkseigener Betriebe,* VVB), which functioned as executive bodies for the State Planning Commission. These VVBs were given greatly increased authority and independence, which made them somewhat comparable to large subsidiaries of diversified American corporations. Placed under new management of mostly younger men with industrial experience, the VVBs as intermediate decision-making bodies were henceforth to guide, coordinate and control the production of their subordinate VEBs within the framework of a less rigidly defined central plan. A VVB could use some of its earnings, which it primarily derived from its VEBs, to finance industrywide investment and research programs or

63. Since this article was signed by E. Liberman, this reform movement is usually, though incorrectly, termed "Libermanism" in the West.

other activities conducive to interplant cooperation or to establish industrywide incentive and bonus funds, but it also had to cover the deficits of its unprofitable subordinates. Not only did the managers of VVBs become more directly involved in the performance of their units, but so did those in charge of VEBs—whether they were VVB-directed or, as was the case with the smaller VEBs, subject to control by the district economic council. The individual VEB became legally and economically an independent unit, with greater scope for decision making with regard to product mix, industrial technology, internal organization and, to a smaller degree, expansion of productive capacity. The rights and responsibilities of the VEB management vis-à-vis its supervisors, however, remained somewhat poorly defined, essentially reflecting the dichotomy on which the NÖS reform rested—devolution in management within a system of central planning.

Once such a polymorphic setup of management and economic organization was established, a new system of indirect economic controls had to be introduced to guide management interests in the direction desired by the central planning authorities. After some experimenting, a so-called self-contained system of economic levers *(geschlossenes System ökonomischer Hebel)* based on material incentives for the individual was introduced by the spring of 1965. To ensure the proper functioning of the economic levers, the following preconditions had to be fulfilled first: a reform of the industrial price structure and a revaluation of industrial assets. Industrial prices, still largely in the straitjacket of the 1944 price system, were utterly distorted and generally far too low to encourage either more economy in the use of scarce inputs or a more rational assessment of costs. A three-stage price reform between April 1964 and January 1967 brought new, substantially increased, fixed prices,[64] which in essence, however, still reflected government priorities more than real costs, even though some reformers had advocated variable prices influenced by the trends on the world market.[65] The price reforms brought with them the additional advantage of basically eliminating the need for direct state budgetary support for the production unit. A similar administrative facilitation also resulted from the decree of September 1964, which obligated VVBs and VEBs to finance their investments largely from internally generated funds or through repayable bank loans instead of by subsidies from the state budget; the primary aim of this was to reduce waste in future investment ex-

64. For example, increases of 70 percent for coal, nonferrous metals, and pig iron, and 40 percent for lumber, leather and chemical products.

65. How realistic prices within the communist economic system were is amply illustrated by the fact that trade among Comecon countries was frequently conducted on the basis of Western prices. Authorities in the selling country hunted for hopefully high-priced invoices of Western suppliers, while the buying country searched for evidence of bargain-basement prices.

penditures. For already existing fixed capital, the same effect was expected from a revaluation of assets, so as to provide a basis for the recalculation of depreciation, and also to give central planning authorities better insight into the distribution of capacities.[66] To encourage production units to release excess assets and to induce a less wasteful use of plant and equipment, a 6 percent charge on the value of the entrusted capital assets was introduced, and it was not to be treated as a cost component but had to be borne out of profits.[67]

The fact that profit became the main criterion of each production unit's performance was another important reform aspect. While volume of output or value of output had previously been used, giving rise to the above mentioned side-effects, profits which could only be raised by producing and selling what customers wanted and/or by reducing costs were henceforth to serve as a measure of achievement. On the basis of a new law of contract, delivery deadlines, higher standards of quality, styling, and customer service became objects of agreement, and their nonfulfillment or other substandard performance became subject to fines deductible from profits, thus curtailing the pecuniary rewards that had been introduced as part of a new profit-based wage and premium system. Latitude in the pursuit of material interests by management and staff was, however, carefully limited by a reduced number of mandatory plan figures (the value of sales or, occasionally, output; the total wage bill; payments into the state budget; and investments) which limited the operation of the price mechanism and effectively maintained central control. Indeed, a certain recentralization, which took place in the late sixties, partially reduced the effective operation of the self-contained system of economic levers. Apart from the introduction of additional planning coefficients, some even delineated in physical terms, the classification of certain projects as "structurally determining" (*strukturbestimmend*) from 1968 on considerably reduced the elbow-room of lower echelons regarding investment decisions.[68] The

66. Gross fixed assets in GDR industry were revalued by 52 percent.

67. The paying of charges on capital was truly a novelty, since in the understanding of the Marxian labor theory of value prices are solely determined by production costs reflecting the socially necessary labor. Permitting fixed charges on capital was a step in the right direction but insufficient to reflect relative scarcities and to lead to an efficient resource allocation on the basis of opportunity costs. A communist economic system can indeed abolish interest and rent as income categories but not their usefulness as allocation devices.

68. Such projects were those that would show a high degree of economic efficiency or automation, that would use domestic materials to a maximum extent, or produce attractive export products. Though it was clear that this essentially meant catching up with the Third Industrial Revolution, greater details were difficult to obtain, due to a more restrictive information policy since 1968. The buttoned-up GDR regarded such projects as secrets not to be divulged to the class enemy.

partial recentralization of such decisions reflected a considerable uncertainty at the production-unit level as to how to direct activities according to unaccustomed economic criteria. The lack of experienced modern management, thoroughly familiar with cost-benefit analyses of investment projects and production processes as well as marketing techniques, stemmed from two decades of neglect in business administration research and formed one of the major obstacles to reform, which only a time-consuming learning process could remove. The limited reserves of the GDR economy, resulting from past mistakes in structural policy, current obligations to other Comecon countries and the general malfunctioning of the central planning system, seemed to permit no extended adaptation period for reform, and triggered the return to centralized comprehensive planning as part of a new policy from 1967 onward, called the "Economic System of Socialism" (*Ökonomisches System des Sozialismus,* ÖSS). While NÖS was not given sufficient time to outlive the problems of its infancy, gain maturity and prove its advantages, the GDR economy as such could, after 20 years of existence, no longer claim adolescence, and had to face up to a prosperity comparison with the FRG.

5

The Standard of Living in the German States

To compare the living standards in the GDR and FRG is, like all such endeavors, a difficult undertaking and will not be attempted here in detail. Some facts and figures on the per capita consumption of a few foodstuffs, industrial goods, and services in the late sixties will simply be provided, since the GDR leadership had already eagerly advocated such an inter-German comparison a decade earlier.

By the late sixties the daily diet in the GDR, as in the FRG, stood at 3,000 calories per person, but consisted of somewhat more carbohydrates and fats and less high-protein foodstuffs.[69] The per capita consumption of coffee, fresh and tropical fruits amounted to only half of the FRG level and suffered wide seasonal fluctuations. Year-round availability as well as consistent product quality have a bearing on consumer satisfaction. Of industrial goods in daily use, footwear can serve as a good example. Whereas the average person in each state owned 3.4 to 3.8 pairs of shoes during the late sixties, only one percent of the

---

69. Flour and potato consumption in the GDR in the late sixties was a good one-third higher, while meat and egg consumption was about one-eighth lower than in the FRG.

shoes offered for sale to the GDR public—according to official GDR sources—met so-called "world market standards" as set by the West European consumer. Deficiencies and differences in quality in general were even more pronounced with regard to consumer durables. While the supply per household of television sets, radios, movie cameras, slide projectors and small electrical kitchen appliances was about the same or slightly lower in the GDR, the lead of the FRG was much more pronounced with regard to refrigerators, washing machines and cars.[70] The lack of suitable private means of transportation in the GDR ranked as a major shortcoming since Germans, as in the old tribal days, continued to be noted for their wanderlust. A good third of the population in each state spent their vacations away from home. While about half of all vacationers in the FRG went to a foreign country, frequently by plane, only some 15 percent of GDR holidaymakers could go abroad—and then only to another Communist state, and usually by land.[71] When staying at home, those living in the FRG increasingly enjoyed more individual living space.[72] Although after years of neglect, GDR regime leaders finally gave some priority to housing construction in the sixties, residential dwellings were older in the GDR[73]—partly due to the fact that wartime destruction of housing had been somewhat heavier in the FRG—and though buildings, like women, usually grow more charming with age, they have fewer physical amenities.[74]

For nearly all these goods and services the average industrial laborer in the GDR had to work much longer than his more fortunate compatriot in the FRG. Though the price structure in the GDR was consciously designed to favor the low income groups, such "field-kitchen ideology" added up to very little. In the category of foodstuffs and semiluxuries, the working time necessary to earn the income to buy some staples was indeed significantly shorter, but for the majority of basic commodities it was substantially longer.[75] A similar two-tier price

70. Appliances and vehicles per GDR household in 1969 as a percentage of FRG level: refrigerators, 57 percent; washing machines, 79 percent; cars, 30 percent; but: motorcycles 570 percent.

71. Yugoslavia was excluded, since it offered too convenient escape routes to the West. All journeys to Western countries were, of course, prohibited, and only occasionally permitted to married people whose next of kin had to stay behind.

72. Living space in square meters per capita for the GDR and the FRG: 1950, 14.7, 14.9; 1961, 17.2, 19.7; 1968, 18.6, 23.0.

73. According to the last housing census in the early sixties, housing of pre-1900 vintage and that built after World War II amounted to 45 percent and 10.5 percent, respectively, in the GDR, compared to 25 percent and 34 percent in the FRG.

74. The proportion of houses without central heating, bath or indoor toilet in the mid-sixties was 64 percent in the GDR and 25 percent in the FRG.

75. In 1969 the work necessary to purchase such articles as rye bread, potatoes, or white cabbage was about 50 percent less than in the FRG, but 40 percent more for meat,

structure existed with regard to household necessities, services, utilities and fares,[76] while in the categories of clothing, textiles, shoes, and especially durable consumer goods, the working time necessary in the GDR was substantially longer.[77] Altogether, by the late sixties, the standard of living in the GDR, though the highest in the Communist bloc,[78] reached—according to Western estimates—at best the level of the early sixties in the FRG, which remained the most relevant comparison for the population. In spite of the fact that as early as the mid-fifties many citizens in the GDR were better off than in 1936, when living standards in the two halves of Germany had been roughly comparable, per capita consumption of goods and services seldom reached 70 percent of the FRG level throughout the fifties and sixties. From 61 percent in 1950, the GDR figure rose to 72 percent in 1955, but dropped to 66 percent the following year, to recover to 72 percent again by 1959/ 60. The first half of the sixties brought continuous decline to 61 percent in 1965, followed by years of stabilization at this or at a slightly higher level.

This relatively high standard of living for a communist country resulted from the large share of the GNP the GDR leadership devoted to private consumption for quite a while. Being the most Western country in the communist bloc—geographically and historically—the GDR was to function as a showcase of communism for its own and the neighboring peoples, as well as present an economic challenge to the ideological enemy, especially the FRG. There the share of personal consumption in GNP amounted to about 60 percent throughout the fifties, and to about 56 percent in the sixties. While only 50 percent of GNP in the GDR was used for personal consumption in 1950, the share increased quickly to about 60 percent in 1955 and 1960, then falling gradually to about 54 percent in 1970. With the erection of the Berlin Wall in August 1961, the GDR leadership ended the contest and almost immediately availed itself of the chance to increase investments at the consumers' expense. The comparatively low fixed capital investment ratio of about 15 percent in the early fifties rose to about 18 percent in

---

75 to 85 percent more for wheat flour, butter and sugar, 150 percent more for eggs and tobacco, and 460 to 550 percent more for tropical fruit and coffee.

76. To pay for items like railroad tickets, dry cleaning, hair dressing, or soap, less work was necessary than in the FRG, but the opposite was true for utilities, radio and TV charges.

77. For suits, dresses, shoes, and bed linen, 50 to 90 percent more; for stockings, ties, and shirts, as much as 260 to 420 percent; for vacuum cleaners and bicycles 70 to 90 percent; for wristwatches, typewriters, and electric ranges, 170 to 200 percent; for television sets, cars, and refrigerators, 420 to 530 percent longer.

78. By the mid-sixties, private per capita consumption in the GDR was about 50 percent higher than in the Soviet Union.

1960 and 23 percent in 1970, compared to FRG figures of close to 20 percent in the late forties, 22 to 23 percent in the early fifties and about 25 percent since the mid-fifties. While, in relative terms, fixed investments in the GDR eventually approached the level of the FRG in the late sixties, capital efficiency continued to lag behind—not least due to the inadequate allocation mechanism of a planned economy.[79] Misdirection of capital was clearly reflected in rising stocks of mainly unsalable goods, which accounted for only about 2 percent of the GNP in the mid-fifties but rose to an enormous 3.4 percent between 1964 and 1967.[80] The altogether smaller shares devoted to private consumption and capital investment in the GDR were set against larger shares for other uses. A residuum, containing allocations for state administration, defense, public services and external contribution, amounted to about 35 percent of the GNP by 1950, under 25 percent in 1955, 20 percent in 1960 and 23 percent in 1970. The exact composition of this residuum is unknown since no balances of payments were published and foreign trade items were assessed at lower values than domestic production and consumption.[81] Estimates of the GDR's share of world trade run at 1.6 percent or about one-sixth of the FRG figure, compared to an industrial production of under 25 percent, a population of about 28 percent and a gainfully active population of 32 percent of the FRG level in the late sixties. While the foreign trade of the GDR thus reached about half the FRG level on a per capita basis, the intensity of foreign trade, i.e., the relation of foreign trade to national income, was very roughly similar in both states at that time. The share of the government budget and its structure have been kept a strict secret, a fact which does not permit an evaluation of the importance of collective consumption for the individual standard of living.[82] From what is known about the "communist achievements" in the field of social policy in the GDR, they—like the application of central planning in a highly industrialized economy in general—present little that either an economist or a trade unionist can get excited about, though a communist, with his different frame of reference, sees it quite differently.

79. Western estimates of the productivity of industrial capital in the GDR in relation to the FRG run at 76 percent for 1960 and 86 percent for 1968, probably partly showing the result of the economic reforms in the GDR and the impact of the 1966/67 recession in the FRG.

80. During the sixties stocks amounted to 1.35 percent in the FRG and 2.5 percent in the GDR.

81. It is nevertheless obvious that the high share of this residuum in the early fifties reflected the large payments of reparations and occupation costs to the Soviet Union.

82. Collective consumption, as a means of forestalling "embourgeoisement" of the populace, was regarded as superior to catering to the wishes of the individual consumer; in this, as in many other aspects, Nazis and communists are truly brothers.

Bibliography

Bröll, W. "Über den Stand der Wirtschaftswissenschaften in der DDR," *Deutschland-Archiv* 2 (1969).

Bröll, W. *Die Wirtschaft der DDR: Lage und Aussichten*. Munich, 1973.

Deckers, J. *Die Transformation des Bankensystems in der Sowjetischen Besatzungszone/DDR von 1945 bis 1952*. Berlin, 1974.

Deutsches Institut für Wirtschaftsforschung. *DDR-Wirtschaft: Eine Bestandsaufnahme*. Frankfurt/Main, 1971.

Gleitze, B. *Ostdeutsche Wirtschaft, Industrielle Standorte und volkswirtschaftliche Kapazitäten des ungeteilten Deutschland*. Berlin, 1956.

Hamel, H., ed. *BRD-DDR: Die Wirtschaftssysteme, Soziale Marktwirtschaft und Sozialistische Planwirtschaft im Systemvergleich*. Munich, 1977.

Immler, H. *Agrarpolitik in der DDR*. Cologne, 1971.

Jochimsen, R. "Die gesamtwirtschaftliche Entwicklung in der DDR." *Geschichte in Wissenschaft und Unterricht* 17 (1966).

Leptin, G. *Die deutsche Wirtschaft nach 1945: Ein Ost-West-Vergleich*. Opladen, 1970.

Miller, D., and Trend, H. G. "Economic Reforms in East Germany." *Problems of Communism* 15 (1966).

Müller, H., and Reissig, K. *Wirtschaftswunder DDR: Ein Beitrag zur Geschichte der ökonomischen Politik der SED*. Institut für Gesellschaftswissenschaften beim ZK der SED, ed. East Berlin, 1968.

Obst, W. *DDR-Wirtschaft: Modell und Wirklichkeit*. Hamburg, 1973.

Pritzel, K. *Die wirtschaftliche Integration der Sowjetischen Besatzungszone Deutschlands in den Ostblock und ihre politischen Aspekte*. 2nd. ed. Berlin, 1965.

Sass, P. "Wirtschaftsentwicklung und Wirtschaftspolitik in der DDR." *Gewerkschaftliche Monatshefte* 19 (1968).

Schnitzer, M. *East and West Germany: A Comparative Economic Analysis*. New York, 1972.

Stolper, W. F. *The Structure of the East German Economy*. Cambridge, Mass., 1960.

Thalheim, K. C. *Die wirtschaftliche Entwicklung der beiden Staaten in Deutschland*. Opladen, 1978.

U.S. Congress, Joint Economic Committee. *Economic Developments in Countries of Eastern Europe*. Washington, D.C., 1970.

Zauberman, A. *Industrial Progress in Poland, Czechoslovakia and East Germany: 1937–1962*. London, 1964.

CHAPTER 7

The Economy of
the Federal Republic
of Germany

1

The Social Market System—Doctrine and Reality

The Concept of Neoliberalism

After 1945, like the Soviet Union, the United States, as the bellwether of the Western Allies, also attempted, albeit somewhat belatedly, to demonstrate the excellence of its political order through the superiority of its economic system. Along with broad programs of political and economic reform, "reeducation" was to emphasize the outstanding merits of free enterprise, and the American military governor was bound to work for the ultimate establishment of the American business philosophy in Germany by favoring its basic tenet, the free market doctrine, as much as possible. In accordance with the Potsdam Agreement the breakup of German cartels and trusts, initially pursued primarily for security reasons,[1] was, with increasing East-West tension, soon to serve the buildup of an American-style economic system. In July 1947 the military governor was instructed that it was not the intention of the United States "to impose its own historically developed forms of democracy and social organization on Germany," but was also ordered to "give the German people an opportunity to learn of the principles and advantages of free enterprise" and advised to

1. The general deconcentration and decartelization law for the U.S. zone, of February 1947, still referred to economic concentrations as a military and political threat in three of its four clauses, and only the fourth obliquely touched on potential economic drawbacks.

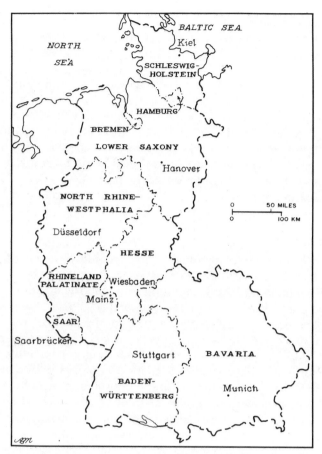

5. *The Federal Republic of Germany and her ten states in 1970.*

"refrain from interfering in the question of public ownership of enterprises in Germany except to ensure that any choice for or against public ownership is made freely through the normal processes of democratic government." Soon the American information service for the German public switched from merely emphasizing the advantages of Western democracy without attacking communism in principle or depicting the "ugly reality" in the East to a far more aggressive stance, stressing especially the detrimental effects of a planned economy and nationalization.

Demands for nationalization of a considerable part of the means of production were, indeed, widespread among the German population. The Social Democrats, representing mostly workers and about one-third of the total electorate, were traditionally committed to nationalization. The equally strong Christian Democrats (with their primarily petty bourgeois and bourgeois backing), though vacillating between individualist and collectivist positions, finally thought it advisable, in their Ahlen Program of February 1947, to advocate public ownership of "enterprises of monopoly character," particularly in the coal and iron industries. Public entities such as the national, state and local governments, as well as cooperative associations and the workers employed in these works, were to share in ownership. Sufficient leeway was to be left, however, for the vitally important entrepreneurial initiative. When, for example in Hesse in the American zone, a constitution containing a nationalization clause was adopted by a democratically elected state assembly, it could not be vetoed by the military governor. Its effect was blunted, however, by his insistence that no measure be taken which would prejudice the future decisions of the national German government.[2]

Western democracy was in for an even greater embarrassment in the British zone, where nationalization laws, duly passed in the heavily industrial state of North Rhine-Westphalia, were vetoed irrespective of the official nationalization commitment previously made by the London Labor government. Since Washington had spoken, London had to fall in line and the case was closed. A continuation of the German nationalization debate became quite pointless, thus freeing energies for the fundamental discussion as to whether governmental guidance or the market mechanism was to regulate economic activity henceforth.

The feuding camps were almost identical to those in the nationalization controversy, since the Social Democrats advocated democratically controlled governmental guidance of the economy, while the Christian Democratic Party, again undecided for quite a while, eventually (with the increasing East-West conflict) came out strongly for the competitive profit system.[3] Free-enterprise ideas had their most solid backing in the Free Democratic Party, which, with its strong big-business elements, should have been the darling of the Americans, but the preference of this liberalist party for political centralism thwarted such a cosy relationship. To ensure an adherence to the American concept of federated states and economic centralism,[4] following the dismissal of the first German director for economic administration of the Bizone on account of anti-American statements in early 1948, a

2. This American condition was not very convincing in the light of the prevailing decartelization and deconcentration policy, which meant very severe interference with German property relations.

3. This wavering attitude of the major conservative party reflected the mood of the consuming public: on the one hand hating rationing, which was associated with the Hitler regime and the immediate postwar years of utter prostration, but on the other hand fearful of price increases as well.

4. It was the American hope that a federally organized Germany would be easier to control and less likely to come under Soviet influence than a Germany centrally governed from Berlin.

new and more trustworthy man, the economist Ludwig Erhard, was handpicked for the job in March 1948.[5] As an academic Erhard had close ties to the neoliberalist school of economics,[6] whose theoretical work served as the main ideological basis in phraseology and substance for the economic policy concept of *Soziale Marktwirtschaft*,[7] the officially pursued economic policy after the currency reform.

Neither neoliberalism nor *Soziale Marktwirtschaft*, however, directly addresses itself to the most important global problems of a modern economy (such as growth, cyclical fluctuations, full employment, foreign exchange or price levels) by offering effective techniques to master them, providing only general principles instead. The neoliberalist creed, rooted in economic and political considerations, emphasizes the need for a well-functioning competitive system as the means of preventing the concentration of public and private power. Dictatorship, state planning and economic controls, as well as private monopoly through industrial cartelization, can be forestalled by the establishment and proper safeguarding of a free market economy. Besides providing the best insurance against the loss of political freedom, the market economy also represents—in neoliberalist understanding—a superior form of economic organization leading to a more efficient allocation of resources.[8] This capitalist wonderland was to be reached by maintaining a certain monetary stability, without which all attempts to achieve a competitive order would be in vain,[9] and by adopting various government measures to assure market competition and economic stability, since an unregulated free market economy of the laissez faire type had historically led to monopolistic practices and cyclical fluctuations. To ensure competition, the government was to restrict, if not forbid, cartels and monopolies, and actively combat any other kinds of restraint of trade, while anticyclical measures, preferably as automatic as possible to avoid arbitrary intervention, were to maintain economic stability. Social cohesion would be fostered by

5. Erhard, who referred to himself as an "American discovery" had been the rather controversial postwar minister of economic affairs in the state of Bavaria for a time, then an adjunct professor of economics at Munich University. Officially, he was sponsored by the Free Democratic Party.

6. The movement—centered upon the University of Freiburg and therefore also known as the Freiburg School—showed an obvious intellectual resemblance to the Chicago School in American economics.

7. This term, coined in 1946, has been translated as "Regulated Free Market Economy" or "Socially Conscious Free Market Economy," reflecting the ambiguous meaning of *Soziale Marktwirtschaft* as a "regulated" (meaning "controlled") and "social" (meaning "just") market economy.

8. Private monopoly and comprehensive state planning were both seen as inefficient, since the one distorted the price structure while the other ran counter to ordinary human incentives, apart from being a technical impossibility.

9. Under deflationary or inflationary conditions alike, money would cease to serve as a proper unit of account and lose its function as an indicator of gain or loss, no longer signalling the efficiency or inefficiency of the enterprise.

mitigating major income inequalities, if they appeared in spite of competition, through a progressive income tax mild enough not to thwart incentives.

Principally then, the differences between the laissez faire liberalism of the nineteenth century and neoliberalism were not very substantial. Both insisted on private ownership of the means of production, and hence autonomy of investment, liberty of contracts concerning prices, wages and interest, private production for private consumption, as well as a tax-financed government acting in accordance with free-market principles. The new version of liberalism was thus seen as laissez faire without the gold standard, but with state responsibility for the global targets of economic development and increased transfer payments. This rather critical evaluation resulted in part from the fundamental insistence of neoliberalism on polarizing the economic and political systems, leaving an alleged choice between individual freedom and independence on the basis of comprehensive competition and widely diffused ownership on the one hand, and a collectivist system on the other. The latter, in its state-controlled form, must necessarily lead to totalitarian planning, while in its private form of cartels and large-scale enterprises depersonalization and "devitalization" would be promoted. Since an admission of government intervention, not in accordance with free-market principles, was thus seen as tantamount to sliding into full planning, and as a "mortal danger" to the independence of the individual, no compromise between the market principle as practiced before 1914 and governmental guidance of the economy as practiced during the interwar years, especially during the Third Reich, was regarded as a viable solution. In reality, however, such a mixed system was precisely what characterized the German economy after the currency reform.

The Restoration of the Market and the Competitive Situation in Industry

While major changes in the existing control system did not constitute a practical suggestion prior to the currency reform, the advent of the latter necessitated a decision as to whether to discard or to continue these economic regulations. Six days after the introduction of the Deutsche Mark, the Economic Council, the quasi-parliament of the United Economic Region, with its conservative majority, passed the "Law Concerning the Principles of Planning and Price Policy after the Currency Reform," which gave the director for economic administration the right to take all necessary measures in the way of regulations and to determine in detail which goods should be free of price control. With regard to the proper timing of liberalization, the occupation authorities and most German experts held that decontrol could possibly endanger the new currency, as sudden and unpredictable upward adjustments of prices might result in a price-wage spiral and lead to open inflation and increased inequality of income; only after a respite would it be advisable and safe to remove price ceilings and rationing. A thorough liberalization to quickly follow the currency reform was, however, advocated by the industrialists, especially joined by Erhard, the director for economic administration, who lacked confidence in the technical feasibility of effective controls after the years when gray and black markets had undermined, indeed eroded, the morale of businessmen, consumers, and civil servants. Convinced of the superiority of free markets, the advocates of liberalization expected that decontrol would unleash productive energies and achieve infinitely more than the best designed and administered governmental guidance of the economy ever could. Consequently some 90 percent of the existing price regulations were repealed as of July 1948 by the German administration, as part of a policy of selective decontrol which lifted regulations in sectors where controls were difficult to enforce, where price increases would have relatively little impact on the immediate cost of living, and where a quick entrepreneurial response to the new opportunities could be expected. This signified, in principle, the freeing of most manufactured articles in daily use,[10] while of the basic foodstuffs potatoes were the first to be freed from rationing in October 1948, and sugar the last, in April 1950. Rents, utilities, public transport fares and freight rates, major industrial raw materials (iron, coal, oil, some non-ferrous metals) remained subject to control, as did all international transactions and the capital market. The labor market was, however, liberalized a few months later in early November 1948, when the wage freeze was abolished and free collective bargaining was restored. These speedy decontrols, just days after the currency reform, circumvented a strict order of the Allied Control Office that it had to consent, in advance, to any alteration of the fixed prices, by simply abolishing most price controls altogether.[11] The appalled Allies were either furious, as were the French and British, with their controlled and barely convalescent economies, or simply nervous, in the case of the Americans.[12] Soon, however, this policy of selective decontrol proved its success, since it led neither to an exorbitant and socially unacceptable increase

10. Clothing and shoes remained loosely rationed but were freed from price control.

11. Noticeably pleased with his successful surprise move, Erhard stated in his memoirs: "The Allies never seemed to have thought it possible that someone could have the idea, not to alter price controls, but simply to remove them. To assume such courage in a German so soon after the end of the war did not fit into the administration's way of thinking just after an overwhelming victory."

12. There is an apocryphal anecdote that the U.S. military governor, General Clay, objected "Herr Erhard, my advisers tell me you are making a terrible mistake," and was answered, "Don't listen to them, General, my advisers tell me the same."

in living costs nor to a too severe restriction of entrepreneurial activity.

To encourage private capital formation and longer working hours, various tax incentives were introduced to indirectly lower the income tax burden, which the Allies had raised to confiscatory levels as an anti-inflation measure in 1946, and insisted on retaining for the time being. The virtual exemption of overtime earnings from the income tax provided strong work incentives, while self-financing was initially promoted through generous depreciation allowances and tax privileges for the reinvestment of profits. During the years immediately after the currency reform, these and similar measures generated a driving power in the business community comparable to the famous spirit of *"Enrichez-vous par l'épargne et le travail"* (Enrich yourself through thrift and work) in early industrializing France. Men of action amassed huge fortunes, while workers had to put up with relatively meager wages and almost nonexistent saving possibilities for years. The even less fortunate and socially weak were maintained at a rather bare minimum through a comprehensive social security system, while the strong (and frequently ruthless) were given the opportunity to work for themselves. That their success would eventually improve living conditions in general was the economic reckoning and political promise of neoliberalism. This goal was indeed achieved later, but only at the price of quite substantial inequalities in private property. Though ownership of assets provided an almost insuperable headstart, the individual businessman could not be sure of success, since tight monetary and fiscal policies in general permitted no surfriding on an inflationary wave to easy profits in a sellers' market. Though there were periods, e.g., during the booms of 1948 and 1950, when a sellers' market prevailed, giving producers the doubly unwholesome benefit of sure profits and lenient tax laws, the general trend during the early fifties saw the economy move towards a buyers' market, providing strong incentives for industry to go after at times hard-to-come-by export orders. Domestic profits, however, were not only curtailed by DM-conscious customers, but also through the action of competitors.

The state of competition in the German economy had been somewhat improved by the Allied deconcentration measures in the coal, steel and chemical industries, in banking and a few other fields, but since the breakup of companies had frequently not considered established and technologically or organizationally sound integration, strong incentives for reconcentration remained. Throughout the fifties and sixties, total German industrial production was supplied by some 100,000 enterprises, of which about 60,000 were small units with less than 20 employees, some 35,000 were medium-sized with 20 to 199 employees, and only roughly 7,000 were large enterprises with a work force of 200 and more. By the late sixties the share of these three categories in total industrial employment and sales was about 5, 25, and 70 percent respectively. It was precisely the very large companies, frequently those enjoying an international reputation, which by far, and to an increasing extent, represented the most important factor in German industry, the fifty largest concerns expanding their share of total industrial turnover from 25 percent in 1954 to 42 percent in 1967. Many of these large units not only dominated swarms of smaller suppliers and subcontractors,[13] undermining their economic maneuverability and competitive behaviour, but also tended to contribute to the restraint of competition among the industrial giants through the establishment of joint subsidiaries. The floating of jointly owned companies as well as mergers and takeovers increased, particularly during the sixties, amalgamations leading to a market share of over 20 percent rising from an annual average of 15 in 1958/59 to 53 in 1965/67.

In almost all branches these tendencies resulted in an increase of the concentration ratio,[14] which by the mid-fifties was already around 70 percent in shipbuilding, oil and tobacco processing, about 60 percent in the automobile industry and in rubber and asbestos processing, close to 50 percent in the pig iron-producing and glass industries, slightly under 40 percent in the chemical, electrical equipment and nonferrous metal industries and mining. A relatively low concentration ratio of 20 to 25 percent existed in the foundries, steel construction, plastics-processing, leather-manufacturing and shoe-making, precision instruments and optical goods industries, and an even lower ratio of 10 percent or less in metal-working, paper, wood, and food-processing, textile and garment industries. By the mid-sixties the share of sales of the four largest enterprises amounted to about 50 percent in some trades, like shipbuilding, the electrical, chemical, rubber and asbestos industries, and even 80 percent in the automobile industry and oil processing.

Stern neoliberalists had to view such an expansion of big business over the years with more than mixed feelings, but the political support they were able to generate turned out to be quite insufficient to stop economic concentration. The voters were intelligent enough not to want a return to the petty bourgeois economic relations of the early industrial period. The need to keep abreast of international developments, especially the creation of larger economic areas, necessitated a certain coordination and cooperation on the domestic market.

13. In the mid-sixties, the electrical giants AEG and Siemens each had some 30,000 suppliers, while the largest chemical concern, Bayer, and Mercedes-producing Daimler-Benz each placed orders with about 17,000 firms.

14. Often defined as the share of the ten largest enterprises of each industry's total turnover.

At a time of rapid, capital-intensive technological progress, the world-wide trend towards larger production units in factories and greater concentration of capital assets in enterprises could hardly be halted in a single country. Because neither considerations of political principle nor neoliberalist doctrine were much heeded,[15] no economic Luddism occurred.

Preventing the misuse of economic power, and the collusion of a few enterprises to the detriment of the consumer, had been the tasks of the Allied decartelization laws of 1947, which affected a much wider range of industries than the deconcentration measures, though they were implemented less vigorously. The general prohibition of cartels denied them the aid of the courts, without which the more rigid forms of cartels, such as sales syndicates or quota arrangements, could not exist. The lesser types, like those concerning price-maintenance ar-rangements or agreements on terms and conditions of sales, were re-ported to persist in some branches in one informal way or another during the early fifties and thereafter, while bitter competition char-acterized other industries.

The continued existence of mild cartel-like arrangements partly reflected the fact that, throughout Germany's industrial history, the academic and governmental attitude toward economic concentration in general, and cartels in particular, had in principle never been one of hostility. Quite in contrast to the Anglo-American view, which con-nected competitive markets with equilibrium and monopolistic situa-tions with indeterminacy and disorder, it was held that unrestricted competition was "destructive" and that cartels were an "element of or-der." Apart from special-interest groups favoring cartels and largely apathetic and unorganized consumers, labor unions usually expected better job security from cartels than from unrestricted competition, or regarded the former as an intermediate stage in the industrial evolu-tion toward socialism, while small producers frequently viewed cartels as protection against being competitively beaten down or swallowed up by larger firms. If one does not subscribe to the demonization of economic bigness and industrial concentration as an act of faith, there is indeed precious little evidence that in the long run cartelization exerted a detrimental influence upon the growth of the German economy. It is usually held in primers on economics that monopolistic practices lead to the double outrage of excessive profits and decreasing efficiency through curtailment of production and investment. Given a

15. The political implications of highly concentrated economic power, especially for the proper functioning of the democratic process, cannot be discussed here, though it is well known that business leaders and the rich usually subsidize the conservative and bourgeois parties.

certain concentration of private assets, higher profits mean higher savings, which in macroeconomic terms can either be invested or hoarded, the latter practice resulting in chronic unemployment. The absence of such chronic unemployment during the many decades when cartels existed in Germany should indicate that the profits were indeed rechanneled into the economy, contributing to research and innovation in capital-intensive industries. Furthermore, the harm cartels might have exerted was probably lessened by the fact that only limited deviations from competitive conditions were possible. Since the German economy was solidly embedded in the world market—though at some times less than at others—domestic producers were exposed to foreign competition, and if profits were still excessive they must always have tempted domestic outsiders to enter the industry. These two factors, and the countervailing power of other cartels, set rather narrow limits on a cartel's profit potential, not to mention what foreign observers have often called the compulsive work habits of many German businessmen, creating strong centrifugal forces within a too-complacent cartel.

Practical historical experience prevented Germans from seeing cartels as quite the monsters that the Allies and neoliberalists thought them to be. In wise foresight, therefore, the occupation powers had stipulated that their laws containing a prohibition of cartel arrangements could be replaced only by a German law which would also subscribe to such a general prohibition. These Allied laws of 1947 not only went contrary to German legal tradition but contained—for the Germans at least —the blemish of citing as the main purpose in breaking up cartels a desire to reduce Germany's industrial power. It should not be surprising that the German cartel law, finally adopted in 1957 after years of vigorous debate and political infighting,[16] resembled a Swiss cheese, prohibiting cartel agreements in principle but, due to industrial lobbying, granting so many exceptions (e.g., for cartel arrangements on trade conditions, rebates, rationalization programs, product types, foreign trade and adjustments due to structural crises) that the prohibitive essence often slipped through the numerous holes. Although the holes were larger, the new law went considerably beyond the old cartel decree of 1923, not the least in that henceforth a national agency, the federal cartel office *(Bundeskartellamt)*, was to watch for abuses of monopolistic power.[17] While little could be done about "breakfast car-

16. On the cartel issue the otherwise often allied industrialists and neoliberalists opposed each other.

17. During the first ten years of its existence, the agency launched some 4,500 investigations into suspected violations; it dropped about 3,800 cases, since in 1,400 instances the contested practice had been discontinued, and fines were imposed on only seven occasions.

tels" and other "gentlemen's agreements," by the mid-sixties only about 130 cartels had been officially approved and been given the protection of the courts, compared to some 3,000 around 1930. Various areas, like agriculture, housing, transportation, banking and insurance were, however, totally exempted from the cartel law. In these sectors the state itself generally organized cartel-like arrangements.

Regulated Sectors of the German Economy

In agriculture, market regulations had been maintained following the currency reform to ensure an equitable supply for consumers in the face of insufficient domestic production and in the absence of adequate foreign exchange to finance additional food imports. Special agencies, entrusted with the monopoly on foreign trading in agricultural products, had to maintain the low inland prices through substantial subsidized imports, while later, when world market prices had sunk below the German level following the Korean boom, these agencies served as a support for German agriculture. Since agricultural policies had for decades emphasized output and given only secondary consideration to production costs, German agriculturists could not be expected to face foreign competition immediately, so that a certain degree of protection was necessary on social political grounds. The structural weakness of German agriculture resulted from the small size of the farms, the fragmentation of landholdings, and the consequently limited degree of mechanization. After years of improvisation and haphazard protection, the Agricultural Law of 1955 established as principal objectives of future agricultural policy a steady increase in productivity, sufficient to generate an adequate food supply at reasonable prices,[18] and the reduction of the disparity between agricultural and nonagricultural incomes. The measures to be taken included direct subsidies of prices and inputs; support to improve the agricultural structure, including consolidation projects, mechanization and product marketing; and assistance to encourage the earlier retirement of farmers and the passing on of the farm, and migration from the farms in general. The consequent changes in agriculture, frequently termed "revolutionary," reflected the success of the "Green Plans" pursued in the FRG since the mid-fifties and the administrative efforts of the EEC. During a transitional period after 1958, national agricultural policy goals were gradually meshed with those of the Community, whose objectives coincided to some extent with the German aims expressed in the Agricultural Law of 1955.

Next to agriculture, housing was another regulated sector of the

18. This goal did not mean agricultural self-sufficiency, which amounted to only 70 percent anyway.

German economy, for in light of the pronounced postwar scarcity of dwellings, rent control had to be maintained after the currency reform. This not only discouraged landlords from making repairs and improvements, thus worsening the housing shortage, but also stifled new construction. Thus the Housing Construction Laws of 1950 and 1956 provided for tax and interest concessions to promote privately financed building projects, and earmarked considerable budget funds for the construction of public housing. Apartments in the latter type were allocated by the housing offices, which admitted primarily low-income occupants, while the subsidized private housing was merely subject to rent control. The first decontrols began in 1960, and led in successive stages to a free housing market in large parts of the country. Although the number of dwellings doubled to over 20 million units between 1949 and 1969,[19] the market remained tight and new laws were required to protect tenants from overly greedy landlords.

Another branch of the service sector, the transport industry, was also directed to only a small degree by free-enterprise principles, since the state exerted considerable influence on the organization and operation of the various carriers. As the federal railroads were to serve the interest of the community by, for example, charging commuting workers and students below-cost fares and maintaining service in and to economically weak and out-of-the-way regions, it was considered necessary to regulate the activities of the private carriers. Bus lines and the commercial forwarding trade were especially licensed in order to prevent the overburdening of the relatively insufficient road network and to secure an adequate transport volume for inland navigation. The number of family-owned and operated barges had substantially increased when, after 1945, many boatmen had moved to the calmer waters in the West. Assistance to these small-scale enterprises was part of a general and broadly based policy to foster the economic wellbeing of the so-called middle classes, which were understood to form a stabilizing element for society. Various government programs to promote small and medium-sized industrial and handicrafts enterprises were intended to equalize the starting condition in branches where large companies, due to their economies of scale, quicker adoption of technological progress, larger advertising budgets, greater capital resources and cheaper credits, were threatening the smaller units with extinction. This decline of smaller units, in economic and technological terms at least a partly rational development—but politically inopportune and socially undesirable in a *"Soziale Marktwirtschaft"*—was retarded and softened by such assistance measures as tax privileges,

19. Housing construction represented on average 5.3 percent of GNP between 1950 and 1969, compared to 2.6 percent between 1925 and 1938.

credit guarantees, subsidies for the promotion of management consulting, further professional training, technical know-how, or advertising and, above all, by loans at reduced rates of interest for the establishment and expansion of small business enterprises. In principle, however, the allocation of capital by the normal market mechanism was the task of the financial establishment.

The more than 10,000 institutions of the postwar German banking system[20] could basically be classified into three groups, each of which was specialized for certain tasks: the agricultural and industrial credit cooperatives, which accounted for almost 90 percent of all establishments by the mid-sixties, but managed a mere 15 percent of the total volume of banking business; the savings banks, with shares of 8 and 54 percent respectively; and the commercial banks, with 3 and 31 percent, respectively. While the primarily rural credit cooperatives provided credit for farmers and small businessmen, the mostly community or county-owned savings banks had a more urban clientele, but they were also oriented toward local needs (small-scale lending, financing of housing and community projects). The twelve central institutions of these savings banks, which had originally operated merely as clearing houses and reserve depositories for the savings banks, increasingly shifted over the years in the direction of becoming full service banks.[21] Such banking activities, including international business, had previously been the sole realm of the investor-owned commercial banks.[22] Of its three types (the private bankers, the regional banks and the nationwide Big Three banks), the latter attract special attention by virtue of their sheer size, since they managed almost one-seventh of the total bank business (over one-fifth of all deposits and loans, over one-third of all sight and time deposits) in the mid-sixties.[23] Around 1960 they owned about two-thirds of all bank holdings in companies other than banks, and controlled about 70 percent of the shares represented in the stockholders' meetings of some 400 major companies. Their influence on large businesses via proxy vote or direct holdings, via credit relations, stock and bond issues, and representation on supervisory boards, provided them with such a key position in the German economy that they have been called "the prefects" of German industry. Although the Big Three could and frequently did act as efficiency audi-

20. Their number decreased from about 13,000 in 1952 to 11,000 in 1966.

21. In the late sixties the two largest of these (of the Rhineland and of Hesse) held second and fifth place respectively among all German banks, which meant eighth and forty-third rank respectively among the 50 largest banks outside the United States.

22. As a countermove, commercial banks expanded their branch networks into smaller communities in the sixties, competing with local savings banks on their traditional turf.

23. The Big Three banks, the Deutsche, the Dresdner and the Commerz, were reestablished in 1957/58, and ranked sixth, twentieth and twenty-ninth among the 50 largest banks outside the United States in 1970.

tors, industrialists had considerable leeway in choosing their banking partners. Their options increased with the trend towards despecialization in banking, the increased competition in this field through the appearance of foreign banking subsidiaries in Germany, and the 1967 abolition of the government-controlled cartel which regulated credit commissions and interest rates for debtors and creditors.[24] Government control through a special federal agency was, of course, continued in order to watch over the observance of sound banking practices, while control over conditions governing the available quantity of money had been entrusted to the central bank.

The State in a Mixed Economic System

As in other Western market economies, the regulation of money and credit in Germany has been used by the government to pursue specific economic policy objectives, and the control of monetary policy has been vested in the central banking system. By directing the supply and use of money by means of the standard instruments of monetary policy (discount rate, minimum reserve requirements, and, since 1955, open-market operations), consumer and investment spending, i.e., the effective private demand for goods and services, can be influenced, and the change in the total flow of these expenditures affects production, employment, and prices. The central bank is required to advise the government on all matters of importance in the area of monetary policy and to support the government's general economic policies, particularly in the area of currency stability. Though owned and controlled by public authorities, the German central banking system of the postwar period legally enjoys far-reaching independence from state interference in its activities. While its predecessor, the Reichsbank, became a totally subservient tool of the Nazi government, the *Bank Deutscher Länder*, founded by the Allied authorities in March 1948, was given considerable legal autonomy and a substantial degree of operational independence from the federal government established one and a half years later. This remained so when, in 1957, a restructuring of German central banking took place, and the decentralized system of the *Bank Deutscher Länder* gave way to a new organizational setup that increased the influence of the federal government. The new bank, the *Deutsche Bundesbank*, was still one of the most independent central banks in the world. Government members were entitled to attend the deliberations of its highest decision-making body, the Central Bank Council, but they had no vote and only enough power to delay the making of a decision for a maximum of two weeks. Conflicts between

24. Foreign banking institutions benefitted greatly from the fact that, even before the formal declaration of general convertibility in late 1958, the DM had actually been convertible for some years.

the two have occurred at times, though rarely. In 1956, for instance, when the central bank, acting as guardian of the currency, restricted credit in order to control the ongoing boom, the government, prodded by the industrialists, was highly displeased. Much more compliant as instruments of governmental policy were, of course, the various banking institutions owned by the state,[25] of which the *Kreditanstalt für Wiederaufbau,* the fourth largest credit institution in Germany in the late sixties, was the most important.[26] At no time, however, did these state banks or the German banking system in general exercise anything resembling the economic control on the business community that was, for instance, exerted by government-owned credit institutions in France.

Public ownership and the entrepreneurial function of the state were maintained in the postwar period in certain areas where such activity had been traditional. Nationwide transportation (railroads, inland waterways, air lines) and most local transportation systems, telegraph, telephone and postal communications, radio and television networks, as well as the overwhelming proportion of the utilities, were owned and operated by public authorities at various levels.[27] Government ownership also extended to manufacturing, though this was not the consequence of any conscious nationalization policy but rather inherited from previous governments. In the early fifties the state held a share of over 20 percent of national production of coal, coke, crude oil, pig iron, and steel, around 50 percent of automobile construction, and iron ore, lead, and zinc production, and roughly 70 percent of aluminum smelting, apart from further substantial interests in other branches like shipbuilding, housing and the chemical industry. State ownership was either direct, as in the case of Lufthansa airlines (founded 1953) or the Volkswagen works, or indirect through holding companies, such as VEBA and VIAG;[28] the former primarily controlled subsidiaries producing coal, coke and lignite, and electricity, while the latter held the federal government's interests in firms in the steel, aluminum and chemical industries. By the late sixties, the federal

25. For example, the Industry Credit Bank, the Equalization of Burdens Bank, and the Berlin Industry Bank, which either provided loans to industrial and trading enterprises or financed economic development in certain problem areas.

26. Founded in 1948, the Reconstruction Bank's initial purpose was to provide medium and long-term loans to financially weak industries (like coal and steel) encountering difficulties in borrowing from other credit institutions. Later on the provision of export credits and of long-term loans to developing countries within the framework of the German foreign aid program became a major function.

27. About 60 percent of electricity production and over 90 percent of gas production and electricity distribution were state-operated in the fifties.

28. VEBA = *Vereinigte Elektrizitäts- und Bergwerks AG* (United Electrical and Mining Co. Inc.); VIAG = *Vereinigte Industrie-Unternehmungen AG* (United Industrial Enterprises Co. Inc.).

government alone had an interest in some 3,000 enterprises despite some previous privatization.[29] In 1959 shares of the PREUSSAG were partly sold to the public under attractive conditions, followed by similar moves with regard to the Volkswagen company in 1961 and the VEBA in 1965. Essentially a means of influencing the electorate on the part of the conservative CDU government, rebates were granted to the less well off classes to encourage the idea of share-ownership in a system of "people's capitalism."[30] The state did not, however, totally divest itself of ownership in these companies, but maintained its influence on management and generally retained at least a theoretical option of using its industrial holdings to exert some countervailing power in oligopolistic markets. Basically, however, the wholly or partially state-owned companies in Germany are run in a businesslike manner as private enterprises, competing for capital, labor and customers in the market place, and their management pays the penalty for poor performance by being replaced.

Besides its entrepreneurial function, the state plays a much larger role in the economy as an administrator. Federal, state, and local governments constitute the three-tiered hierarchy of the German administrative system. According to the Basic Law, the FRG consists of ten states, plus the specially related state of West Berlin, each with its own assembly. A state is further subdivided into districts, while the smallest unit of administration is the municipality. Since each of these bodies has its responsibilities and powers laid down in the Basic Law, authorities on the federal level were put in charge of such national matters as foreign affairs, defense, social relief charges resulting from the war, currency and foreign trade relations, and post and telegraph services. The realm of the states encompasses such domestic areas as the police, justice, public health, education and cultural affairs, radio, television, and the like. Competing federal-state legislative jurisdiction[31] covers a variety of fields, of which the regulation of economic and social matters is of special interest in this context. Since in a small country[32] many economic and social problems have tended to become national affairs calling for a nationwide solution, there has been a trend toward a certain centralization of legislative powers over the years. While the

29. In 1969 the federal government owned one-fourth or more of the stock of some 650 companies.

30. Some 1.5 million small savers bought VW shares, while about twice that number acquired VEBA shares; since in both cases the shares were offered at about half of their real value, the individual investor made a windfall profit of a few hundred dollars. These measures have been frequently interpreted as dissipation of public property to provide a scanty fig-leaf for the social unchastity of *Soziale Marktwirtschaft*.

31. The states retain the right to legislate unless the federal parliament preempts the field.

32. The FRG has the area of the state of Oregon, but 30 times its 1970 population.

states of the FRG do not have the power that state governments in the United States do, the basic unit of local government, the community, has been responsible for a much wider range of activities than its average American counterpart. These have included the operation of such local enterprises as public utilities, buses, streetcars, slaughterhouses, savings banks, hospitals, museums, theaters and orchestras among others.

To fulfill its administrative obligations, each level in this three-tiered governmental hierarchy was assigned specific public revenues: local authorities received the trade tax and the landed property tax, plus contributions from the state budget; the states were given the general property tax, inheritance tax, motor-vehicle tax, and the major part of the tax on personal and corporate income; the rest going to the federal treasury, along with all customs duties, the general-turnover tax and various excise taxes. To equalize the tax burden carried by the various states and municipalities, some of which were more industrialized and therefore obviously richer than others, funds had to be transferred between states and to local governments. The public sector in the FRG as a whole, i.e., federal, state and local authorities, has been of more importance than in the United States, although less than in France or Sweden. Measured with respect to national income, the proportion of government purchases of goods and services rose from 23 to 28 percent between the early 1950s and late 1960s. The total share of the public budget remained at approximately 37 percent, with 34.7 percent in 1955 and 41.5 percent in 1967 representing the low and high extremes. The federal government's share amounted to half, that of the states to a third, and the rest going to the communities. This sizeable share in national income, however, could only with great difficulty be used for a consistent fiscal policy, for the budgets of the federal and state governments were autonomous and independent of each other. Deliberate changes in government expenditure and taxes to control economic fluctuations by influencing public demand or private consumption and investment were rarely possible, owing to the fragmentation of responsibilities. Furthermore, German budget policy was hampered by the Basic Law's restriction on deficits, permitting public debts only for productive purposes, thus only allowing the accumulation of surpluses to dampen hectic upswings. Freezing budget funds usually turned out to be an extremely difficult undertaking, since in a parliamentary democracy all sorts of lobbyists quickly show an appetite for the cake on the shelf.

The Share of Nongovernmental Organizations in Economic Policy Making

Leaving out such elected bodies as parties, parliaments, and governments, the representation of private interests in the FRG, as a society honoring the right of free association, has been the domain of various semipublic or private organizations, which have at times considerably influenced the shaping of economic policy. The Chambers of Industry and Commerce, of Handicrafts, and of Agriculture, as public-law entities entrusted with certain governmental functions, represent the regional concerns of their members. Their central institutions in particular have occasionally been able to influence economic policy decisions but, due to their rather heterogeneous composition, not, in general, as readily as the more specialized interest organizations. These economic associations *(Verbände)*, legally organized as private-law societies, unite members of the economic community who share similar interests to plead their cause among the general public and vis-à-vis the government. Pressure groups of nonbusinessmen (like those of the war victims, veterans, taxpayers, tenants, savers, consumers, and other similarly less potent groups) typically have a large membership but limited influence, quite in contrast to the powerful economic associations representing individual branches or entire sectors of the economy. Among the most influential are the Federation of German Industry and the Farmers' Federation, either of which could claim to be "primus inter pares" among a host of others, such as the associations of wholesale and foreign traders, retailers, bankers, insurers and carriers, all of them with hundreds of subgroups and regional federations. Usually these collective organizations encompass within themselves a great many competing units whose conflicting interests have to be integrated. Since formal procedures for the formation of the collective will were frequently lacking from the outset, such organizations have been repeatedly criticized for their low degree of internal democracy, as well as for the opacity of their relations with the political parties and their corresponding influence on official economic policy.

A legal midposition (between the chambers as public-law entities and the private-law economic associations) is held by the trade unions and the employers' associations, which, though private-law entities, have been empowered with certain competencies under public law, like participation in such public bodies as industrial courts, labor offices, and social insurance institutions. Management associations and unions— the "social partners" as the Germans call them—act as independent parties in the collective bargaining process, the results of which represent important macroeconomic data for other economic policy makers. This complete freedom of action, i.e., depoliticalization on principle as well as discontinuance of previously practiced governmental supervision, and the considerable modifications in the organizational structure of the unions, represented the most conspicuous changes in Germany's postwar labor market. While the employers more or less revived the Weimar setup of their organizations, the labor leaders of the postwar period, remembering how fragmentation into some 200 unions representing different denominational, political, and craft interests had weakened their cause during the 1920s and early 1930s, established a unified nondenominational, nonpolitical body, the German Trade Union Federation (*Deutscher Gewerkschaftsbund,* DGB), with its 16 constituent industrial unions, in 1949.[33] These industry-based organizations, which represented all the workers in a particular industry (e.g., the metal industry) or related trade groups (e.g., construction and building materials), abolished the multiplicity and diffusion of the past and ended, or at least internalized, demarcation and comparability disputes. The new unions, built up from scratch, showed themselves incomparably better suited to the modern age than those inherited from the nineteenth century in some other European countries, since they facilitated a national wage policy and long-term economic budgeting by management, expedited mediation, and reduced strikes and lockouts, apart from strengthening the bargaining position of the unions in the bilateral monopoly of countervailing powers. Though the outcome of negotiations between bilateral monopolists is not entirely determinable in principle—even if one of the contestants is "limping" due to a lack of solidarity on his side, reflecting the existing employment situation—attempts to "objectify" the bargaining process have been made; but they have been greeted with little enthusiasm by the two "social partners." The solutions brought forth by various economists have failed to convince either side.[34] The institutionalization of objective expertise in general, which would have made compulsory arbitration by the state possible, must have made each bargaining side conscious of past impotence and fear future redundance.

Unions and employers not only agreed in jealously safeguarding their independence and autonomy against any public intervention but also reached common ground with the DGB's eventual acceptance of the *Soziale Marktwirtschaft.* Inspired by Marxist thinking, the DGB's Munich Manifesto of 1949 had demanded the transfer of such key sectors as the iron, basic chemicals and power industries, mining, the main transportation systems and all credit institutions to public ownership. The repeated rejection of nationalization and comprehensive economic planning by the majority of voters in the federal elections of the fifties led Social Democrats and unionists to a modification of their

33. The DGB did not succeed in securing the adhesion of the Civil Servants' Union and the Union of Salaried Employees.

34. The pet theory of the employers has been the "productivity formula," i.e., the linking of wage increases to productivity improvements, which would maintain the existing income distribution. The unions, at least in the mid-fifties, were quite taken by the "doctrine of an expansionary wage policy," according to which higher labor costs would compel entrepreneurs to quickly introduce new cost-cutting methods, and thus not lead to higher prices.

aims regarding the economic order, and to their acceptance of *Soziale Marktwirtschaft*. After 1959 the Social Democratic Party advocated "as much competition as possible, as much planning as necessary." The DGB followed suit in 1963 stating that "every economy needs planning within a frame of reference which, in principle, is based on competition." That some sort of macroeconomic planning was indeed advisable was learned by the conservative parties and their supporters in the business community during the shocking recession of 1966/67, which led to a CDU-SPD coalition government and general support for the creation of additional economic policy instruments. While unionists and Social Democrats on the one hand, and employers and the conservative parties on the other, could henceforth differ about the desirable extent of governmental guidance of the economy—without questioning the principle necessity for such macroeconomic planning—labor's request for participation in microeconomic decision making remained a heavily contested issue.

The trade unions' request for codetermination in the actual management decisions had had a long history. Immediately after the Second World War—as after World War I, when workers' councils were established to provide some say in the conduct of business—the unions had again attempted to increase their voice in company management. However, since the Allies vetoed the respective laws passed by various state assemblies, because workers' participation in management was viewed as severely impeding entrepreneurial freedom, this question of "Industrial Democracy" was postponed until after the foundation of the Federal Republic. Though capital had come, to some extent, to appreciate the active cooperation of labor in the joint fight against dismantlement, only the threat of a strike made the conservative majority in the federal parliament pass the Law of Codetermination for the mining and iron industries in spring 1951. Henceforth, the supervisory boards which appoint and supervise the managing boards in these industries were to have equal representation from labor and capital, plus one neutral member to be selected by both groups. Furthermore, on the boards of management, which were responsible for the day-to-day conduct of business, the workers' interests were to be represented by way of an executive labor director. Labor had the right to veto a nominee to this position, whose responsibility encompassed social and personnel matters, and who was granted an equal voice in all other company affairs. However, the labor director in reality seldom turned out to be a narrowminded labor lobbyist, but was usually an advocate of the long-term interests of both the enterprise and its employees. This attempt to give labor an institutionalized position in company management was, however, too unrepresentative to permit a definitive evaluation. By 1952 the newly established European Coal and Steel Community had already absorbed important managerial responsibilities, and prevented a possible policy of joint management-labor collusion in the shrinking coal-mining industry that would have been detrimental to the consumer. Labor's participation in other industries was regulated by the Works Constitution Law, which was passed in the fall of 1952, again under a strike threat. The law entitled works councils to a voice in determining the social, personnel and, in rare cases, economic policies, in all enterprises with more than 20 employees.[35] As, furthermore, in stock companies delegates representing labor were to make up only one-third of the supervisory board, while no representative was required on the managing boards, this law fell far short of union aspirations.[36] The realization of further demands was not conceivable before the late sixties, when the conservative majorities in the federal parliament and in the state assemblies were increasingly eroded and sometimes lost.

The question remains whether the term "market economy" adequately describes the economic reality in the Federal Republic of Germany at that time. Codetermination limiting entrepreneurial independence; the existence of a bilateral monopoly in the labor market, and of a system of relations, contractual and otherwise, between powerful semieconomic and semipolitical organizations; increasing concentration in industry and banking; the persistence of cartels and cartel-like arrangements; lasting controls over entire sectors of the economy; the considerable entrepreneurial activity of the state, and the further extension and refinement of its regulatory and redistributing operations—all this, surely, would have not only astonished but probably distressed the ideological founding fathers of the German economic system. But whatever *Soziale Marktwirtschaft* was lacking in doctrinal purity—from the neoliberal point of view—has been compensated for by actual performance.

2

The German Economic Recovery and Its Mainsprings

Following the currency reform of June 1948, the economy of the three Western zones, which became the Federal Republic, recovered very quickly. Within a few years the defeated and destroyed country

35. Codetermination was granted for economic decisions affecting job security, such as relocating or closing of the plant, mergers, and drastic changes in production systems, equipment or methods of work.

36. Altogether, the participation of labor in the operation of a German enterprise is quite substantial by Western, particularly American, standards.

rejuvenated itself, rising phoenixlike from rubble and ashes to provide a standard of living at or even above the prewar level.[37] The nearly half a decade following the currency reform has quite often been referred to abroad as the years of the German "economic miracle." Though many Germans frequently expressed their disapproval of the term "economic miracle," insisting instead on an "economy without miracles,"[38] the performance of their economy was nevertheless astonishing, though in no way unique.

Indeed, in the four years between mid-1948 and mid-1952, the German GNP rose nominally by over 80 percent, and by 67 percent in real terms, while industrial production increased by 110 percent. Yet changes of that magnitude and speed had occurred twice in Germany during the previous two decades: negatively between June 1929 and June 1932, when industrial production had fallen by about half, and positively during the recovery from the depression, between 1933 and 1937, when industrial production had risen by about 80 percent. Furthermore, by contemporary international standards, the German economic comeback after 1948 was not exceptional, since in per capita production Germany was still about 12 percent behind France and 3 percent behind Great Britain in 1952. However, these and other European countries had a headstart of about three years, as their peacetime reconstruction had not been delayed until the middle of 1948.[39] Apart from a belated start, the economy in Germany was much more "kaputt" than those of other West European countries, owing to various postwar burdens (among them partition, dismantling, forced exports, production prohibitions, and refugees) placed upon the war-devastated country. Germany's transformation from a starving outcast to an esteemed economic giant is partly told in the table on the next page.

This splendid performance, especially during the immediate post-currency-reform years, not only surprised observers inside and outside Germany but very soon also enticed economists to study "Germany's comeback in the world market" and to explain the "mainsprings of the German revival."[40] In the following pages, some of the causes of this recovery will be outlined briefly by analyzing the role of capital, labor, markets and policies, particularly up to the mid-fifties.

37. Private per capita consumption reached the level of 1936 in 1951, while in 1948/49 it was about 25 percent lower.

38. This *("Wirtschaft ohne Wunder")* was the title of an omnibus volume published in 1952, containing articles by neoliberal academics and politicians.

39. In 1948 the index of industrial production (1938=100) stood at 121 in Belgium, 116 in Great Britain, 113 in the Netherlands, 110 in France and 99 in Italy, compared to 45 during the first half year and 60 during the second half year in Germany.

40. These, incidentally, were the titles of two books that appeared almost simultaneously in 1955; the first written by the chief architect of the German recovery, Minister of Economics Erhard, the other by Yale economist H. Wallich.

B. *Economic Development of the Federal Republic of Germany, 1950–1970*

Year	Gross National Product in Stable Prices — Index	Gross National Product in Stable Prices — Percentage Change From Previous Year	National Income[1] in Current Prices — Billions of DM	National Income[1] in Current Prices — DM Per Capita	Cost of Living — Index	Cost of Living — Percentage Change From Previous Year	Industrial Production — Index	Gainfully Employed Persons Yearly Average — In Millions	Unemployed — In Percent of Employees[2]	Balance of Foreign Trade — Billions of DM	Year
1950	100	—	75.2	1 602	100	—	100	20.4	8.2	-3.0	1950
1951	111	10.9	91.1	1 921	107.8	7.7	116	20.9	7.7	-0.1	1951
1952	121	9.0	103.8	2 174	110.0	2.1	124	21.3	6.4	0.7	1952
1953	130	7.9	112.1	2 328	108.1	-1.8	135	21.8	5.5	2.5	1953
1954	140	7.2	121.1	2 486	108.2	0.2	151	22.4	4.7	2.7	1954
1955	157	12.0	139.5	2 834	110.0	1.6	173	23.2	2.7	1.2	1955
1956	168	7.0	154.4	3 100	112.9	2.5	189	23.8	2.2	2.9	1956
1957	177	5.8	168.3	3 337	115.2	2.0	197	25.3	1.9	4.1	1957
1958	183	3.3	180.1	3 528	117.7	2.2	203	25.5	1.7	5.0	1958
1959	196	6.9	194.0	3 757	118.8	1.0	219	25.8	1.1	5.4	1959
1960	226	8.8	235.7	4 252	120.5	1.4	246	26.2	0.6	5.2	1960
1961	238	5.4	258.0	4 593	123.2	2.3	263	26.6	0.5	6.6	1961
1962	248	4.1	277.5	4 882	126.9	3.0	274	26.7	0.4	3.5	1962
1963	256	3.5	295.8	5 154	130.7	3.0	282	26.8	0.5	6.0	1963
1964	273	6.6	324.3	5 593	133.8	2.3	309	26.8	0.4	6.1	1964
1965	288	5.6	355.3	6 060	138.3	3.4	327	26.9	0.4	1.2	1965
1966	296	2.9	377.1	6 375	143.1	3.5	331	26.8	0.5	8.0	1966
1967	296	-0.2	376.0	6 342	145.2	1.4	322	26.0	1.6	16.9	1967
1968	319	7.3	416.9	7 006	147.3	1.5	359	26.0	0.8	18.4	1968
1969	344	8.2	460.6	7 669	151.5	2.8	405	26.4	0.5	15.6	1969
1970	364	5.8	529.2	8 725	157.0	3.7	431	26.7	0.5	15.7	1970

Source: Federal Ministry for Economic Affairs, *Leistung in Zahlen* (Bonn, 1968 and 1973).
[1] Changes on computation make for approximately 2 to 4 percent higher figures since 1960.
[2] Key day: September 30.

Material and Human Production Factors

For its economic reconstruction Germany needed investable funds, which could come from either foreign or domestic sources. Up to October 1954 the Federal Republic received about $4.4 billion in foreign aid from the Western Allies. While the American GARIOA assistance ($1.7 billion) and its British counterpart ($0.8 billion) stressed relief, the ERP and post-ERP aid ($1.9 billion) emphasized reconstruction, since its allocations primarily consisted of industrial inputs, especially raw materials. The total foreign aid received, which in 1948 and 1949 amounted to about one billion dollars for each year, and in 1950 to half a billion dollars, was not, however, very substantial in quantitative terms. Even during the top year of 1948/49, it hardly accounted for 5 percent of the German national product.[41] The quantitative importance of Allied aid as a source of investable funds is reduced still further when the various burdens placed upon Germany by the Allies are considered. Their total at the time far exceeded the foreign aid which Germany received.[42]

Although strictly speaking there were no reparations from current production, dismantlement had cut into the existing stock of capital. The Inter-Allied Reparations Commission in Brussels had set the value of dismantled plants, shipped to 18 recipient nations, at RM 0.7 billion (at 1938 prices), or about DM 1.5 billion. Since valuation had been based on rather severe depreciation standards, and dismantling had frequently meant the destruction of adjacent installations and buildings, the cost of dismantlement to Germany was considerably higher than the benefits derived by the recipients. This loss of productive potential, which in many cases could not be used at the time for lack of fuel or raw materials anyway, was only to be felt later when capacities were fully employed. The enforced low-priced exports of coal, scrap and timber increased domestic scarcity, undoubtedly retarding German reconstruction, while also representing a heavy loss of foreign exchange. In their economic effects, these forced exports were analogous to external restitutions, which were especially important in the French zone. France had been the sole nation among the Western Big Three under German occupation, and thus a source of goods and services to Germany during the war. Moreover, she had not been invited to the

41. The first Marshall Plan year ran from April 1948 to June 1949. According to the London Debt Agreement of February 1953, only about half of the total postwar aid of approximately DM 16 billion had to be repaid, thanks to an American waiver. Although repayment by 1982 was envisaged, the Federal Republic prematurely repaid her debt of about DM 7 billion.

42. This had been the gist of the claims made by the first German director for economic administration of the Bizone. They led to his dismissal at the beginning of 1948. Between 1946 and 1949 an estimated 11 to 15 percent of the national income of the Western zones went for occupation costs and reparations.

Potsdam Conference by the actual victors and thus did not feel bound by their agreement. In addition to severing the Saarland from Germany and incorporating this small but economically valuable region into the French economy,[43] France used her zone of occupation, basically an agricultural and heavily wooded area, to feed and house a disproportionately large segment of her army and their dependents, and for forced deliveries of timber and other products, to such an extent that France was importing as much from this small area as she had from the entire Reich in 1938.

To maintain their armies in Germany, the Western powers had in the early 1950s stipulated an annual levy for occupation costs of over DM 7 billion, which in economic terms could be regarded as a substitute for German defense expenditures. For the FRG, this represented a slightly smaller proportion of the national income than the military budgets of the three occupying powers during the early fifties.[44] Though it meant a substantial burden for an economically disorganized country, no transfer of foreign exchange was involved. Indeed, the presence of Allied troops, receiving their pay in dollars and pounds, was actually an important source of foreign currency, since the soldiers spent part of their pay within the country. Germany's foreign exchange position suffered, however, from the loss of $1 to 2 billion worth of external assets (especially foreign subsidiaries, patents and trademarks) and their earnings. Balance-of-payments problems, however, did not result from the broad restitution and general indemnification program undertaken at Allied request, since all the respective payments, which had been expected to reach DM 8 billion but by 1970 amounted to almost three times that figure, were to be made in German currency without transfer obligation.[45] With few exceptions, therefore, the burdens placed upon Germany taxed domestic resources but did not seriously undermine her balance-of-payments position, which was greatly strengthened by the Marshall Plan. This, indeed, was the main contribution of Allied, particularly American, aid, providing Germany

43. On the basis of a plebiscite, the Saar returned to Germany on 1 January 1957.

44. The 1951/53 expenditures for defense (in percentage of gross domestic product) amounted to 6.5 in Germany compared to 4.7 in Italy and 2.2 in Japan, and were not even dissimilar to those of the Western European hegemonial powers with worldwide colonial interests: Britain (7.8 percent) and France (10.0 percent). The corresponding figure for the United States (11.7 percent) is inflated as a result of the Korean war, since between 1948 and 1951 only 4.8 percent was spent annually on military expenditures. Only later, when Germany's economic expansion was well underway, did she carry a relatively lighter defense burden, usually spending around 3 to 4 percent between 1956 and 1969, compared to the corresponding figures for France (over 5 percent) and Britain (6 to 8 percent).

45. Sales of the resulting blocked DM (negotiable at discounts ranging from about 50 percent in 1951 to small fractions in 1954) tended, of course, to depress the DM's exchange rate somewhat.

with the foreign exchange to acquire vital foodstuffs, raw materials and other imports.[46] Indeed, in this qualified sense foreign aid deserves to be ranked beside currency reform and decontrol as the third major basis for Germany's quick reconstruction.

The sale of imported commodities to German consumers and producers under the Marshall Plan generated so-called "DM counterpart funds," which could be used by the German government through the *Kreditanstalt für Wiederaufbau* to finance investments in bottleneck areas. Since such counterpart investments averaged about 4 percent of gross investment between 1948 and 1953, their significance—like that of foreign aid in general—was qualitative, providing the government with the main source of financing for its centralized investment planning. Budget funds for this purpose were very limited, following the thoroughgoing decentralization of the public authorities by the Allies. While Germans kept their belts tightened in order to reach the high gross investment levels of 20 to 24 percent of the GNP attained between 1949 and 1953/54,[47] relatively small funds were allocated as part of a centrally guided investment program. Since authorities on the local and state levels felt the pressing need of housing and public works most severely, such high priority investments were both foreseeable and desirable. Bottleneck industries like coal, iron and the utilities, with their set price ceilings and consequent inability to finance themselves internally or to attract external funds, were at first the main beneficiaries of counterpart funds. After 1952 they received additional investment assistance from nearly all other industrial sectors that had profited from their low sales prices. The long-debated law concerned required the raising of one billion DM, for which the contributors received bonds of the debtor industries, and provided for the distribution of these funds through a special bank.

Banking in general fulfilled an important task in supplying funds, particularly right after the currency reform, when many businesses needed short-term loans to finance their expansion. Since the currency reform had contracted the banks' balance sheets to 10 percent or less, they were eager to expand their credit volume again to cover at least their operating expenses. Neither these nor the central bank could for a time afford to be overfastidious in their choice of borrowers. The favorable economic climate, however, generally prevented these loans from going bad. The rapid rise of time and savings deposits soon opened possibilities for engaging in large-scale lending on medium and long term. The traditional method of prefinancing capital in-

46. Aid-financed share in total imports: 1946/47, 70 percent; 1948, 65 percent; 1949, 43 percent; 1950/51, 16 percent; 1952/54, 2 percent.

47. None of the major European countries reached the German investment ratio at the time.

vestment through short-term credits and subsequent consolidation through the issue of securities could not, however, be used for a long time, as the capital market only slowly recovered. It provided about 10 percent of gross investment between 1949 and 1952. The issuing of securities was generally subject to government approval; industrial bonds were limited to 6½ percent interest so as to make 5 percent mortgage bonds possible at a time when the free market rate would probably have been around 8 percent. This was done in order to keep the cost of mortgage money somewhat in line with the return of low-rent housing. Other methods for subsidizing public borrowers, usually involving tax privileges, made the floating of industrial bonds or common stocks an extremely expensive form of company financing, and encouraged internal financing through the retention of profits. Self-financing, which from the point of view of its effect on the national economy usually receives ambivalent ratings,[48] provided over 80 percent of all investable funds during the first year after the currency reform and at least half during the early 1950s.

High profits, particularly right after the introduction of the DM and during the Korea Boom of 1950/51, meant involuntary consumer saving, while tax concessions encouraged the investment of profits instead of their distribution. Capital formation was fostered by means of accelerated depreciation allowances on expenditures for the replacement of war-damaged equipment and the construction of new residential and commercial buildings. After 1951 many of these tax privileges were discontinued or limited, as the socially undesirable distributive effects on income and wealth became noticeable. Instead, to encourage individual saving, the acquisition of government bonds and special housing bonds, the granting of direct loans for shipbuilding and construction of dwellings were made income-tax deductable. Saving through public and private bonds generally carried tax concessions for some time after 1952. From 1953 onward the propensity to save of lower-income receivers, for whom the prevailing fiscal concessions had been of little consequence, was stimulated through the offer of direct bonus schemes. Partly as a consequence of these measures, the fledgling securities market developed quite satisfactorily,[49] and by the late 1950s the rate of interest in the German capital market was about 5 percent, and thus roughly at the level prevailing in the leading foreign financial centers. The policy of encouraging the formation of wealth among private households was not quite as successful, and only in the

48. On the one hand, internal financing is said to lead to a less thorough examination of investment projects than is the case with external funding; on the other it is said to make possible the pursuit of new and uncharted courses involving greater risks.

49. Volume of the securities market in billion DM: 1950, 1.6; 1952, 4.3; 1954, 12.5; 1960, 53.4; 1970, over 200.

1960s was there a real breakthrough in private saving and a decline in compulsory saving.[50] Initially, however, given the general capital shortage in the economy and the preference for the market mechanism, budget surpluses and entrepreneurial self-financing were the only feasible methods of capital accumulation in the face of a dry securities market, limited and relatively expensive bank credits, and slim corporate equities. The policy of favoring corporate saving, as at first pursued in the FRG, not only to a certain degree permitted governmental channeling of funds in desired directions by means of tax concessions but also provided the basis for future external financing through the building up of equities, as well as creating strong incentives for the individual businessman. That this altogether decentralized form of national capital formation quickly led to a large increase in the national product resulted partly from the fact that the substantial existing stock of plant and equipment, though in part inoperable due to damage, dismantlement and wear and tear, permitted the quick commencement of operations once a relatively small amount of capital had been strategically applied. On the other hand, the fast growth of commodity production reflected the policy of German management to invest particularly in fields characterized by a low capital-output ratio and quick returns.

Other factors played an equally important role in the economic reconstruction of the FRG. For instance, German management had traditionally contained a larger proportion of professional executives among its industrial leaders than the other major industrial countries in Europe. In connection with Germany's most significant contribution to the modern industrialization process, i.e., the creation of science-based industries, engineers, technicians and scientists had been liberally admitted into managerial ranks. The general respect for university learning also opened the doors of executive suites to other nonowners earlier and more easily than in most countries. Among these were graduates with a legal or economics background, who brought to business conduct an even greater degree of rationality and professional expertise. This trend was further encouraged by the banks, which— as the main purveyors of funds and middlemen to the securities market—often insisted upon selection of men most fit for management positions. While most of the small and medium-sized businesses have remained family-owned and run, even after the Second World War, the large companies have remained the domain of professional managers. Their realm was actually widened by the political and economic challenges of the time; defeat, occupation and reconstruc-

50. Percentage share in total saving in 1950, 1960, and 1970: Households, 17, 26, 38; enterprises, 46, 42, 38; public authorities, 37, 32, 24.

tion called as much for a creative entrepreneurial response as the opportunities presented by the Common Market required a willingness to
innovate. Accordingly, talented young people who might previously
have been inclined to pursue careers in the civil service or the armed
forces found promising professional opportunities in industry since,
especially in the early years of the FRG, positions in these traditional
occupations were very limited if they existed at all. Many former officers also entered the business world after the war, and it was no coin-
cidence that many of them rose to leading positions. After all, some
principles of military organization, particularly the staff-line pattern
of organization, which combines hierarchical structure with functional
specialization, have also proven useful in the guiding, coordinating and
controlling of the activities of enterprises with a mass or continuous
flow production of standardized goods. Germany's demilitarization
can generally be said to have freed considerable human resources for
business careers. That foreign, and in particular British observers,
habitually praise German managers is a well-known platitude, but it
is probably just as valid as the cliché of the German's extraordinary
industriousness.

The long list of virtues, often called "Prussian," which foreign
authors like to assemble, usually includes as typical German characteristics a love of order, a talent for effective organization, the strong inclination to save and invest, a pronounced spirit of inventiveness and
enterprise and, above all, a willingness bordering on a craving for
work. It cannot be the task here to unravel the threads entwined in the
fabric of German mentality—a doubtful undertaking in any case—but
a few facets of the German character, familiar to foreign observers, will
be presented. It is usually held that work is not just a job for the typical
German, not just a means of earning his living, but a task to be fulfilled,
and not seldom the central aspect of his life. Working long and hard
proves one's toughness, and such toughness was also an utter necessity
for centuries in a country rather poorly endowed by nature. Forced to
be frugal, especially on the barren soil of Prussia, the tradition of starving oneself rich *(sich grosshungern)* developed. The metaphysical preoc-
cupation of the German with getting to the root of things makes him a
true radical and leads to thoroughness and high quality of work in the
material world. The Faustian urge to "produce" *(schaffen)* and to "find
out" *(herausfinden)* is pursued in an orderly, systematic fashion; the
German penchant for organization may give rise to pedantry and per-
fectionism at times, but it has been very helpful and probably an indispensable prerequisite for scientific research and technological inven-
tion. Possibly as a protection against the plumbing of boundless
philosophical depths, discipline is highly valued by the German, who
has developed a great ability to impose, and to submit to, order and

system. Each of these traits cannot be dealt with in detail here, but if these characteristic features do, indeed, exist, the total collapse of the political, social and economic system in May 1945 must have intensified them. If a Spartan mentality was advisable for the Germans in case they intended to rebuild their economy, such an attitude was an absolute must for the millions of returning soldiers, the bombed-out, and all the others whose means of livelihood had disappeared. This was particularly true of the refugees and expellees who had to begin from scratch in a new environment.

In 1950 every fifth person in the FRG had recently taken up residence there. This inflow of over nine million people presented a major problem at the time as well as a considerable opportunity for the future. From the very first, and for years afterwards, the refugees and expellees constituted a major hindrance to reconstruction, since the newcomers placed an additional burden on such already overstrained facilities as housing, hospitals, schools and transport installations. At the same time the general unemployment and underemployment, due to lack of raw materials and productive equipment, prevented an appropriate productive contribution by this additional labor force for a long time. The real capital available per person was lowered by this influx, thus reducing the productivity of labor, while the need to channel more investable funds into nonproductive employment, e.g. housing, hospital and school construction, slowed down the growth of the productive capital stock in the following years, and consequently of per capita income. Apart from this negative impact on national income, the fact that the state faced higher expenditures for social and welfare purposes due to the refugees, and therefore had to claim a larger share of the GNP, exerted similar adverse effects because of the disincentives of high taxation upon economic activity. The stream of refugees, furthermore, reduced the degree of self-sufficiency in agricultural products. This necessitated additional food imports and had a negative impact on the German balance of payments, which was compensated, however, by the pressure of refugee labor on German wages, thus helping the exporting industries. The German foreign trade position was also improved over the years by refugee entrepreneurs resuming their previous economic activity on the basis of their know-how and reputation, by opening plants which were either highly export-intensive or which showed an import substitution effect through the harmonization of the partly upset production structure in the FRG. Increasingly, as the general reconstruction progressed, the refugees and expellees became an asset instead of a liability to the German economy. The refugees not only had a somewhat larger share of persons of working age than the indigenous population; they were also more mobile due to their lack of local ties and thus willing to move to where there was employment. Since many of the weak and sick had succumbed to the rigors of expulsion and the hardships of the westward trek, the survivors represented the more sturdy and alert, who were eager to improve their lot and confront the well-established, and at times complacent, indigenous members of the economic community with new ideas and methods. Such competition was not confined to entrepreneurial circles but was also prevalent among workers, and the availability of refugee labor tended to act as a depressant upon wages.

The German worker's restrained wage demands and his steady and industrious efforts were the invaluable contributions he made to his country's reconstruction. Just like the laborers in neighboring countries, he was prepared to work long and hard; there is little statistical evidence, however, that he did anything exceptional in this respect. Compared to the average of almost 50 working hours in 1938 and during most of the war, the work week in 1946/47, with its 39 hours, was rather short. After the currency reform, working time became longer (a weekly average of 42 hours in 1948 and 46 hours in 1949), but remained stable throughout the first half of the fifties once the 48 hour level had been reached in 1950.[51] Since there is also little quantitative proof of greater work intensity, the "hard work" thesis has been generally rejected as an unsatisfactory explanation for the rapid German reconstruction. Unusual labor efforts would have been rather strange in the face of the widespread unemployment, which averaged approximately 9 percent in the four post-currency-reform years. This unemployment was primarily structural in nature, reflecting the basic facts that the population of the FRG had risen by 25 percent within a few years and that the exigencies of the time (the need for shelter, food and heating) had led to a substantial geographic misallocation which only a lengthy relocation process could rectify.

In the face of this general abundance of labor, which increased by an average of almost 5 percent in each of the five post-currency-reform years, wages rose markedly. The index of real weekly earnings of all workers rose by 80 percent between mid-1948 and mid-1953, which meant the surpassing of the 1938 level by one-fifth. This substantial rise was, however, insufficient to increase labor's share in the national income, which actually declined from about 58.6 percent in 1950 to about 57.4 percent in 1952, but recovered to 59.4 percent in 1954. There was very little the union leaders could or wanted to do about this development, since the centralization of the trade union movement had not only increased labor's bargaining power but also placed greater responsibility for the common good on its representatives. Freed from

51. The statistics, of course, do not take into consideration such spare time activities as repairing one's home or cultivating one's garden plot, nor the time-consuming foraging tours before the currency reform.

the need to pursue a more aggressive wage policy, which usually is a must in cases of interunion competition, the labor leaders could successfully recommend short-term wage sacrifices to achieve long-run income benefits. The rank and file were, for their part, well aware of the recent improvements in their standard of living, which had been assisted by the interim maintenance of price control and rationing of many basic necessities immediately after the currency reform.

Apart from a general reluctance to endanger the budding economic reconstruction through more vigorous wage-bargaining, there were also other reasons for the unions' reserve. Necessity made caution the better part of wisdom, if one considered the total depletion of strike funds by the currency reform and the existence of a fairly large reservoir of the unemployed, and thus of potential strike-breakers. Other factors which also injected a downward bias into wage bargaining included the practice of concluding collective agreements on a regional basis. These had to orient themselves on the cost situation of marginal producers, and not on the profit position of the branch leaders, if shutdowns were to be avoided. This pursuit of nonwage objectives—e.g., job security, vacation time, codetermination, and also currency stability, under the eyes of an inflation-conscious membership—was a general characteristic of union policy during the early reconstruction period. It took years before the first big postwar strike was called, and even the six months' walkout of the metal workers in Schleswig-Holstein in 1955 did not seriously impair industrial harmony in Germany.[52] Labor's restraint—whether due to a statesmanlike sense of responsibility among union leaders or a proper understanding of the harsh realities among the rank and file—contributed greatly to Germany's recovery. Moderate wages enabled the buildup of plant and equipment to take place, ensured the stability of the new currency, and permitted Germany's return to the world market through competitive exports.

Markets and Political Measures

For an international trading country like Germany, access to foreign markets, whether as buyer or seller, was of particular importance. The restoration of international economic relations, however, took longer after 1945 than after the First World War, since the war years had been preceded by a phase of economic disintegration during the 1930s. The creation of new institutions such as the International Monetary Fund and the International Bank for Reconstruction and Development, the so-called World Bank, both in 1944, and the General

52. In that year the days lost through strikes were 5 per 100 employees in Germany, 17 in Great Britain, 25 in France, 55 in the United States and 61 in Italy.

Agreement on Tariffs and Trade in 1947, was necessary to establish a framework for international negotiation and cooperation. While these institutions, with their worldwide membership, aimed at restoration of the world economy, the Organization for European Economic Cooperation (OEEC) was more restricted in scope. To make the Marshall Plan aid more effective, the American government had insisted on close cooperation among the recipient countries and the OEEC, which, though not functioning as a supranational planning body, was to provide the framework for the removal of trade restrictions and the creation of an effective inter-European payments system.

Even before the founding of the Federal Republic, the United Economic Region of the Western zones had already become an OEEC member, thus participating in the required abolition of all quantitative trade restrictions for about half of her imports from other OEEC countries by mid-1949. For a time, thereafter, Germany played a leading role in further liberalization, and had freed 60 percent of her imports by the fall of 1950. Balance-of-payments problems during the Korean war necessitated the suspension of trade liberalization in February 1951, however, and it was not resumed until January 1952.[53] This relatively rapid recommencement of liberalization was partly made possible through the well-directed working of the European Payments Union (EPU), founded in July of 1950, which replaced bilateral balancing of international payments by a multilateral clearing system. Furthermore, within a framework of agreed quotas, the EPU provided automatic credits to member countries with an adverse trade balance. Germany became the first recipient of such a special credit (beyond the set quota) in order to pay for her excess imports in the fall of 1950.

For Germany the liberalization of trade and the multilateralization of payments opened the doors to nations producing foodstuffs and raw materials, which accounted for about 45 percent and 30 percent, respectively, of German imports in 1950. Foreign food supplies were particularly vital, given the loss of Germany's breadbasket and the population increase of about 25 percent; contemporaries were surprised that no higher agricultural imports were needed. Until the early fifties the difference was partly made up by an increase in domestic food production of somewhat over 10 percent, and a general lowering of consumption standards compared to the prewar diet; consequently self-sufficiency was able to reach 65 to 70 percent. As with food, Germany also had been a longtime importer of raw materials, given her poor endowment of natural resources, apart from coal. The self-sufficiency policy of the Third Reich, with its emphasis on domestic extraction of oil and ores and the production of synthetic gasoline,

53. The liberalized proportion rapidly advanced from 57 percent of imports in 1949 to 81 percent in August 1952 and 90 percent in April 1953.

rubber, fibers and plastics, had not been able basically to alter this situation, although it had strengthened Germany's raw materials base. Wartime destruction, dismantlement and production prohibitions prevented the regular and adequate provision of German industry with domestic raw materials before mid-1949. The Korean war not only tightened these bottlenecks again, particularly in coal and steel, but also aggravated the almost continuous difficulties of German industry in obtaining enough foreign raw materials such as textile fibers, nonferrous metals, natural rubber, crude oil and leather. On the whole, however, the Korean crisis was advantageous to Germany's foreign trade, since exports showed a surplus for the first time during the second half of 1951 and almost balanced imports for the entire year. For once, the country was not involved in a military dispute, and existing industrial capacities and scarce raw materials were not needed for armament programs, and were thus free for highly profitable export production in the face of increased international demand and reduced foreign competition. In this situation Germany was favored by her traditional industrial structure with its emphasis upon capital-goods industries.

The partition had left 63 percent of the Reich's industrial output of 1944 in the Western zones, which by 1946 housed 71 percent of the German people. At least with regard to such broad groupings as basic-materials industries (67 percent), capital-goods industries (62 percent) and consumer-goods industries (60 percent), the industrial structure looked relatively well-balanced. But this was not always the case. In some branches, e.g., clothing, glass, electrical, precision and optical equipment, production capacity was limited, whereas in others, e.g., leather and shoe manufacturing, and the steel producing and processing industries, production facilities were more than ample. A few highly specialized branches were almost totally lacking, e.g., the production of hosiery, gloves, certain types of textile and office machinery, and some stages of paper and chemical production. Nevertheless, the Western part of the country was better equipped industrially than the Soviet zone to begin successful reconstruction and more capable of catering to international demand. Germany's ability to supply machinery, industrial equipment, vehicles, and certain electrical and chemical products accounted to a considerable extent for her remarkable comeback on the world market. She could offer these commodities at attractive prices owing to her comparatively conservative domestic economic policy, the general undervaluation of her currency and a variety of export promotion schemes[54] on the part of the federal government, which also provided realistic policies in general.

54. Assistance was rendered to the export industries through tax credit subsidies, credit insurance, export credits and similar devices, which at the time were among the usual tools of export promotion used in Europe.

Events on the international political stage in particular played a role of overwhelming importance in Germany's recovery. The relatively rapid breakup of the anti-Hitler coalition into rival ideological camps once the war had ended enabled the Germans east and west to metamorphose from hated enemies into appreciated allies. While the price of partition was stiff, the loss of national unity permitted the contemporary generation to rebuild their divided country quickly once the repressive spirit of the Potsdam Conference had given way to Cold War ideology. Without the East-West split, there can be no doubt, the occupation policies of the Big Four would have been harsher, or at least less benevolent, and would have lasted longer and pressed harder upon the Germans. In this sense, the latter turned out to be the main, though not the only, beneficiaries of the Cold War, which has come to be regarded as the most decisive single factor in Germany's recovery. The presence of Western troops not only saved three-quarters of all Germans from possibly being overrun by communist aggressors, and from sharing the fate of the many non-Russian peoples that became captive nations within the Soviet satellite system, but was also conducive to internal political stability once the FRG had been established. The permanent stationing of Western forces in Germany narrowly circumscribed the sphere and facilitated the settling of social and political conflicts within the country, a completely different picture from the years after World War I, with their long series of relatively weak governments and repeated revolutionary and secessionist attempts.

In political terms German voters contributed their share to internal stability through their lasting renunciation of extremism both of the right and of the left, and their solid support of democratic parties either of a bourgeois-conservative or of a social democratic-laborite stamp.[55] Conservative cabinets under Adenauer (up to October 1963) and Erhard (until November 1966) were able to restore confidence in the state apparatus and to revive a certain paternalistic spirit of government, epitomized in the father figures of *"Der Alte"* and *"Der Dicke."*[56] The provision of political order and stability, made possible by the active cooperation of a loyal social democratic opposition, was no small task in a country where, within slightly more than a quarter of a century, constitutional monarchy, democratic parliamentarism and strong-man dictatorship had thoroughly disillusioned the public. But this was an essential condition for entrepreneurial activity, a workable social contract, and the confidence of the business partners abroad.

Order for a conservative government meant, of course, the pursuit of an economic policy which was solidly probusiness. In line with

55. In this respect the German voters showed significantly more political maturity than those in postwar Italy or France, thus making up for past follies.
56. That is, "the Old Man" (Adenauer) and "the Fat One" (Erhard).

neoliberal ideas on the importance of monetary stability for a competitive market system, the conservative government accorded top priority to stable prices, and the central bank pursued a restrictive course during boom periods to prevent losses in the DM's purchasing power. This policy was so effective that the relatively low level of prices in Germany led to the buildup of substantial trade and payments surpluses after 1952. The increasing stability of the DM raised hopes for a revaluation, resulting in a large inflow of speculative money, particularly from 1957 onward. The Advisory Council to the Minister of Economics had already proposed a revaluation of the DM in that year, but this step was not taken until the spring of 1961. In the meantime the *Bundesbank* pursued an ambivalent policy between internal and external monetary stability, but finally in November 1960 acknowledged that the balance-of-payments position had to take priority over domestic price stability. The slight revaluation brought the problem of "imported inflation" under control for only a relatively short time, however. From 1963 on, massive trade and payments surpluses accumulated again in Germany, primarily as the result of the inflationary policies of her Common Market partners. Increasingly, therefore, Germany pressed for monetary cooperation among the major trading nations inside and outside the Common Market.

After the DM had become convertible at the end of 1958, monetary policy in general proved itself less suitable for influencing business activity. Up to then tax and expenditure policies had hardly been employed as anticyclical devices, since the main fiscal objective had been to keep the budget balanced. Between 1952 and 1956 everincreasing budgetary surpluses, resulting from underestimated revenue and overestimated future defense commitments, were "frozen" at the central bank as an act of "good housekeeping." The buildup and eventual dissolution of this "Julius Tower"[57] after 1956 unintentionally provided anticyclical effects, at first by dampening the boom of 1955/56, later by somewhat mitigating the downswing of 1957/58. From about 1960 onward, however, the budget was used more consciously, though on a very small scale, for anticyclical purposes in the face of a less effective monetary policy. Apart from certain regulations to manipulate tax revenues, the government was empowered to block budgetary expenditures for stability purposes and did, in fact, make use of these provisions during the early sixties. But from 1962 onward the federal government's room to maneuver became smaller with the development of permanent budget deficits. In 1965, an election year, federal expenditure and revenue moved so much further apart that by the fall

57. The nickname was derived from a fortress tower where the Prussian kings had kept their war treasure.

a law for safeguarding the budget had to be enacted to reduce expenditures substantially enough to avoid an especially large budget deficit. Chancellor Erhard's obvious inability to balance the budget contributed greatly to his cabinet's fall the next year.

Erhard, generally assumed to have been quite luckless as chancellor, was much more successful as minister of economics.[58] Although neoliberal philosophy required that taxation should be as neutral as possible in its impact on the market, he nevertheless advocated special tax concessions, usually to encourage capital formation, in the abnormal situation of early reconstruction. By bending one neoliberal principle, another could be upheld: an interventionist tax policy allowed the avoidance of public investment planning at the enterprise level. While justified as long as there was an imbalance of production factors, a number of these tax privileges were maintained too long and eventually outlived their original purpose of encouraging investment. Instead, many of these tax concessions merely contributed to the concentration of income and wealth and a certain polarization of society that neoliberalism allegedly wished to avoid.

The share of gross wages and salaries in the national income rose between 1950 and 1970 from 58.6 percent to 66.7 percent, a 14 percent increase.[59] It would, nevertheless, be hasty to conclude from this increase that labor made slow but steady gains, since the proportion of receivers of such income in the gainfully active population rose during the same period by 22 percent, from 68.5 percent to 83.4 percent. That labor experienced a relative loss of position was also reflected by the fact that the weekly gross earnings of a male industrial worker rose 340 percent during these two decades, while the per capita GNP rose 440 percent. On the other hand, income differentials tended to decrease, and according to UN studies Germany was neither among the countries with constant income distribution over the years (as in Britain, Denmark and the Netherlands) nor among those with increasing inequality (like Finland and, particularly, France), but showed instead a trend towards greater equality with respect to income earned in the market.[60] It is difficult to determine the extent to which the rather complicated German tax structure contributed to income redistribution in favor of the lower-income groups. Recent studies on tax burdens have found that between 1950 and 1965 income from wages and salaries, property, and other income after taxes, tended to move to-

58. He held this position in all Adenauer's cabinets until 1963.

59. For statistical purposes the high renumeration of top managers was treated as salaries, and the meager earnings of small but independent businessmen as entrepreneurial income.

60. German income distribution in percent before taxes and transfer payments by fifths in 1950 and 1967: lowest fifth, 4, 8.7; second lowest fifth, 8.5, 13; third fifth, 16.5, 17.1; fourth fifth, 23, 23; highest fifth, 48, 38.2.

ward more rather than less equality. A similar redistributive effect must have resulted from transfer and other public expenditure payments under the comprehensive social security system. Besides old-age, disability and survivors' benefits, the German system also includes sickness, maternity, work-injury and unemployment compensation, family allowances, war pensions and related assistance as well as equalization-of-burdens payments and other forms of social help. This meant that by the late sixties German transfer payments, expressed as a percentage of national and personal income, were higher than in all other major Western European countries save France and far exceeded those in the United States and Japan. It is still difficult, however, to establish the precise redistributive effect of the German social welfare system, since most of the costs were financed by social security levies, which, like taxes, were paid partly by the beneficiaries and partly by the employers, while the rest came from state subsidies stemming from direct and indirect taxation. It also remains unclear what exact relation there existed between the development of personal assets and the trend toward more equal income distribution, particularly given the rise of new men and the decline of established families.

The virtual absence of official data—in itself a suspicious fact— permitted economists to claim that employed persons held 35 percent of all assets in 1950 compared to only 17 percent in 1965. By the mid-sixties some 15,000 millionaires, representing about 3 percent of all those paying property taxes or about one-twelfth of one percent of all households, owned 41 percent of all taxable assets, while almost half of all property-taxpayers had individual fortunes of under DM 100,000, owning merely 12 percent of the total. Furthermore, their assets consisted mostly of real estate and savings accounts and only to a small extent of shares and assets in enterprises. This undoubtedly reflected among other things the ownership policy of the conservative government, which had encouraged such forms of wealth formation since the early fifties, though the degree of encouragement was still narrowly limited up until the mid-sixties. At that time, Erhard's former chief adviser Müller-Armack, who had popularized the term "*Soziale Marktwirtschaft*," had to admit: "It seems to me now to be time to give greater prominence to the social goals of the Social Market Economy." Though he could point to the growth of mass income, as well as to the fact that real wages and salaries in Germany were the highest of all the Common Market countries, he conceded that wealth formation through uncontrolled and lavish tax privileges had been permitted for too long.

Apart from high real wages and comprehensive social welfare programs, secure jobs especially contributed to the improved standard of living of the masses. Although the Basic Law—in contrast to the

Weimar constitution and the constitutions of some of the states—did not explicitly acknowledge a moral right to work, in reality a state of permanent full employment had existed since the mid-fifties, when the unemployment rate fell below 4 percent.[61] The extraordinarily low rate of unemployment in the FRG (whether by European or American standards) was in no way the result of deliberate government policy. Above all other economic policy objectives the conservative government regarded the maintenance of the DM's purchasing power in domestic and foreign trade as its primary economic objective, and its tight monetary and fiscal management implied a rejection of full employment policies. The German neoliberals maintained that such desirable goals as full employment or rapid economic growth would result in the long run from the steadfast pursuit of internal and external monetary stability. In the face of the successful development of Germany's economy, it was difficult to contradict them. Less explicit, however, was the neoliberal success with regard to redistribution and social welfare, which the advocates of *Soziale Marktwirtschaft* also accepted as economic policy objectives in their own right. The policy adopted in 1948 of giving men of action the opportunity to work for themselves in the hope that their success would also improve living conditions in general had certainly worked, and had led to an outstanding provision of goods and services for private and public consumption. Nevertheless, critics have frequently asked whether the Social Market Economy really deserves the epithet "social," given the exorbitant inequality in private wealth, the fact that progress towards a wider distribution of income has been small and too slow, the limited diffusion of economic power, and the uncontrolled influence on official economic policy exerted by noisy, well-financed pressure groups and cliques. It seems as if social advance has been slower than economic progress.

3

The Phases of Progress

The German Roller Coaster

German development in the two decades after the currency reform was characterized by a tendency for growth rates to decline, superimposed by fluctuations of such regularity that four complete

---

61. It is held that in American terms, German statistics understate the unemployment rate by about 0.8 percent.

business cycles can be detected:[62] 1950–54, 1955–58, 1959–1963, and 1964–67. This declining economic trend[63] corresponds well with theoretical growth concepts which suggest that in an economy characterized by an imbalance in production factors (a relatively small capital stock and a large labor supply), the consequently high productivity of capital will encourage extensive investment, resulting in a steep rise in the national product. The broad expansion of the capital stock, however, will in time lead to a diminution of the productivity of capital and a consequent reduction in future rates of investment and for this reason to slower economic expansion. Eventually the capital stock reaches a level from which its further growth (and that of the national product) will be determined by the increase in technological knowledge and population. Such reasoning can, indeed, explain the initially steep and subsequently flattened increase in the German GNP. In the late 1940s, capital was relatively scarce while labor was abundant, encouraging high investment and resulting in fast economic growth. Over the years the capital stock widened, while the labor force grew at a much slower rate due to the reduced influx of refugees and the declining natural population growth. Modern methods came to be used more and more, thereby closing the technological gap, so that henceforth new investment would merely represent the normal increase in technological knowledge.

This tendency for growth to decline was superimposed by fluctuations of common character and causation. Each cycle began with an upturn phase lasting about two years, started by a more or less sudden upsurge of demand, leading to overutilization of productive capacities, rapidly rising prices and profits, and thereafter steep wage increases. As the initial flood of demand levelled off, sellers' markets increasingly gave way to buyers' markets; utilization of capacity and employment declined and for two to three years the German economy would pass through a phase of sluggish growth,[64] to be followed by a new demand-induced cyclical upswing.

Changes in demand were the main cause of these rhythmic fluctuations, which in all four cases (1950, 1955, 1959, 1964) started mainly in the exporting industries.[65] This pull which foreign demand exerted on

62. Since the classical business cycle, with its absolute decline in economic activity, has become the exception, the term is frequently used nowadays to describe the motion pattern of a growing economy.

63. The average growth rate in the cycles: 8.8 percent, 7 percent, 5.7 percent, and 3.6 percent.

64. "Sluggish" here means in relation to the growth rates during the preceding boom, and not in relation to the simultaneous performance of other countries.

65. To a lesser extent other sectors of demand played a role, e.g., in 1950 the outbreak of the Korean war influenced domestic demand as well; in 1954/55 private invest-

the German economy did not necessarily come as a deus ex machina but was to a considerable extent induced.[66] The preceding recession had not only brought a certain pressure to bear on German prices and shortened the delivery time for German products—both attractive developments for foreign customers—but German producers had tended, in the face of unsatisfactory domestic demand, to intensify their export activities.[67] Increased export orders stimulated not only the respective branches but also—through the acceleration principle—the producer-goods industries to a great extent. The generally increased demand soon positively affected—through multiplier processes—the consumer-goods industries, which in their turn placed orders for additional plant and equipment. High profits, resulting from lower costs—due to better utilization of capacities—and the general excess of demand, provided the necessary funds for investment projects. Credits, for a time still at the relatively low interest rates stemming from the previous slowdown phase, also facilitated entrepreneurial expansion.

A new phase of sluggish growth began in each cycle (1952, 1957, 1962, 1965) as the consequence of decreasing demand for capital goods. The initial clustering of orders for plant and equipment, their technical indivisibility and lengthy gestation period probably broke the investment boom in each case. In all likelihood, businessmen abstained for a time from further increasing their production facilities and curbed their demand for capital goods until they had better information on the fate of their recently enlarged capacities. Better empirical evidence is available on the restrictive monetary policy pursued by the *Bundesbank* to curb inflationary tendencies once each boom got under way. The reduction of funds available from outside sources and declining possibilities of self-financing investments due to wage increases, typical for the later part of each expansion phase, resulted in each case (but particularly in 1952, 1956, and 1965/66) in shrinking demand for capital goods. While in all these years public authorities did not pursue a well-devised anticyclical budget policy to diminish the boom by raising taxes and postponing government expenditure,[68] a stabilizing ef-

---

ment increased substantially in view of the forthcoming cancellation of certain tax privileges; in 1959 publicly supported construction expenditures were a contributing factor.

66. Nevertheless there did exist an element of good luck, since in each case German and foreign business cycles were not fully synchronized.

67. Such a willingness to export can by no means be taken for granted and frequently did not exist among industrialists in other European countries, who preferred to curb production during a period of slackening demand at home.

68. It is true, however, that at times some budget allocations for public construction were partly blocked. A deflationary effect was also achieved, albeit accidentally, when the "Julius Tower" was formed in 1955/56.

fect, however, emanated in 1955, 1959 and especially 1965/66 from the domestic price increases, which slowed down exports and intensified imports.

The ensuing deflationary process in each cycle not only broke the investment boom and concomitant inflationary tendencies, thus leading to equilibrium, but usually overshot the mark by turning into a recession. In the face of declining demand, entrepreneurs tended to adopt a policy of "wait and see," by limiting further expansion of their activities, thus in time actually converting their own pessimistic expectations into reality. It was probably thanks to the relatively constant private consumption that a serious contraction was avoided,[69] but this stabilizing effect was insufficient to usher in a revival of business. Nor would this be brought about by an increased demand for capital goods stemming from new investment projects sensitive to interest rates. In every case it was an increased foreign demand that drew the German economy into the expansion phase of a new cycle, since up to the mid-sixties no major fiscal policy measures were taken to stimulate the economy.[70] This reflected partly the fact that, in the face of high growth rates of 8 to 10 percent during a speedup phase, their levelling off to 5 to 7 percent during the following slowdown phase was regarded as a welcome calming down of excessive economic activity and a return to internal and external economic stability. However, when in the mid-sixties the upswing phase brought an average growth rate of only 6 percent and contraction began to mean virtual stagnation (or even absolute decline, as in 1967 when German GNP fell by 0.2 percent), a deliberately expansionist fiscal policy had to be adopted to prevent the recession from becoming a depression.

Though it would be possible to present the history of Germany's economic performance during the fifties and sixties by using these four growth cycles as organizing concepts, a slightly different classification, which partly emphasizes political events, is often employed, distinguishing a reconstruction phase from 1948 to 1951, a consolidation phase from 1952 to 1958, a "falling-in-line" phase from 1959 to 1966, and the years between 1966/67 and 1970.

The Phase of Reconstruction (1948–1951)

The first years after the currency reform of June 1948 were devoted to rebuilding. This period ended in 1951 when dismantling was

69. During the contraction phase the ratio of wages (and of consumption) to national product tends to increase. Furthermore, falling prices raise the real value of cash balances and increase the propensity to consume (Pigou effect). Lastly the habit-persistence effect makes for the maintenance of the habitual standard of living in spite of temporarily decreasing incomes or unemployment.

70. The work creation program of 1950 turned out to be superfluous with the beginning of the Korean boom.

officially discontinued. Throughout the entire year, industrial production had surpassed its 1938 prewar level, and Germany's balance of trade nearly squared for the first time. Before this was achieved, many difficult problems had had to be solved. In the production sphere, damaged plants, public installations and buildings, but also destroyed or run-down machines, tools, and office equipment had to be repaired or replaced altogether. In the consumers' realm, replacements had to be found for residential premises, furniture, household goods and clothing lost by those bombed-out and expelled. This huge demand for goods, which had been increasingly piling up for almost a decade, pressed upon a liberalized but still narrow market, driving prices sky-high. Although pre-currency-reform hoarding of commodities had been considerable, stocks were quickly depleted. Within six months, by December 1948, retail prices of manufactured consumer goods rose by 18 percent, food prices by 29 percent and the total cost-of-living index by 15 percent (due to the compensating effect of stable rents and the lowering of some excise taxes and rates). Strong voices demanded the reintroduction of controls, and in mid-November the unions called a one-day work stoppage to demonstrate against the official economic policy. However, the bizonal administration did not change its course, and by the end of the year the economic climate had shifted from a "price boom" towards a "quantity boom" as a result of the slackening demand. Apart from a general policy of keeping money tight, the conversion of RM-balances into DM-accounts came to an end, thus curbing consumer spending. Tax revenue increased quickly as a consequence of the upswing in economic activity, thus reducing the need for the deficit-financing of government expenditure in the context of the initial allocation of currency. Wages remained essentially stable, not least due to the realistic attitude of the unions.

While the flood of demand abated, the supply continued to increase, since the index of industrial production (1936=100) rose by 46 percent, from 54 in June to 79 in December. This expansion reflected the sudden use of already existing, but partly inoperable facilities made possible by the acquisition of a few essential spare parts or machines. Nevertheless, the reconstruction did not merely confine itself to the rebuilding of previous installations. It also—not infrequently thanks to dismantling—included a transition to more modern methods, an adaptation of individual plants and of the production structure in general to the partition of the once integrated German economy, and an adjustment to changes in the world market.

By the turn of the year 1948/49, the incipient slackening of worldwide economic activity accompanied the stabilization of the German market, which increasingly tended to become the buyers' domain. The earlier momentum was broken, and for the next fifteen months growth slowed down considerably. While the index of industrial production (1936 = 100) continued to rise by a respectable 22 percent, from 81 in January 1949 to 99 by March 1950, prices began to drop off, and the cost-of-living index fell by almost 9 percent from its peak in December 1948 to its lowest point in May 1950. Declining prices dampened entrepreneurial propensity to invest, and encouraged consumers to postpone purchases in expectation of a further downward pressure on prices. The beginning of liberalization of foreign trade increased imports, but had few discernible effects on German exports, since the many production prohibitions and restrictions had only recently been lifted[71] and the dollar trading policy of the JEIA caused several countries to discriminate against German exports. Thus only German raw materials encountered a brisk demand and in 1949, for instance, 40 percent of exports to Great Britain consisted of scrap iron and sawn timber, while 90 percent of exports to France consisted of coal and lumber.

As a result of the relatively slow pace of economic progress, German unemployment quickly increased, from an annual average of 4.2 percent in 1948 to 8.3 percent in 1949 and 10.3 percent in 1950. That the introduction of the DM and the concomitant return of entrepreneurial thinking in terms of costs would terminate the false full employment of the prereform economy and lead to some unemployment had been a foregone conclusion, but its alarming proportions caused considerable concern. Unemployment was particularly high, and rising, in those predominantly agricultural states with a large proportion of refugees and expellees.[72] This was potentially politically dangerous, because after all unemployment had helped Hitler to power. Requests were made, therefore, especially by the social democratic opposition and the unions, to use an expanded money supply and budget deficits for a vigorous full-employment policy. Such proposals were countered by the conservative government with the argument that after two inflations within one generation, monetary stability was of the utmost political and economic importance, and would surely be jeopardized by such expansionist policies. Since the unemployment was primarily structural and not cyclical in nature—as reflected in the relatively low unemployment ratios in the industrialized and highly ur-

71. Under the Washington Agreement of April 1949, production prohibitions had been transformed into production restrictions for heavy machine tools, electronic tubes, aluminum and magnesium, while production restrictions were lifted for precision instruments, optical goods, electrical appliances and equipment, private cars, trucks, tractors, heavy motorcycles, pharmaceutical products, coal-tar dyes, heavy chemicals, copper, zinc, lead, and cement.

72. Unemployment in percent in 1948, 1949 and 1950 in Schleswig-Holstein 6.5, 21.5, 25.2; in Lower Saxony 4.6, 13.2, 17.0; in Bavaria 7.3, 12.5, 13.9.

banized states, with their smaller share of new immigrants[73]—its causes, not merely its symptoms, had to be cured. Eventually there would have to be a new migration of the refugees, expellees and bombed-out from the agricultural states, with their limited employment opportunities but considerable housing space, to the industrial centers. This, however, could not be accomplished just then, owing to the limitations placed on industrial expansion by shortages of coal, steel and energy, the absence of adequate housing in industrial areas, the lack of industrial skills and the physical handicaps of many unemployed. Under such conditions, stimulation of the economy would not essentially lead to greater employment but primarily to higher prices, and would contribute to a further worsening of Germany's balance-of-payments position.

In view of the huge deficit in foreign exchange and the scheduled rapid decline of American aid, Germany actually had to increase her exports in order to be able to pay her own way. In mid-September 1949, Germany followed the example of various other European countries and raised the exchange rate of the dollar from DM 3.33 to DM 4.20. As this devaluation was less than that instituted by Britain or France, it reduced the competitiveness of German goods in these countries, while at the same time—in connection with a further generous import liberalization, as recommended by the OEEC—facilitating the access of foreign commodities to the German market. As a result Germany's balance of payments quickly deteriorated, increasing the central bank's reluctance to finance large-scale work-creation programs. Political and social considerations, however, required such a policy when, in early 1950, the unemployment level reached the two million mark. The deficit-financing of public expenditure for housing construction was planned and tax cuts were scheduled to become effective in June. Ironically, this was the month when a communist act of aggression in a distant part of the world relieved the bourgeois government of the FRG of its serious economic difficulties. Before the planned palliatives could become fully effective, the outbreak of the Korean war initiated an upswing which lasted until mid-1951.

It is true that already about three months before the communist attack on 25 June 1950, a new economic upswing seemed to be in the making, since the index of industrial production (1936 = 100) rose from 99 in March to 110 in June, and unemployment fell from 12.2 to 10.0 percent. However, the autobiographic claim of the then minister of economic affairs, Erhard, seems to have been somewhat over-

73. Unemployment in percent in 1948, 1949 and 1950 in North Rhine-Westphalia 3.2, 3.9, 4.8; and in Baden-Württemberg 2.0, 3.3, 4.3.

optimistic. He maintained that "even without Korea" the German economy would have continued to develop, and would even have increased the rate of its growth.[74] Such an evaluation takes insufficient account of the Allies' revision of their policy of industrial and technological "disarmament" of Germany in view of the Korean war. Already at the foreign ministers' conference in New York in September 1950, the general production prohibitions concerning the manufacture of small firearms and cut-and-thrust weapons were transformed into mere restrictions, but the manufacture of aircraft, naval vessels and all kinds of other war material remained forbidden, although a more lenient policy was adopted with regard to the construction of merchant ships. Most important, the 11.1 million ton ceiling on annual German steel production, though not officially lifted before mid-1952, was no longer strictly enforced, making possible an output of 12.1 million tons in 1950 and 13.5 million tons in 1951. The Agreement on Industrial Controls of April 1951 brought further alleviations: production prohibitions on synthetic rubber and fuel were changed into capacity controls; production restrictions on heavy machine tools, aluminum, synthetic ammonia and chlorine were abolished, and those for shipbuilding (except naval vessels) and ball bearings were transformed into mere capacity controls. At about the same time the general supervision of research in the chemical industry had also been lifted.

The Korean war did at first create some problems for the FRG, despite a gradual expansion in her assortment of exportable goods. German industrialists, especially sensitive to wartime shortages, almost immediately started building up their stocks of foreign raw materials. This, together with an increased import demand resulting from the previously planned stimulation measures and the hoarding of private households, soon led to a substantial external trade deficit. The anti-boom campaign of the central bank, belatedly started in October and with little active support from the government's fiscal policy, did not impress the hoarders in the face of the new situation caused by the military intervention of Red China in Korea in November 1950. Because about three-quarters of Germany's imports came from EPU countries, the widening trade deficit forced her eventually to suspend the previous liberalization policy and to resort to administrative import restrictions. By the second quarter of 1951, however, the balance-of-payments crisis was essentially under control, owing to the cresting of

74. Erhard claimed that the Korean boom created more difficulties than benefits for the German economy and provided almost no positive impulses. In fact, however, the upsurge of world demand at least quite substantially accelerated Germany's reintegration into the world economy.

the worldwide raw materials boom and the continued fast growth of German exports.[75] Altogether Germany profited by the Korean crisis, since greater industrial production and exports had been achieved at the price of a relatively small rise in the cost of living and wages (8 and 20 percent respectively) and a temporary deliberalization of trade of less than one year. By the second half of 1951, the economic upswing had on the whole run its course and a phase of reduced growth followed, primarily as a reaction to the excesses of the previous boom. Again requests for a more expansionist economic policy were made, but fiscal and monetary policies remained restrictive, leading to some idle production factors and declining living costs. The government argued that the German balance-of-payments position was still vulnerable, and that a certain capacity reserve would be desirable in view of a potential rearmament boom once Germany had joined the European Defense Community. Neither, however, materialized.

The Consolidation Phase (1952–1958)

The six years from 1952 onward were a period of relative tranquility compared to the preceding time of hectic developments. Germany's economic upsurge continued with few tendencies towards higher prices throughout the fifties,[76] and her GNP in real terms increased between 1952 and 1958 at an annual average rate of 7.6 percent,[77] while the unemployment ratio fell from 6.4 percent to 1.7 percent leaving virtually no further reserves on the labor market. Besides substantial economic progress, these years of the "Golden Fifties" also brought considerable improvements in Germany's political position. Largely as a result of the communist invasion in Korea and the general intensification of the Cold War, the status of the Federal Republic underwent a rapid change from former enemy to future ally. Within a few years the FRG was accepted as a sovereign state among the Western nations, which began to pool their resources and to coordinate their policies in such supranational bodies as the European Coal and Steel Community (ECSC), the North Atlantic Treaty Organization (NATO), and finally the European Economic Community (EEC).

As early as the spring of 1952, the occupation powers had granted internal independence to the FRG, though the respective contractual agreement did not become fully effective until 5 May 1955. The Germans fulfilled their part in this elaborate and protracted diplomatic

75. During the three half-year periods between July 1950 and December 1951, German exports rose by 55, 27 and 25 percent, in each case compared to the level of the preceding half-year.

76. Percentage rise of cost-of-living indices, 1950/1959; Germany 19, United States 22, Italy 39, Britain 49, France 66.

77. Average annual growth of real GNP: United States 2.2 percent; Britain 3.2 percent; France 4 percent; Italy 5.1 percent.

bargain by joining NATO four days later. An agreement had previously been reached with France on the Saar question, while since August 1952 the FRG, together with the Benelux countries, Italy and France, had accepted permanent joint control of all national coal and steel industries in the ECSC.[78] Within a short time the High Authority of the ECSC removed tariffs and quotas on the intra-Community trading of coal, steel, scrap and iron ore, reduced allowable subsidies, and took various steps to abolish discriminatory freight rates. Common guidelines were worked out regarding price and investment policies and measures were taken to regulate competition and concentration and to influence production and productivity. The high level of demand for the products of these bottleneck industries facilitated the work of the High Authority for many years and led to far less interference with production and employment than had originally been anticipated. Beginning in 1957/58, however, coal surpluses put pressure on the mining industry, particularly in Belgium and Germany, and the steel slumps of 1958 and 1961 only aggravated the situation. The necessary economic policy decisions remained within the competence of the individual governments, not the Community. These problems in these branches revealed the limitations of partial or sectoral integration in the face of different fiscal systems, social security regulations, monetary and business-cycle policies and the many other economic policy measures available to the national governments.

Efforts to establish a more comprehensive economic union became a reality when, in March 1957, France, Italy, the FRG and the Benelux countries signed the twin Treaties of Rome creating the European Atomic Energy Community (Euratom) and the EEC. Both came into force on 1 January 1958. Euratom, though providing a useful organization to save the six member nations time and money through cooperative research, turned out to be of little economic importance because structural changes on the international fuel market deferred the time when atomic energy would be a paying proposition. The EEC, by contrast, gained momentum very quickly, covering the whole of the six nations' economies and, therefore, involving a much wider transfer of sovereignty rights. Nevertheless, the Rome Treaty had delegated the major decision making not to the EEC Commission in Brussels, the executive body representing Community interests in general, but to the Council of Ministers, as the spokesmen for the individual national interests. Since the treaty merely outlined the objectives, common rules and timetables for the envisioned economic integration, the formula-

78. Previously only the German industries had been under international control; with the formation of the ECSC the 11.1 million ton ceiling for Germany's steel industry was officially lifted.

tion of detailed policies had to be established in years of tough bargaining among the member nations by balancing, for instance, greater advantages to the French in agriculture against increased benefits to the Germans in industry or higher gains to the Benelux countries in commerce and transit trade. Since the principal idea had been to go beyond a mere trading bloc and to create a genuine economic community, steps had to be taken to abolish internal barriers to the commodity trade and the free movement of labor and capital, to coordinate financial and general economic policies, and to adopt a common approach to agriculture, transportation and foreign trade. In short, a common concept had to be developed and appropriate regulations issued which would make possible a close intertwining of the national economies. "To establish the foundations of an even closer union among the European peoples"—in the words of the treaty's preamble—a period of twelve years was allowed, for instance, for the gradual reduction of all tariffs between the six nations. However, the Six moved ahead much more quickly than originally planned, owing to the general prosperity, the favorable reaction of the business community, and the changed position of France.

For Western Europe as a whole, the fifties were a period of economic growth, and the regained economic strength of the area showed itself when its principal currencies officially returned to full convertibility against the dollar in late December 1958. Economic expansion and optimistic conclusions as to the future course of economic activity facilitated tariff reductions. Business circles which had had reservations about, or had even opposed the creation of the Common Market, rushed to meet the inevitable, immediately preparing to confront the forthcoming competition on the home market and to establish themselves in time in foreign markets which would soon be easily accessible. Since the business world acted as if the customs frontiers were to fall soon, and not in the distant future, the governments were able to accelerate the tariff reductions. This was also promoted by a new situation in France, in the early years often unable to go through with her own proposals for integration because of political and economic weakness. Under De Gaulle, who came to power half a year after the creation of the Common Market, France's economic conditions improved so much that the reduction of tariffs could be speeded up. Thus it can largely be said that prosperity—in all the EEC countries—made the Common Market, and not the other way around.

The Gaullist formula of *"L'Europe des patries"* ("A Europe of Fatherlands") and the French dislike of supranational bodies, however, brought other uncertainties for the future of the European Community. A reluctance to delegate sovereign rights to supranational institutions had also been one of the reasons for Britain's remaining outside the EEC and for her leadership in creating the European Free Trade Association (EFTA).[79] Established in May 1960, the EFTA threatened to become a rival trade bloc, possibly leading in the future to a two-tier system of West European economic integration: the "Outer Seven" versus the "Inner Six." Since such an economic division would probably be detrimental to Germany's exports, of which in 1960 almost identical shares of slightly under 30 percent went to the EFTA and EEC countries, she became an early champion of British entry into the Common Market.

German exports throughout the "Golden Fifties" developed quite impressively, actually rising by almost 120 percent in the six years after 1952, when a favorable balance of trade was achieved for the first time. In 1953 the German cost of living declined somewhat from its peak during the Korean War boom, but soon commenced to rise again, though by only 9 percent between 1954 and 1958. This increase, small in comparison to other major European trading nations, permitted attractive German export prices, which were further reduced by the general undervaluation of the DM, leading to large balance-of-trade surpluses and growing foreign exchange reserves.[80] Probably of more importance for Germany's success in foreign trade was the desire and the readiness of her industrialists to export, after a good decade of enforced absence from international markets. Analyzing sales possibilities in external markets, adjusting one's assortment to the demand of potential foreign customers, setting up appropriate marketing organizations abroad, reestablishing old, though interrupted, trade relations, as well as making new contacts within a changed world market, was time-consuming and hard work, but increasingly began to bear fruit during the "Golden Fifties." Furthermore, it is generally reported that while industrialists in some economically saturated countries tended to increase productive capacities primarily in response to a pressing demand for their products, German entrepreneurs frequently did not wait for such inducements, but expanded their plants while hunting for new and mostly foreign outlets to keep their additional capacities sufficiently employed.

The Volkswagen company presents a good example of increased production and sales. The "Beetle," designed in 1934 on Hitler's orders to popularize private motoring in Germany,[81] had served mainly military purposes, and some 70,000 functioned as the German jeep during

79. Other members were Sweden, Norway, Denmark, Switzerland, Austria, and Portugal, which, however, together represented only slightly over 40 percent of the bloc's population.

80. On the import side, Germany benefitted from the drop in international raw-materials prices.

81. The car's official name was the *"KdF-Wagen"* ("Strength-Through-Joy Car").

the war. By 1945 two-thirds of the Volkswagen plant was war-damaged, and the remainder was spared dismantling only because a British commission of automobile experts had reported that "the vehicle does not meet the fundamental technical requirements of a motor car. As regards performance and design it is quite unattractive . . . too ugly and too noisy . . . to build the car commercially would be a completely uneconomic enterprise . . . it would mean no undue economic competition on the world markets against British products." Reconstruction thus permitted, daily production amounted in 1946 and 1947 to somewhat under 30 Beetles, in 1950 to over 300, in 1955 to over 1,000 and to around 4,000 by late 1960. That was the year Detroit introduced its compact car to the American buyer to meet the challenge of the VW, half a million of which had by then been imported into the United States. To sell "Hitler's baby" to Americans had been an arduous task and in 1950 when imports began, only 330 VWs had been sold in a market that absorbed 5 to 6 million cars annually. By 1953 only a total of about 2,000 VWs had been sold; however, some 6,600 were sold the next year, 30,000 in 1955, 50,000 in 1956 and eventually over 300,000 in 1970 which then represented slightly over 6 percent of the market. By that time the Beetle was seriously threatening to break the record of the famous Model T, of which, before and after World War I, Ford had sold over 15 million, and which Hitler had called "a splendid example." Just as the "Tin Lizzy" in its time had been the main means of American motorization, so the Beetle played a similar role in postwar Germany, where the number of private cars per 1,000 inhabitants rose from 11 in 1950 to 79 in 1960 and 236 in 1970.[82]

Not only the automobile became an article of mass consumption during the fifties, taking over from the bicycle, the motor-scooter and the motorcycle. Many consumer durables, such as television sets, automatic washing machines, and various other electric household appliances, also increasingly lost their luxury character. Such articles began to attract the attention of the German consumer in the years after the currency reform, once he had eaten his fill, clothed himself properly, and acquired new furniture. While successive spending waves benefitted the particular industries concerned, other branches manufacturing new products, like plastics, fully synthetic fibers, precision instruments and optical equipment also gained ground once their production prohibitions and/or output limitations had been lifted. However, industries which had traditionally been concentrated in the west and previously supplied the entire German market, stagnated and encountered considerable adjustment difficulties, while branches

82. An ordinary industrial laborer had to work seventy weeks in 1950 to buy the cheapest VW, while in 1970 twenty weeks sufficed for the same purpose.

which had been underrepresented in the west at the time of the zonal division experienced very fast growth. Besides these manifold shifts in the traditional industrial structure, the geographic distribution of industry also changed somewhat during the fifties. Particularly around Munich, Stuttgart and Frankfurt, new industrial centers sprang up or grew faster than the Rhine and Ruhr regions, since abundant coal supplies and suitable rail connections had lost much of their location-creating advantage with the rise of the power station, the truck and, eventually, the pipeline. Industries hitherto unrepresented in the west, like those producing glassware or stockings, were set up by refugee entrepreneurs, frequently in rural areas, and often with their former employees. This contributed to the dispersal of industry, and to the economic integration of the expellees as well.

By about 1960 the economic (and also social and political) integration of expelled persons into their new environment had been basically achieved, and for the first time their unemployment level remained below the national average. This was chiefly the result of the resettlement of many of them from the rural areas where there were few jobs to the industrial centers. By 1960 only about one-third of the once independent farmers had found self-employment in agriculture. Apart from the agricultural middle class, the owners of small and medium-sized handicrafts businesses and tradesmen were hit hard by the loss of their homeland. Here too, only about one-third had been able to return to their previous independent activity by the late fifties.[83] To a considerable extent, this reflected the shortage or total lack of equity capital, necessary for any entrepreneurial activity, though the government attempted to provide financial support through loans, tax privileges, and particularly by an equalization of burdens. In accordance with the relevant law of 1952 a special Equalization Fund had been established, which was financed, apart from state subsidies, by levies on the devaluation profits from credits and mortgages, made in connection with the currency reform, and a general property levy of 50 percent on all assets owned on the day of the currency reform. Since the levies were to be paid in yearly installments until 1978, the creeping inflation and initial under-assessment meant that only about 10 to 20 percent of the private property held in June 1948 was actually redistributed. Throughout the fifties the Fund in principle only made payments to those in need of aid on social grounds (e.g., relief allowances or household goods indemnities) and financed activities of national economic interest (particularly assistance to refugee enterprises and work-providing projects). From 1961 on, however, payments were made on the basis of incurred losses,

---

83. In 1957, for instance, the proportion of wage and salary earners among working refugees was 91 percent, compared to 73 percent among the indigenous population.

though on average the compensation only covered 15 percent of the lost assets. Compared to German recipients, foreign claimants, once victims of Nazi terror, usually fared much better, especially since with the strong position of the DM, difficulties in transferring the restitution payments had vanished.

The "Falling-in-Line" Phase (1959–1966)

The hardening of the DM reflected the much slower rise of prices and the faster growth of the GNP in Germany than in some other major trading countries throughout the fifties. However, from the late fifties onward, through the better part of the sixties, German price and production performance rather closely resembled that experienced by other major industrial nations. Germany not only lost her leadership in the Western growth league,[84] but also increasingly encountered price difficulties as well,[85] and thus tended to move roughly in unison with the other West European nations.

Yet the goal of German monetary policy had not changed, and the *Bundesbank* continued its previous policy of maintaining the purchasing power of the DM, or at least of keeping its annual loss at as low a level as possible in the hope of protecting the German island of price stability in a sea of creeping inflation. With the establishment of full convertibility of the DM in late 1958, however, the *Bundesbank* had lost part of its autonomy in making monetary policy. Thus, when the primarily export-led boom of 1959 got under way,[86] quickly leading to price and wage increases in the face of a completely dry labor market (the unemployment rate was under 1 percent), the *Bundesbank* took its customary restrictive measures. The discount rate, which after repeated reductions stood at the unprecedented low level of 2.75 percent in January 1959, was raised to 3 percent in September, 4 percent in October, and 5 percent in June of the following year. In addition the rediscount quotas of the commercial banks were cut by 20 percent in October 1959 and greatly reduced again in March 1960, and stiffer minimum reserve requirements were set in November 1959, and January, March and June 1960. These fairly drastic restrictions still could not curb the boom. The relatively high level of interest, compared to rates abroad, made German borrowers attractive customers for foreign lenders, and encouraged the inflow of foreign funds. The German banks repatriated their foreign short-term assets and bor-

84. Average annual growth of the real GNP 1959/1966: FRG 5.5 percent, France 5.5 percent, Italy 5.9 percent, United States 5 percent, Great Britain 3.3 percent.
85. Annual average increase in the cost of living: 1952/58, 1.2 percent; 1959/62, 1.9 percent; 1963/66, 3 percent.
86. Construction activity was also encouraged by the low mortgage rates and publicly assisted housebuilding.

rowed funds abroad, thus replenishing domestic liquidity and further feeding the boom. The still comparatively inexpensive output of the German export industries guaranteed ongoing sales, further bloating Germany's exchange reserves.

The German foreign exchange cushion, which had grown from DM 1.1 billion in 1950 to DM 13 billion in 1955 and almost DM 32 billion in 1960, meant that Germany's spectacular export gains threatened to import inflation into the German economy by both withdrawing goods and services from the home market and increasing the domestic supply of money. At the same time Germany's external imbalance tended to disrupt the whole system of European payments, and requests had already frequently been made by her trading partners during the second half of the fifties either to allow domestic prices to rise, or to make long-term foreign loans, or to revalue the DM. The first suggestion for working off the balance-of-payments surplus could not really be followed, given the inflation consciousness of the German public. Long-term capital exports were, indeed, encouraged and undertaken. From 1957 on, official loans were made to several European governments and international institutions, while in 1958 the first industrial bond issue since before World War I was floated by a foreign company in Germany. The first annual decline in reserves (by 10 percent) in 1959 did not, however, indicate a basic reversal in the trend of the German balance of payments, but reflected some atypical influences, and in 1960 exchange reserves were DM 5.5 billion, or 21 percent above the record set two years before. Since mere palliatives had proven insufficient, and basic correctives were necessary if something was to be done about Germany's embarrassing international imbalance, the government revalued the DM by 5 percent, setting the new parity at DM 4.00 to the dollar on 6 March 1961.

By that time Germany's foreign exchange reserves were second only to those of the United States and over twice as large as those of the British, and stabilized for the following years, until 1967 at an average of DM 32 billion, with a spread of 29.6 to 33.4 billion. The revaluation could only partly take credit for this development, however, since the price competitiveness of German exporting industries was not seriously undermined. Tendencies already at work for some time, particularly physical constraints, such as labor scarcity, further accentuated by the erection of the Berlin Wall in August 1961, a shortening of the average working week, longer paid vacations in 1962, and greater difficulties in recruiting skilled foreign workers in the face of Europe-wide full employment, slowed down the growth of the German GNP from its unsustainable earlier pace to a continental European average of about 5 percent during this "falling-in-line" phase. In international capital transactions, German trends also began to resemble those in other major industrial countries.

German direct investments abroad started somewhat slowly. They had, indeed, been prohibited by the Allies until 1951, but even after that German businessmen remained reluctant to rebuild foreign holdings after two confiscations within a quarter of a century. Furthermore, high domestic returns on capital provided little incentive to search for lucrative investment opportunities in foreign countries. Consequently direct investments of only about DM 0.4 billion were made up to 1955, followed by increments of an annual average of DM 0.5 billion up to 1959, of DM 0.8 billion between 1960 and 1962, of slightly over DM 1 billion between 1963 and 1965, and of DM 2.5 billion up to 1970. While these increases in foreign investments represented an annual growth of more than twice the American or British figure, by the late sixties total German holdings abroad only amounted to 5 percent of American, 24 percent of British and 60 percent of French investments in foreign countries, reaching the level of nations like Canada or Switzerland. On the other hand, foreign nationals invested over DM 21 billion in Germany during the sixties, which was about the amount German investors had spent abroad throughout the fifties and sixties. On an annual basis, German direct investments did not surpass those of foreigners in Germany until 1968. Of the foreign holdings in Germany in 1970, one-half belonged to Americans and the other half to Europeans, more or less equally divided between the EFTA and EEC countries. In the same years, half of the German foreign assets were in Europe (at a ratio of three to two between EEC and EFTA nations), about one-tenth in the United States and one-fifth in Latin America. Though Asian and African countries each accounted for only 10 percent of German foreign assets in 1970, the FRG received the highest praise in the Pearson Report of the International Bank for Reconstruction and Development for her contributions to developing countries, which in 1967 amounted to 1.24 percent of her GNP.[87] Apart from financial contributions, German development aid to a considerable extent consisted of technical and vocational assistance.

Industrial know-how was also transmitted to the millions of foreign workers who sought gainful employment in Germany after the late fifties. A proportion of them sooner or later returned home, and the skills and knowledge they had acquired in Germany then benefitted the economies of their home countries. In 1955 the foreign labor force in the FRG amounted to only some 80,000 workers, mostly Dutch or

---

87. This figure compared quite favorably to the UN-suggested rate of 0.94 percent, the American contribution of 0.65 percent, or the 1.26 percent of Switzerland, the most generous country of them all.

Austrian nationals, but by 1960 some 300,000 foreigners, half of them from Mediterranean countries, were employed, constituting 1.5 percent of all wage earners. Freedom of movement as a consequence of the Common Market meant that South Italians were the first to arrive, soon to be followed, however, by Greeks, Spaniards, Turks, Portuguese and Yugoslavs, so that by 1970 about two million foreigners— *Gastarbeiter* (guest workers) as the Germans call them—were registered, representing almost one-tenth of all employed persons. The FRG required these additional workers and their economic importance was considerable. Already existing productive capacities could thus be better utilized; no costs of upbringing and elementary education had to be borne for this additional labor force; its favorable age structure meant overproportional contributions to the social insurance system; and the tax revenues generated by these additional producers and consumers were larger than guest-worker-induced expenditures. The substantial subsistence payments to families in the countries of origin acted like capital exports and were desirable in the face of Germany's persistent external imbalance, while the inflow of foreign labor tended to curb the upward tendency of domestic wages, thus raising the price competitiveness of German export industries. In the long run, though, the curbing effect of the guest workers on wages was less than had been hoped or feared. For the permanent residence of so many foreign workers brought an additional demand for labor, since it increasingly made the expansion of the country's infrastructure necessary and also provided the domestic consumer-goods industries with additional customers. The more abundant supply of labor probably also slowed down desirable changes in the economic structure, particularly the substitution of capital for labor through rationalization, while the existence of a larger pool of unskilled workers tended to affect factory work and industrial training. While the German industrial worker frequently passed through an apprenticeship and received a certificate of proficiency which attested to his skills, the guest workers, coming quite often from a purely agricultural background, and with considerable language difficulties, could only take up less skilled jobs. Since modern technology often permits a division and simplification of complex tasks, various industrial activities can be "deskilled" and thus be left to semiskilled workers who have attended group training for a few weeks or months. German industrial training and factory work have thus occasionally acquired certain American features.

The FRG imported not only labor but also technical (and organizational) know-how. The United States was the main source for the import of such knowledge, receiving almost one-half (or about ten times the British share) of German expenditures for foreign patents and licences by the late sixties. While at the time this to a considerable extent reflected Germany's "electronic gap" and consequent attempts to narrow it, there had existed for about two decades a substantial inflow of industrial know-how, not least through American subsidiaries in Germany. In consequence the German balance of licence fees showed on average an annual deficit of about DM 50 million during the first half of the fifties, followed by a quick increase to a new level of about DM 450 million around 1961, which was maintained until about 1967. German industry tried to regain the general standard in conventional technology which had been lost during the war and the immediate postwar years, when Germany's participation in the normal process of technological diffusion had been interrupted. The quick and extensive introduction of modern technology, reflecting the preparedness of management and labor to accept new methods, was greatly facilitated by the high ratio of investment to national income throughout the fifties and sixties, as well as by the restoration of an efficient price system after June 1948. It substantially accounted for the general productivity increase of 119 percent for the economy as a whole between 1950 and 1966.

In agriculture the increase was an impressive 147 percent, though it essentially remained a problem branch. In contrast to industry, which contributed 53.4 percent of Germany's gross domestic product and employed 48.5 percent of the total labor force in 1969,[88] agriculture's share of the gainfully employed was 9.1 percent for a contribution of only 3.7 percent to her GDP. Although Germany was one of the world's largest import markets for agricultural commodities by the late sixties,[89] her farmers were not in a position to take full advantage of the favorable demand situation. By the mid-sixties, German net food production, i.e., excluding food production on the basis of fodder imports, was about 140 percent above the prewar level as the result of very substantial improvements in production techniques.[90] The continuation of an almost century-old agricultural policy, however, prevented the adequate production of high-grade foodstuffs, since high fixed prices for grain and largely liberalized markets for animal products undermined the ability of domestic stock raising and dairy farming to compete successfully with imports. This meant that the German farmer often had to leave the supplying of an increasing demand for

88. The share of industry was substantially lower in other countries: France 48 percent; Great Britain 46 percent; Japan 39 percent; Italy 39 percent; United States 36 percent.

89. Imports of agricultural products represented 19 percent of total imports, while farm exports comprised only 3 percent of the value of all exports.

90. During the fifties and sixties, employment in agriculture decreased from 5 to 2.2 million, and the number of farms fell from 1.9 to 1.2 million. Vast increases occurred in mechanization (the numbers of combines rose 160 times, of milking machines 50 times, of farm tractors 11 times), while the average farm size increased from 7 to 10.3 hectares.

the products of animal husbandry to his foreign competitors. Such a policy was not only in the interests of the larger farmers, with their relatively intensive grain production,[91] but also of the export industries. The latter favored the largest possible import gap in agricultural products which would have to be paid for by industrial exports. German production of foodstuffs increased from 34 million tons of grain-equivalent units[92] in 1950/51 to 57 million tons in 1969/70, of which animal products represented 73 percent and 81 percent respectively. Most of this slight shift in production came during the sixties, when the impact of the "Green Plans" and of the EEC's agricultural policy were felt. Their principal objectives, to increase agricultural productivity and to reduce the disparity between agricultural and nonagricultural incomes were, indeed, to a considerable extent achieved, although the EEC authorities argued in their memorandum of 1969 that both processes should be accelerated.[93] While the Commission in Brussels proposed the rapid creation of very large, highly mechanized production units,[94] German agricultural experts argued in favor of continuing the more evolutionary process towards a diversified agricultural structure with mixed occupational opportunities. To increase part-time nonagricultural employment for farmers, in their view, would effectively check the trend towards surplus production in the Common Market, and be conducive to a better economic and residential structure in Germany through the industrial development of her rural regions.

Regional backwardness was not, however, a serious problem in Germany in comparison with many other EEC countries, since the FRG had started with a relatively balanced economic area and her less developed regions in general had been growing faster over the years than the more advanced ones. Up to about 1957 the traditional centers of German industry and commerce expanded fastest, in particular North Rhine-Westphalia and Baden-Württemberg, while the growth rates in some relatively backward agricultural states, such as Bavaria, Lower Saxony and Schleswig-Holstein, were below the national average. From 1957 onward, however, growth in these three states was usually above the national average, while that of North Rhine-Westphalia tended to be below. This reversed trend partly reflected the success of the Federal Government's regional development program of 1951. It aimed at counteracting the wholesale exodus of population from pre-

91. While in the base period 1963/67 German farmers achieved wheat and rye yields of more than twice the American level, compared to other intensive farming countries such as the Netherlands they were approximately one-quarter behind.

92. The grain equivalent of a plant product is determined by its nutrient content, that of an animal product by its nutrient requirement.

93. During the first decade of the Agriculture Law of 1955 the average remuneration of labor almost tripled in industry, but quadrupled in agriculture.

94. Farms of at least 80 to 120 hectares, with 40 to 60 cows or 450 to 600 pigs.

dominantly agricultural areas by raising the average income through the creation of new, usually industrial, employment opportunities. Expenditures for improving the infrastructure, and for long-term credits at conditions attractive to entrepreneurs willing to set up factories, aimed in particular at the zonal border areas[95] to compensate economically for the loss of the natural hinterland there, and also to present a favorable picture on the border with the communist world. Some credit, however, must go to market forces for the diminishing of regional productivity and income differences since the highly industrialized and urbanized centers lost some of their previous advantages for producers and consumers. This was particularly the case in the Ruhr district.

The loss of economic dominance of the Ruhr resulted from the declining importance of heavy industry. While industrial sales quintupled between 1950 and 1968, turnover rose by 4.5 times in the iron producing industry and slightly more than doubled in coal mining.[96] Coal, which had provided almost three-quarters of Germany's energy needs in 1950, held a share of about one-third in 1967, although annual energy consumption had doubled. Up to the second half of the fifties, official mining policy in Germany, as well as in other Western European countries, had been based on the assumption that it would soon no longer be possible to meet growing energy requirements, and various measures were taken to encourage the expansion of coal output. The fairly rapid rise in the use of oil, however, soon radically changed the situation and Germany turned from a major energy exporter into an importer. While the government attempted to assist the hard-hit coal branch by protectionist measures, the industry reduced its labor force from almost 600,000 in 1955 to 300,000 in 1967, and made other, quite substantial adjustments.[97] Since the measures taken did not, however, solve the structural crisis in the German mining industry, a law to reorganize the ailing branch was passed in May 1968. A newly founded private company, the *Ruhrkohle AG*, was to buy all investor-owned mines and was commissioned to shut down the inefficient units. The owners' financial interests were safeguarded through a federal guarantee of the price to be paid for such mines. If the attempt to put the branch on a sound financial basis succeeded, the German coal consumer would pay the price of the mines acquired and closed; if it failed,

95. A strip of land about 25 miles wide running the whole length of the border with the GDR.

96. A more detailed analysis would show that sales of the iron industry stagnated between 1960 and 1968, while turnover in coal-mining, after constant figures during the first half of the sixties, actually declined after 1965.

97. The average performance per miner and shift rose during the same period from 1.6 to 3.3 tons, which eventually meant the highest output in Western European coal-mining.

the German taxpayer would provide the necessary funds. This was a lucrative solution for the mine owners and partly reflected a desire to maintain Germany's sole large energy base, as well as the eagerness of the new conservative-social democratic "Grand Coalition" government to dispose of a troublesome structural problem in the face of serious, previously unknown cyclical difficulties.

The Years between 1966/67 and 1970

By the mid-sixties, foreign observers were wondering whether the days of German economic triumphs were numbered and the "Economic Miracle" was coming to an end. In October 1966, the London *Economist* asked whether one could detect any creeping symptoms of the "English sickness" that might soon infect the German economy, and added that the three biggest dangers were a serious price inflation, a sharp reduction of investments, and an adverse balance of payments.

In 1966 the German GNP in fact grew by 2.9 percent in real terms, and industrial production by only 1.2 percent, in both cases the lowest postwar growth ever, while the cost of living increased by 3.5 percent, the highest rise since the Korean war year of 1951. Unemployment remained at a low 0.5 percent, but total employment for the first time showed declining figures (down 0.3 percent) and short-time work rose somewhat. From the middle of 1966 onward, a more pessimistic evaluation of the economic climate prevailed among businessmen, who increasingly felt that their order books were too thin and their stocks of finished products too large. Moreover, their profit expectations had been substantially curtailed through wage hikes, which during the upswing of 1964/65 had already outstripped productivity increases at both the start and the finish of the boom.[98] Since this wage trend continued in 1966,[99] entrepreneurs undertook expenditures in plant, equipment and stock more hesitantly, contributing to a fall of 1.8 percent in total investment compared to the previous year. Investment financing also became more difficult, since the *Bundesbank*, fearful of further price increases and forced to carry the whole burden of demand restraint alone, pursued an even more restrictive policy in 1966,[100] permitting the money supply to rise by only 1.4 percent above the level of the previous year. Since in 1965—an election year with substantial increases of federal expenditure and tax reductions— budget deficits had fueled inflationary tendencies, federal fiscal policy

98. Previously wages had, in fact, outrun productivity in most years since 1950, but disparities were minimal up to 1955, and thereafter wage increases were matched or even outstripped by rises in productivity during the early phase of each economic upswing.

99. Wages rose by 7.2 percent, productivity by merely 3.1 percent.

100. Already in 1965, when prices rose by 3.4 percent, the discount rate had been raised from 3 to 4 percent. In mid-1966 an increase by another 1 percent followed.

became less expansionist in 1966,[101] at a time when monetary policy had already led to a pronounced recessionary situation. States and municipalities even pursued a procyclical policy, and slightly reduced their capital expenditures. Entrepreneurs, unions, central bank and nonfederal public authorities, though as independent economic decision makers all partly responsible for the downswing, in a quick process of "passing the buck" finally placed the blame on the federal government as the guilty party. There it remained, and it became customary to speak of the "Erhard Recession."

On 1 December 1966 the Erhard cabinet was replaced by a "Grand Coalition" government supported by the conservative and social democratic parties and headed by Chancellor Kiesinger. Under the new leadership the situation got worse before it got better, and 1967 brought an absolute decline in the real GNP by 0.2 percent and of industrial production by 2.7 percent, a tripling of the unemployment rate to 1.6 percent,[102] a substantial increase in short-time work, and a reduction of the number of guest workers from 1.3 to 0.99 million. By the second half of 1967 the worst was over, however, and the economic climate began to improve. This was partly due to the restoration of confidence in the solidity of the federal government's financial policy, which had been badly shaken during the preceding few years. The orthodox elimination of the budget deficit was achieved through expenditure cuts, especially in the sphere of public consumption, and by increases in revenue, particularly through the reduction of tax concessions. But since such actions would have accelerated the downhill movement of economic activity and made for future deficits, a pump-priming program was introduced in the spring of 1967, which provided for additional investments in the national railway system, postal services and road building. The anticyclical impact of these federal capital expenditures was, however, more than counterbalanced by contractions in budgetary spending by state and local governments. Furthermore, since the implementation of the federal investment program became effective with a considerable time lag, and private enterprises initially reduced their stocks for tax reasons—in expectation of the introduction of a value-added tax at the beginning of the next year[103]—total investments in 1967 were about 13 percent below

---

101. The index of federal expenditure (in stable prices) rose in 1965 by 10.7 percent, in 1966 by 4.1 percent.

102. At times, the unemployment rate during the 1966/67 recession stood as high as 3.2 percent.

103. According to an EEC harmonization directive, the value-added tax became mandatory in all member countries on 1 January 1970. Its earlier introduction in Germany and the corresponding demise of the turnover tax reflected export considerations.

the level of the previous year. Neither special depreciation allowances for private capital expenditure, nor the development of wages more or less in line with productivity,[104] could overcome the hesitancy of private enterprises to invest. The *Bundesbank* was equally unsuccessful, although it had begun to ease credit restrictions as early as late 1966, had quickly reduced the discount rate in four steps from 5 percent to 3 percent during the first half of 1967, and increased the economy's total money supply by 10.4 percent over the previous year.[105] It took a new fiscal policy to bring about a change in the entrepreneurs' assessment of the economic climate.

To put federal fiscal policy back on a sounder footing the Law for Promoting Stability and Growth in the Economy was passed in June 1967. Referred to as the "Magna Charta" of modern medium-term management of the economy, the law provided the federal government with a number of new tools, some of them unique.[106] While previously the federal government, the eleven state governments and the approximately 25,000 municipalities made up their budgets independently of each other, thus making fiscal plans covering several years and a combined and coherent fiscal policy almost impossible, the new law brought about a certain centralization of fiscal powers and the first steps towards growth planning. Instead of the annual and uncoordinated budgets of the past, five-year finance plans and medium-term public investment programs became mandatory at all levels, and the federal government was required to submit an annual report outlining its economic and fiscal policy objectives for the next year within the framework of an overall five-year projection. Various new instruments of cyclical policy were created, or assumed more concrete form. Federal and state governments were required to make reserve deposits with the *Bundesbank*. The federal government was authorized to limit the power of the states and municipalities to go into debt, and could borrow up to DM 5 billion to finance additional federal expenditures; it also received authority to manipulate depreciation and investment allowances, and to vary income and corporation taxes by up to 10 percent in both directions to influence private investment and consumer spending. The enlarged armory of cyclical and growth-policy weapons was to guarantee the attainment of four economic policy objectives: price stability (an annual inflation rate of not more than 1 percent); full employment (an unemployment rate not surpassing 0.8 percent);

104. Wages increased by 3.2 percent, and productivity by 2.8 percent during 1967.
105. Given high liquidity preference of the business community, the cost-of-living index rose by only 1.4 percent during 1967.
106. No other national government could pride itself on a similarly comprehensive set of Keynesian policy instruments at the time.

external equilibrium (a surplus of the balance of trade of 1 percent of the GNP); and an adequate growth rate (4 percent of real GNP annually).[107]

The federal government immediately made extensive use of the new powers, and the fiscal policy measures—through the interplay of multiplier-accelerator processes—gave new impetus to the economic machine, so that 1968 and 1969 became splendid years. The German economy again grew by an average of 8 percent, unemployment fell substantially under the 1 percent mark, and price increases also remained moderate until about mid-1969. Thereafter prices began to rise, and fiscal and monetary policies had to become more restrictive, boom conditions with corresponding inflationary pressures continuing into 1970.[108] The countercyclical policy of the federal government remained timid for quite a while, however, thus displaying the well-known asymmetrical behavior of parliamentary governments, particularly those with a laborite backing, which are eager to introduce expansionist measures but reluctant to take restrictive steps. The new government's principal commitment to maintain a high level of employment and economic activity influenced employers and employees by removing their concern that higher wage demands and price increases could lead to a new recession. A series of wildcat strikes in late summer of 1969[109] brought premature contract negotiations in some industries, which contributed to a rise in wages of 9.7 and 15 percent in 1969 and 1970 respectively, while in those years productivity grew by only 6.2 and 4.4 percent.

The widening gap between productivity and wages clearly shows that one new instrument of medium-term management of the economy, so-called "concerted action" *(Konzertierte Aktion)*, from which much had been hoped, had failed. As one of the two means of moral suasion institutionalized by the Stability Law,[110] "concerted action" sought to bring labor and management representatives together under the chairmanship of the minister of economics. He would then present "data for economic orientation," obviously trying to establish

107. These were the objectives for 1968. Later on less rigid targets were set, e.g., those for 1970: price increases, 1.5 to 2 percent; unemployment, up to 1 percent; export surplus, 1 to 2 percent; growth, 4 to 5 percent.

108. Increase of the cost-of-living index: 1968, 1.5 percent; 1969, 2.8 percent; 1970, 3.7 percent.

109. In general, labor strife was quite minimal throughout the sixties and only 23 working days were lost annually in Germany per 100 employees, compared to 40 in Sweden, 147 in Japan, 223 in Britain and 1,305 in Italy.

110. The other instrument of coordination by information and persuasion was the newly established Business Cycle Council *(Konjunkturrat)*, where representatives of the federal, state and local governments were to discuss all anticyclical fiscal measures to be taken.

guidelines for bargaining between unions and employers. The lack of macroeconomic cooperation demonstrated by the autonomous "social partners" was probably partly an expression of their fear that the right of self-determination in negotiating working conditions, and especially wages, would be undermined.

Since tendencies to price increases were not primarily caused by excessively high demand, but reflected more a cost-push situation, monetary policy, like "concerted action," remained largely ineffective. The *Bundesbank's* strong restrictive measures—the discount rate was raised in steps from 3 percent in April 1969 to a postwar record of 7.5 percent in March 1970—could not curb the boom conditions, the more so as inflationary infection from abroad continued. As a safeguard against such foreign influences, the federal government revalued the DM by 9.3 percent, setting the parity at 3.66 to the dollar on 27 October 1969. A few weeks earlier, the question of whether to revalue or not had been an issue in the September election, which led to a social democratic-liberal cabinet under Chancellor Willy Brandt.

In the new government the architect of the recent economic resurgence, Karl Schiller, continued to play a leading role.[111] His economic policy aimed at combining the neoliberal free-market economy with control of the effective aggregate demand à la J. M. Keynes. As early as 1954, Schiller had advocated the idea of "as much competition as possible, as much planning as necessary," and this principle had been given formal recognition in the SPD's Godesberg Program of 1959. Though the word "nationalization" was struck from official party publications, it remained in the heads and hearts of many Social Democrats. Since the late 1960s the extreme left wing of the party had grown to respectable size, and it came out into the open again when young socialists of Marxist or neo-Marxist persuasion swelled membership ranks once the party participated—at first as junior, then as senior partner—in the federal government. While the party as a whole continued to reject communism, some of its groups gave the impression—at least verbally—that their goal was to transform the economic and social system of the FRG into something not unlike that of the GDR.

The GDR acquired a certain respectability in some circles of the FRG when the respective heads of government met twice in spring 1970. For the first time, more than twenty years after the two states had come into being, talks were held at the highest level. The *Ostpolitik* (policy toward the East) of the Brandt cabinet, guided by the two-states-within-one-nation doctrine, accepted the GDR as a separate entity

111. Schiller, who in the Kiesinger cabinet had been economics minister, became minister of finance as well in the Brandt cabinet.

from the FRG, though the former remained a constituent part of Germany as a whole.[112] Whether such political contacts will lead to a new modus vivendi in Central Europe, whether the flag will be followed by intensified exchange of products, people, and ideas, whether Germany will become the classic case of convergence of two political, social, and economic systems remains to be seen. In any case the Germans—as usual—promise interesting pages in future books on political and economic history.

Bibliography

Albach, H. "New Trends in the Economy of the Federal Republic of Germany." *German Economic Review* 7 (1969).

Arndt, H.-J. *West Germany: Politics of Non-Planning,* Syracuse, N.Y., 1966.

Balabkins, N. *West German Reparations to Israel.* New Brunswick, N.J., 1971.

Behrendt, G. "Ownership Policy in the Federal Republic of Germany." *German Economic Review* 3 (1965).

Blum, R. *Soziale Marktwirtschaft.* Tübingen, 1969.

Bundesministerium für Wirtschaft. *Leistung in Zahlen '67.* Bonn, 1968.

Bundesministerium für Wirtschaft. *Leistung in Zahlen '72.* Bonn, 1973.

Denton, G.; Forsyth, M.; and Maclennan, M. *Economic Planning and Policies in Britain, France and Germany.* London. 1968.

Erhard, L. *Germany's Comeback in the World Market.* New York, 1954.

Erhard, L. *Prosperity through Competition.* New York, 1958.

Erhard. L. *The Economics of Success.* Princeton, N.J. 1963.

Glastetter, W. *Die wirtschaftliche Entwicklung der Bundesrepublik Deutschland im Zeitraum 1950 bis 1975.* Berlin, 1977.

Gutmann, G.; Hochstrate, H.-J.; and Schlüter, R. *Die Wirtschaftsverfassung der Bundesrepublik Deutschland.* Stuttgart, 1964.

Hennessy, J.; Lutz, V.; and Scimone, G. *Economic 'Miracles.'* London, 1964.

Huffschmid, J. *Die Politik des Kapitals: Konzentration und Wirtschaftspolitik in der Bundesrepublik.* Frankfurt/Main, 1969.

Hunold, A., ed. *Wirtschaft ohne Wunder.* Zurich, 1953.

IFO- Institut für Wirtschaftsforschung. *Fünf Jahre Deutsche Mark.* Munich, 1954.

Krause, L.B., ed. *The Common Market: Progress and Controversy.* Englewood Cliffs, N.J. 1964.

Lampert, H. *Die Wirtschafts- und Sozialordnung der Bundesrepublik Deutschland.* Munich, 1970.

Mintz, J. *Dating Postwar Business Cycles: Methods and their Application to Western Germany, 1950–1967.* New York, 1969.

112. This was by no means unimportant legal hairsplitting. Much to the chagrin of other communist countries, for example, agricultural deliveries of the GDR to the FRG, defined as intra-German trade, were not subject to the EEC's external tariff.

Mockers, J.-P. *Croissances Economiques Comparées: Allemagne, France, Royaume-Uni 1950–1967.* Paris, 1969.

Müller-Armack, A. "The Principles of the Social Market Economy." *German Economic Review* 3 (1965).

Nelson, W. H. *Small Wonder: The Amazing Story of the Volkswagen.* Boston, 1970.

Ott, A. E., and Wagner, A. "Materialien zu den Wachstumszyklen in der Bundesrepublik Deutschland." In *Wachstumszyklen,* edited by A. E. Ott. Berlin, 1973.

Postan, M. M. *An Economic History of Western Europe 1945–1964.* London, 1964.

Price, A.H. *The Federal Republic of Germany, A Selected Bibliography of English-Language Publications.* 2nd ed. Washington, D.C., 1978.

Radcliffe, S. *Twenty-five Years on: The Two Germanies 1970.* London, 1972.

Reuss, F.G. *Fiscal Policy for Growth without Inflation: The German Experiment.* Baltimore, 1963.

Roskamp, K.W. *Capital Formation in West Germany.* Detroit, 1965.

Schiller, K. "Stability and Growth as Objectives of Economic Policy." *German Economic Review* 5 (1967).

Schonfield, A. *Modern Capitalism: The Changing Balance of Public and Private Power.* Oxford, 1965.

Sohmen, E. "Competition and Growth: The Lessons of West Germany." *American Economic Review* 49 (1959).

Vogt, W. *Die Wirtschaftszyklen der westdeutschen Wirtschaft von 1950 bis 1965 und ihre theoretische Erklärung.* Tübingen, 1968.

Wallich, H. C. *Mainsprings of the German Revival.* New Haven, 1955.

Winkel, H. *Die Wirtschaft im geteilten Deutschland 1945–1970.* Wiesbaden, 1974.

Many useful articles on this period, as well as on preceding ones, can be found in the 12-volume *Handwörterbuch der Sozialwissenschaften* (Stuttgart, 1956–65).

Glossary of
Economic Terms

Accelerator. The process by which variations in the demand for consumer goods bring about even larger changes in the demand for capital goods to produce them.

Accounting. The recording (bookkeeping) of the transactions of a firm to reveal its financial position and to provide its management with information for control purposes.

Aggregate demand. The total expenditure for all purchases of capital and consumer goods in a given market.

Aggregate supply. The total physical volume of goods and services entering a given market.

Anticyclical policy. Economic measures aiming to counteract the business cycle, the ups and downs of an economy.

Arbitrage dealings. Dealings in currencies between several markets to take advantage of the differences in the prices of the respective currencies.

Autarky. An economic policy aiming at the highest degree of self-sufficiency, i.e., independence from imports.

Balance of payments. A country's financial statement showing all its payments made to and received from all other nations during a given period.

Balance of services. The relation between the total payments into and out of a country concerning services ("invisible transactions"). E.g., "Invisible exports" include interest and dividends of capital invested abroad; earnings from transportation, insurance, and banking services rendered to foreigners; expenditures of foreign visitors within the country.

Balance of trade. The relationship between a country's imports and exports of merchandise ("visible transactions"). If exports exceed imports the balance is termed "favorable" or "active." In the opposite case the terms "unfavorable" or "passive" are used.

Barter trade. The direct exchange of commodities for commodities without the use of money.

Bilateralism. In contrast to multilateralism, a setup of special trade and payments arrangements between each different pair of countries. Every country aims to balance all payments made to and received from every other country.

Bill of exchange. An order for the making of payment of a certain sum of money at a certain date.

Bond. An instrument of long-term debt issued by a public body (e.g., state or municipal government) or private company carrying a fixed rate of interest and being repayable when due.

Book profits. A firm's profit or loss as shown in the books may differ from the real profit or loss due to special accounting procedures (e.g., over- or undervaluation of assets or liabilities). Drastic changes over time in the value of money lead to such book profits or losses if the bookkeeping does not adjust to the changing value of the unit of account.

Budget. Government's statement of estimated or actual expenditure and revenue for a given period, usually a year. If one exceeds the other, a deficit or a surplus exists.

Business Cycle. Fairly regular fluctuations in business activity (economic upswing and downswing, prosperity and recession) when employment, wages, prices, profits and production tend to rise or decline together.

Capital. Besides land and labor, one of the factors of production (i.e., economic goods) used in the manufacturing of other goods. It may be subdivided into fixed capital and working (i.e., variable or circulating) capital. The former consists of instruments of all kinds (plants, machinery, means of transportation, etc.); the latter comprises goods in the process of being prepared for consumption (raw materials, semi-finished and finished articles).

Capital expenditures. Expenditures of a non-recurrent nature (investments) leading to the acquisition of assets.

Capital market. The market for long-term funds (e.g., bonds, stocks, mortgages) as opposed to the money market for short-term loans and bills.

Capital-intensive. Form of production where considerable use of capital equipment (plant and machinery) is made relative to other necessary inputs like labor, land or raw materials.

Capital-output ratio. The amount of capital necessary to produce an additional unit of output. It indicates the capital intensity of an industry.

Cartel. A combination of firms which, although retaining their separate legal identities, combine to pursue a common policy in their joint economic interests.

Central bank. The bank which in any country is the banker of the government and of the commercial banks and also implements the country's monetary policy.

Clearing system. An organizational setup to settle the accounts of mutually indebted companies or states. It may be arranged on a bilateral or multilateral basis.

Commodity exchange. Like the stock exchange where securities are traded, the market for the bulk sale and purchase of food and raw materials (e.g., grain, tropical products, textile fibers, metals).

Compensation trade. See: Barter trade

Consumer goods. Products that reach the final consumer.

Cooperatives. Business enterprises owned and operated by voluntary associations to provide economic benefits (earnings, goods or services) for their members. There are consumer or retail cooperatives, producer cooperatives, particularly in agriculture, credit cooperatives in banking and many other types.

Convertibility. The freedom to exchange one currency for another currency at the going exchange rate.

Cost. The expenditure incurred to obtain the services of a factor of production.

Cost-push situation. In contrast to a demand-pull inflation, a situation where prices are said to rise not due to increased demand (buyers' inflation) but on account of higher production costs (sellers' inflation) resulting from increases in the prices of imported raw materials, taxes, wages, etc.

Countercyclical policy. See: Anticyclical measures

Cyclical. Phenomena which repeat at fairly regular intervals. Economic forces which tend to amplify such repetitions act procyclical as opposed to anticyclical ones which dampen them.

Cyclical fluctuations. See: Business cycle

Debt service. With reference to public debt the payment of currently due amounts of interest and principal.

Deficit financing. The financing of a budget deficit (expenditures exceed receipts) by means of borrowing (i.e., by increasing the national debt). Used as "pump priming" to stimulate the economy.

Deflation. A general decline in prices and money incomes, accompanied by a corresponding increase in the value (purchasing power) of money.

Devaluation. Under the previous system of fixed exchange rates, the sudden cheapening of a currency (in terms of gold or foreign currencies) by the government usually with the intention to improve the balance of payments.

Discount. The sum deducted from the face value of a bill of exchange if cashed before it matures.

Division of labor. Synonymous with specialization (i.e., an overall task is divided into separate tasks so that each individual involved performs only a part of the overall task).

Economic cycle. See: Business cycle

Economic indicators. Statistics sensitive to economic fluctuations such as figures on prices, production, employment, foreign trade, orders on hand in major industries, consumer spending, etc.

Economic steering devices. In line with the actual form of economic organization (*see:* Economic systems) the economy is managed through a varying combination of the market or price mechanism with governmental control.

Economic systems. Denote ideal or real forms of economic organization. There are two ideal or theoretical types: the totally centrally planned system and the free market system. Economic reality presents a mixture of both, more or less inclined to one of the extremes, e.g., a state regulated market economy or a planning system with market elements.

Efficiency (economic). The effectiveness with which factors of production are employed to achieve stipulated economic ends. The lower the cost per unit of output, the greater the economic efficiency of a production setup.

Exchange control. In contrast to free convertibility, government regulates all dealing in foreign currencies.

Equity capital. The equity of a company (or the ownership capital) is the value of its net assets (i.e., once all its debts are deducted).

Factors of production. The various forces which together produce a commodity or service: labor (physical or mental), capital (the result of savings embodied in plant equipment, machinery, etc.), land (resources provided by nature) and entrepreneurship (the service of combining the other three factors and bearing the risk of this undertaking).

Floating debt. That part of the government's indebtedness (national debt) which is borrowed for short-term as opposed to long-term or "funded debt."

Foreign investments. Assets acquired abroad by the citizens or the government of a country, like titles of land, buildings and machinery, public or private securities, bank deposits, etc.

Gross domestic product. See: National product

Gross fixed investment. See: Investment

Gross national product. See: National product

Hyperinflation. An inflation which has got out of control (runaway inflation).

Income elasticity of demand. The response of the demand for a product to a change in the income of the consumer. E.g., if a small change in income produces a relatively large alteration in the demand for a product then the income elasticity of demand is said to be high.

Index numbers. Figures which disclose the relative change of a given economic phenomenon (e.g., foreign trade, production, employment, prices) between one period of time and some other "base period," the latter conventionally being 100. *See:* Economic indicators

Industrial dispute. An industrial dispute is termed a "lockout" if the employers decline to admit the workers into the plants, a "strike" if the men refuse to come to work.

Inflation. A general increase in prices and money incomes, accompanied by a corresponding decline in the value (purchasing power) of money. Deflation denotes the opposite state of affairs.

Infrastructure. The basic underpinnings for an economy which provide essential services for supporting economic activity: transportation networks, utilities, educational and health facilities, etc.

Input. Any goods or services used in the process of production to manufacture an output.

Laissez faire. A policy by which the government interferes very little or not at all in economic affairs.

Liquid assets. In contrast of fixed assets, these are assets either in form of cash and bank deposits or those which can be quickly converted into money, like securities.

Macroeconomics. The branch of economics analyzing the economy as a whole, dealing with aggregates like the volume of consumption, saving, investment, national income, employment, foreign trade, etc.

Market economy. An economic system where the decisions concerning production, distribution and consumption are taken by individual consumers and producers with no governmental interferences. The more of this decision-making the government reserves for itself, the more "managed" or "regulated" such an economy becomes.

Microeconomics. The branch of economics analyzing the behavior of individual consumers and producers (i.e., of the decision-making units like households and firms). It provides the theoretical basis for macroeconomics.

Minimum reserve requirements. Official minimum amount of reserves a commercial bank must keep at the central bank. A means to regulate the supply of money in the economy.

Money supply. The amount of money in an economy like coins, bank notes and current accounts or demand deposits (e.g., checkbook money).

Multiplier. The factor by which an increase (decline) in investment is multiplied to give the total increase (decline) in national income or total employment. This concept helps to explain how economic fluctuations are generated.

National income/National product. The total of all incomes earned, or all goods and services produced, in an economy in a given time period, including net income from abroad. There are four general concepts:

National income at factor cost:

All wages, salaries, rent, dividends, interest and profits before direct taxes are deducted.

National income at market prices:

national income at factor cost plus indirect taxes less subsidies.

Gross national product:

National income (at factor cost or at market prices) plus allowances for depreciation and maintenance.

Gross domestic product:

gross national product minus net income from abroad.

Nationalization. The taking over by the state of the ownership of any means of production.

Neoliberalism. The modern adaptation of the laissez faire doctrine of the nineteenth century reacting against increased state intervention in the economic sphere. It claims that, on balance, the market mechanism works well in satisfying human wants and in allocating resources to alternative uses.

Nominal. See: Real

Oligopoly. A market structure where a small number of large firms produces the bulk of the output.

Open market operations. By selling and buying government securities in the open market, a central bank can influence the reserves of commercial banks and thus the supply of money in the economy and thereby its performance.

Opportunity cost. Faced with a choice between alternatives, the real cost of one chosen alternative includes the foregone benefits from all other possible choices.

Output. Any saleable goods or service manufactured in the process of production.

Planned economy. An economic system where government makes all the decisions concerning production, distribution and consumption.

Portfolio. The list of securities held by an investor.

Price-wage spiral. An inflationary process where an upward trend of prices leads to increases in wages and salaries (because labor resists a loss in purchasing power) which make producers raise their prices even further (on account of increased costs) and so on.

Producer goods. Durable equipment made for the purpose of producing other goods. Synonymous with capital goods.

Productivity. The efficiency with which factors of production are used. With regard to labor it can be measured as the relationship of output per man-hour.

Profit charges. That part of the trade margin which remains after costs.

Proxy. Authorization given by a stockholder to another person to vote on his behalf at a stockholders' meeting.

Pump priming. In analogy to the water pump which does not raise water until the pump is primed, i.e., some water is introduced into its valves and piping, the governmental policy to revive a depressed economy by its own spending. When private spending has been stimulated sufficiently, public spending is to taper off.

Real. If an economic phenomenon is expressed in real terms it means that the changing value of money has been taken into account. E.g., in contrast to money or nominal wages, real wages indicate the purchasing power of a worker's earnings, (i.e., an adjustment to changes in consumer prices has been made).

Rediscount rate/Rediscount quota. The rate at which the central bank acting as lender of last resort will discount bills of exchange presented by commercial banks. A quota to set a maximum ceiling to such lendings. Both are instruments of monetary policy.

Reflation. A monetary policy which could be called "controlled inflation" aiming at an increase of the supply of money in the economy to counteract deflationary tendencies.

Residual income. The difference between the total receipts and the total payments or cost of production of an employer (if positive called profit, if negative called loss) once the salary due to the employer himself for his own work and interest on any of his own capital invested in the business has been deducted. The remainder may be called "pure profit" as reward for taking risk.

Revaluation. Under the previous system of fixed exchange rates, the sudden increase in price of a currency (in terms of gold of foreign currencies) by government action.

Sectors. Production in an economy takes place in three sectors: in the primary sector (agriculture, fishing, mining), the secondary sector (manufacturing industries), and the tertiary sector (service industries like trade, banking, insurance, transportation, and the professions).

Securities. Stocks, shares or bonds issued by government or companies.

Stock. A document indicating that the holder participates in the ownership of a company and has a claim to share its profits. Often used synonymously with share.

Supervisory board. According to German company law, a board of supervisors is elected at the stockholders' meeting to which it has to report on the activities of the board of managers.

Syndicate. The most tightly organized form of a cartel in which the relationship between the producer and buyer is regulated by an intermediary selling agency.

Tariff. A tax levied on imports.

Taxes. Compulsory payments which individuals and companies have to make to the government. Taxes on income or wealth are known as direct taxes, those on commodities or services are referred to as indirect taxes.

Time and demand deposit. Money on deposit in banks may be withdrawn only after giving specified notice of a certain time or immediately on demand.

Trade bill. In contrast to a finance bill, which is a purely money instrument, a commercial or trade bill is used by businessmen in the transaction of actual commodities.

Trade margin. The percentage charge added to the buying price to establish the sales price. It includes costs and profit.

Transfer payment. An income flow for which no goods or services are received in return and which thus effects a change in the distribution of national or international wealth, e.g., welfare payments, development aid, reparations.

Trade tax. The tax levied on the individual plant of an enterprise which is based on its assets, earnings or wage bill.

Treasury bill. The means by which the government can raise short-term or intermediate-term funds to meet financial commitments before tax revenues are in. If not funded at maturity they build up the floating debt.

Undercapitalization. Insufficient provision of an enterprise with plant and equipment given a certain common level of technology.

Undervaluation. A currency is said to be undervalued when its purchasing power on the domestic market exceeds its purchasing power on international markets.

Universal banks. Banks, the business of which is not confined to certain banking activities but comprises its whole gammut with the exception of issuing banknotes.

Value-added tax. A tax on the "value added" (i.e., the difference between the value of the output a firm produced and the value of the inputs purchased from other firms).

Veil of money. Since goods are actually exchanged for goods, transactions in money form a "veil" which at times may hide the underlying real processes. *See:* Real

Velocity of circulation of money. The rapidity with which the money supply in an economy changes ownership (i.e., the average number of times that each unit of money, be it in coins, notes or bank deposits, changes hands in the course of a year).

Vertical combination. The integration or merging of firms active at successive stages of the same production process.

Appendix Tables

1. *Total Population and Population Density, 1910–1970*

	Reich (respective territories)			Federal Republic of Germany		German Democratic Republic	
	Population			Population		Population	
Year	In Millions	Per Square Km	Year	In Millions	Per Square Km	In Millions	Per Square Km
1910	64.6	119	1939	43.0	173	16.7	155
1920	61.8	130	1946	46.2	186	18.6	171
1930	65.1	138	1950	50.2	201	18.4	171
1939	69.3	147	1955	52.4	211	17.8	166
1944	65.3	139	1960	55.4	223	17.2	160
			1965	59.0	238	17.0	158
			1970	60.7	244	17.1	159

Sources: Statistical Yearbook of the FRG, 1968 and 1972; Statistical Yearbook of the GDR, 1973.

2. *Birth Rate, Death Rate, Marriage Rate, Infant Mortality Rate, 1910–1970*

Year	Birth Rate		Death Rate		Excess		Marriages		Infant Death Rate Per 1000 Born Alive	
			Per 1000 Inhabitants							
1910	29.8		16.2		13.6		7.7		162	
1913	27.5		15.0		12.5		7.7		151	
1920	25.9		15.1		10.8		14.5		131	
1925	20.8		11.9		8.9		7.7		105	
1930	17.6		11.0		6.6		8.8		85	
1935	18.9		11.8		7.1		9.7		68	
1938	19.6		11.6		8.0		9.4		60	
1939	20.4		12.3		8.1		11.2		61	
	FRG	GDR	FRG	GDR	FRG	GDR	FRG	GDR	FRG	GDR
1946	16.1	10.4	13.0	22.9	3.2	−12.4	8.8	6.9	97.1	131.4
1947	16.4	13.1	12.1	19.0	4.3	−5.9	10.1	8.7	86.3	113.7
1948	16.5	12.8	10.5	15.2	6.0	−2.4	10.7	9.6	68.9	89.5
1949	16.8	14.5	10.4	13.4	6.4	1.1	10.2	10.1	59.6	78.3
1950	16.2	16.5	10.5	11.9	5.7	4.6	10.7	11.7	55.3	72.2
1955	15.7	16.3	11.1	11.9	4.5	4.4	8.8	8.7	41.9	48.9
1960	17.4	17.0	11.6	13.6	5.9	3.4	9.4	9.7	33.8	38.8
1965	17.7	16.5	11.5	13.5	6.2	3.0	8.3	7.6	23.8	24.8
1970	13.4	13.9	12.1	14.1	1.3	−0.2	7.3	7.7	23.4	18.5

Sources: Statistical Yearbook for the FRG, 1961, 1963, 1972; Statistical Yearbook for the GDR, 1960/61, 1973.

3. *Family Size, 1900, 1960 and 1970*

Year	After 20 Years of Marriage 1000 Couples Had				
	No Children	One Child	Two Children	Three Children	More Than Three Children
1900	100	105	150	147	498
1960*	162	210	302	173	153
1970*	189	231	341	162	77

Source: Wirtschaft und Statistik, Statistisches Bundesamt (ed.), Mainz 1962, 1971.
*FRG only.

4. *Life Expectancy at Birth by Sex, 1901/10–1967/69*

Year	Males		Females	
1901/10	44.8		48.3	
1924/26	56.0		58.8	
1932/34	59.9		62.8	
	FRG	GDR	FRG	GDR
1946/47	57.7	—	63.4	—
1949/51*	64.6	65.1	68.5	69.1
1960/62	66.9	66.9	72.4	71.7
1967/69	67.4	68.0	73.5	73.2

Sources: Statistical Yearbook of the FRG, 1962, 1968, 1972;
Statistical Yearbook of the GDR, 1955, 1973.
*GDR 1952/53.

5. *Age Composition, 1910–1968*

	Percentage of Total Population					
Year	0 to 15 years old		15 to 65 years old		65 years old and over	
1910	33.9		61.2		4.9	
1925	25.7		68.5		5.8	
1933	24.2		68.7		7.1	
	FRG	GDR	FRG	GDR	FRG	GDR
1950	23.6	22.8	67.2	66.6	9.3	10.6
1961	21.7	22.2	67.2	63.7	11.1	14.1
1968	23.3	23.7	63.9	61.0	12.8	15.3

Sources: Statistical Yearbook of the FRG, 1962, 1970.

6. *Population Distribution by Size of Community, 1910–1970*

	Percentage of Total Population, Residing in Communities of . . . Inhabitants							
Year	Under 2,000		2,000–10,000		10,000–100,000		Over 100,000	
1910	40		19		20		21	
1925	35		18		20		27	
1933	33		18		19		30	
	FRG	GDR	FRG	GDR	FRG	GDR	FRG	GDR
1939	30	28	18	21	20	25	32	27
1950	29	29	23	23	21	27	27	21
1960	23	28	22	22	24	29	31	21
1970	19	26	21	20	28	32	32	22

Sources: Hoffmann, *Wachstum,* p. 178; Statistical Yearbooks of FRG and GDR, 1972.

7. *Occupational Activity, 1910/13–1970*

Year	Percentage Proportion of Economically Active Population*		Structure of Employment by Sectors in Percent					
			Primary Sector		Secondary Sector		Tertiary Sector	
1910/13	46		35		38		27	
1925	51		30		42		28	
1933	49		29		41		30	
1939	51		26		42		32	
	FRG	GDR	FRG	GDR	FRG	GDR	FRG	GDR
1950	47	43	25	24	43	39	32	37
1960	48	50	14	19	48	40	38	41
1970	45	51	9	13	49	41	42	46

Sources: Hoffmann, *Wachstum,* p. 35; Petzina, *Grundriss,* p. 776; Statistical Yearbook of the GDR, 1955, 1962, 1972.
*Persons earning or seeking to earn a living by gainful activity.

8. *Percentage Proportion of Self-Employed and Female Labor, Total Economy and by Sectors, 1907–1970*

Year	Total Economy		Primary Sector		Secondary Sector		Tertiary Sector	
	Self Employed	Female	Self Employed	Female	Self Employed	Female	Self Employed	Female
1907	20	34	25	46	17	20	17	40
1925	18	37	22	50	15	23	19	41
1933	22	40	24	51	21	25	21	42
1939	14	37	22	54	9	23	13	40
1950*	15	35	25	54	11	21	17	38
1960*	13	37	32	54	6	25	13	48
1970*	11	36	34	53	5	25	12	45

Sources: Hoffmann, *Wachstum,* pp. 205, 209, 210; Statistical Yearbook of the FRG, 1962, 1972.
*FRG only.

9. *Percentage Distribution of the Industrial Labor Force by Size of Enterprise,*
1907–1970

(A) Industry and Crafts

Year	Employees Per Firm					
	1–5	6–10	11–50	51–200	201–1000	Over 1000
1907	31	7	19	21	17	5
1925	25	8	20	22	18	7
1950*	16	10	20	20	20	14

(B) Industry Only

Year	Employees Per Firm				
	1–9	10–49	50–199	200–999	1000 and Over
1952*	3	12	22	29	34
1961*	2	9	19	30	40
1970*	2	9	19	30	40

Sources: Hoffmann, *Wachstum,* p. 212; Statistical Yearbook for the FRG, 1954, 1962, 1972.
*FRG Only.

10. *Share of White Collar Workers in Gainfully Employed Persons in*
Industry, 1907, 1958, 1970*

Year	1907	1958**	1970**
Percentage	8	18	23

Sources: Hoffmann, *Wachstum,* p. 210; Statistical Yearbook for the FRG, 1972.
 *Industrial and craft establishments with six or more employees; for 1970 with ten or
more employees.
**FRG only.

11. *Average Weekly Working Hours in Industry and Crafts, 1913–1969*

Year	1913	1932	1941	1950*	1960*	1970*
Hours	57	42	50	48	42	39

Sources: Hoffmann, *Wachstum,* p. 18; Statistical Yearbook for the FRG, 1952, 1962, 1972.
*Industry and FRG only.

12. *Consumption of Typical Households in Percentage, 1907–1968*

Year	Foodstuffs	Semi-luxuries	Dwelling	Household Goods, Furnishings, Heating, Lighting	Clothing, Shoes, Textiles, Household Effects	Cleaning, Hygiene	Domestic Services	Education, Recreation	Transport
1907	38.1	14.1	14.6	7.0	15.9	3.1	3.1	1.2	2.8
1927	36.0	13.9	11.3	10.3	16.8	3.5	2.4	2.6	3.1
1937	35.7	14.1	15.2	8.0	12.1	5.0	2.4	3.6	3.7
1950*	36.3	15.6	9.1	8.6	15.6	4.5	1.5	5.2	3.6
1959*	30.2	16.7	9.4	10.5	15.1	4.8	1.3	5.2	6.8

Year	Foodstuffs	Semi-luxuries	Rent, Gas, Electricity, Heating	Home Requirements, Electrical & Other Industrial Articles	Clothing, Shoes, Textiles	Transport	Recreation, Education	Other Services and Repairs
1960								
FRG	38.5	6.8	15.1	16.7	13.2	2.9	3.7	3.1
GDR	43.1	9.7	6.8	18.7	14.9	1.7	5.1	
1968								
FRG	31.8	5.8	20.1	20.2	11.7	3.5	3.8	3.1
GDR	36.7	11.0	5.8	20.7	16.3	2.3	2.9	4.3

Sources: Hoffmann, *Wachstum*, p. 702; Report of the Federal Government (Bonn, 1971).
*FRG only.

13. *Expenditure on Food in Percentage, 1907 and 1959*

	1907	1959
Total Plant Foodstuffs	40.9	31.6
Cereal Products	26.3	10.9
Potatoes	6.2	5.0
Vegetables	2.0	3.3
Sugar	3.6	4.4
Domestic & Tropical Fruit	2.8	8.0
Total Animal Foodstuffs	55.8	63.5
Meats	30.7	38.4
Eggs	3.0	6.0
Dairy Products	20.0	16.5
Fish	2.1	2.6
Other (esp. animal and vegetable fats)	3.4	5.1

Source: Hoffmann, *Wachstum,* p. 703.

14. *Percentage Shares in National Income of Ordinal Groups, 1928–1959*

			Year		
Category	1928	1936	1950*	1955*	1959*
Top 5 percent	27	28	24	18	18
Top 20 percent	49	53	48	43	43
Lowest 60 percent	31	27	29	34	34

Source: Kuznets, *Modern Economic Growth,* p. 209.
*FRG only.

15. *Wages and Salaries as a Percentage of National Product, 1925/29–1965/69*

Period	1925/29	1930/32	1933/38	1950/54*	1955/59*	1960/64*	1965/69*
Percentage	60	63	57	59	60	63	65

Source: Statistical Yearbook for the FRG, 1972.
*FRG only.

16. *Rates of Growth in Major Countries, 1913/60*

Country	Percentage Rates of Growth Per Decade		
	Total Product	Product Per Capita	Product Per Man-Hour
Germany	28.4	17.4	21.6
United Kingdom	20.7	15.5	19.5
France	15.7	13.6	23.0
Belgium	15.1	10.8	18.0
Italy	25.4	17.4	26.1
Sweden	27.5	20.0	25.4
Switzerland	29.8	21.1	26.7
United States	34.5	18.0	26.8

Source: Kuznets, *Modern Economic Growth*, p. 352.

17. *Growth of National Product in Real Terms per Capita, 1913–1969*

(A)

Year	1913	1925	1929	1932	1938	1950*	1959*	1969*
Index	100	100	114	86	137	118	190	276

(B)

Period	1913–25	1925–38	1938–50*	1950–59*	1960–69*
Average Annual Growth in Percent	0.0	2.5	−0.9	6.2	4.0

Source: Petzina, *Grundriss*, p. 770.
*FRG only.

18. *Structure of Domestic Product by Sectors in Percentages, 1910/13–1969*

Period	Net Domestic Product in 1913 Prices		
	Agriculture	Mining, Industry and Crafts	Services
1910/13	23.4	44.6	32.0
1925/29	16.2	47.9	35.9
1930/34	20.5	41.8	37.7
1950/54*	10.6	55.0	34.4
1955/59*	8.2	59.9	31.9

Period	Gross Domestic Product in 1967 Prices		
	Agriculture	Mining, Industry and Crafts	Services
1960			
FRG	4.8	50.7	44.5
GDR	13.1	53.0	33.9
1969			
FRG	3.8	54.4	41.8
GDR	8.9	57.9	33.2

Sources: Hoffmann, *Wachstum,* p. 33; Report of the Federal Government (Bonn, 1971).
*FRG only.

19. *Employment of Capital in Percentages, 1913–1959*

Year	Buildings	Implements and Machinery	Stock-in-Trade	Railroads	Roads
1913	52	22	12	9	6
1939	53	19	13	8	8
1959*	46	30	13	4	7

Source: Hoffmann, *Wachstum,* p. 47.
*FRG only.

20. *Structure of Investment by Sectors in Percentages, 1910/13–1955/59*

	Net Investment in 1913 Prices			
Period	Agriculture	Industry and Crafts	Nonagricultural Housing	Public Buildings, Railroads, Roads
1910/13	13.9	42.9	24.5	18.8
1925/29	10.9	48.3	23.3	17.5
1930/34	38.5	−43.4	53.9	51.0
1935/38	10.1	53.2	14.6	22.1
1950/54*	6.0	61.4	22.9	9.8
1955/59*	4.9	60.8	20.7	13.6

Source: Hoffmann, *Wachstum,* p. 143.
*FRG only.

21. *Government Expenditure, 1913–1970*

(A)

		Administrative Levels in Percentage		
Year	Percentage of National Income	Central	State	Local
1913	16.5	41.1	25.3	33.6
1925	25.2	45.2	23.6	31.2
1928	28.7	50.4	19.7	29.9
1930	30.7	—	—	—
1932	34.0	48.9	20.2	30.9
1933	38.1	51.4	19.6	29.0
1935	38.7	—	—	—
1937	40.9	71.8	10.3	17.9
1938	45.3	—	—	—
1950	35.9	62.0	22.3	15.7
1955	37.7	—	—	—
1958	40.6	63.4	21.2	15.4

(B)

21. (*continued*)

Percentage Structure By Functions

Year	General Adminis-tration	Law and Order	Defense	War-Related Charges	Social and Health Services	Education	Economic Services	Communal Services and Housing	Debt Service
1900	12.3	9.4	24.4	—	8.1	17.6	12.2	5.7	10.3
1910	11.2	9.2	21.0	—	9.7	19.1	12.9	6.2	10.7
1913	8.8	7.9	25.2	—	9.7	18.6	12.7	6.1	11.0
1925	9.8	8.8	4.4	11.6	26.8	16.1	9.6	11.1	1.8
1930	8.2	7.6	3.7	16.5	30.1	15.2	9.1	9.0	6.6
1935	7.0	5.7	24.3	2.0	21.2	10.7	12.2	5.0	11.4
1948	7.9	5.4	24.7	3.6	26.1	11.2	10.0	9.5	1.6
1950	6.7	4.7	17.1	3.0	30.7	10.7	14.2	11.0	2.4
1955	6.7	5.0	11.9	2.1	30.8	12.0	15.9	12.1	3.9
1960	6.2	4.3	12.9	3.5	26.2	12.6	19.0	12.7	3.2
1965	9.2	3.4	12.5	2.2	27.0	11.9	19.8	9.5	4.5
1970	11.9	3.7	9.2	—	28.8	14.9	19.2	5.1	7.2

Sources: Handbuch der Finanzwissenschaft, 3rd ed., vol. 1, p. 742 f.; Andic and Veverka, *Growth of Government Expenditure,* p. 244 f.; *Statistisches Bundesamt, 1872–1972,* p. 231 f.

22. *Share of Exports and Imports in Percentages of Net National Product at Current Prices, 1910/13–1965/69*

Period	1910/13	1925/29	1930/34	1935/38	1950/54*	1955/59*	1960/64*	1965/69*
Exports	17.5	14.9	12.0	6.0	13.3	18.0	16.8	19.5
Imports	20.2	17.0	10.1	5.7	12.9	15.8	15.2	16.9

Sources: Hoffmann, *Wachstum,* p. 151; Statistical Yearbook for the FRG, 1972.
*FRG only.

23. *Structure of Foreign Trade in Percentages of Commodities, 1913–1970*

		Imports		
Year	Foodstuffs	Raw Materials	Semi-Finished Goods	Finished Goods
1913	38	35	17	10
1928	41	28	18	13
1937	38	37	18	7
1950*	44	30	14	12
1970*	19	14	16	50

		Exports		
Year	Foodstuffs	Raw Materials	Semi-Finished Goods	Finished Goods
1913	12	13	11	64
1928	7	12	12	69
1937	1	10	9	80
1950*	2	14	19	65
1970*	4	2	8	86

Source: Petzina, *Grundriss,* p. 782.
*FRG only.

24. *Structure of Foreign Trade by Countries in Percentages, 1913–1970*

(A) Reich

Country or Group of Countries	Country of Origin			Country of Destination		
	1913	1929	1938	1913	1929	1938
Northern Europe (Sweden, Denmark, Norway, Finland)	5.1	7.3	11.3	7.7	10.2	12.8
Eastern Europe (Russia, Poland, Latvia, Lithuania, Estonia)	13.2	6.9	4.3	8.7	6.5	4.2
South-Eastern Europe (Hungary*, Yugoslavia, Romania, Bulgaria, Greece)	8.7	3.9	9.8	13.0	4.3	10.3
Southern Europe (Italy, Spain, Portugal)	5.0	5.5	6.7	5.8	7.5	7.9
Western Europe (Great Britain, France, Belgium, Netherlands, Luxemburg, Switzerland)	21.8	22.1	16.9	39.7	35.9	27.5
Near East (Turkey, Egypt, Persia)	1.8	1.4	3.6	1.4	1.2	4.7
Latin America (Argentina, Brazil, Chile, Mexico)	9.0	8.7	10.7	6.1	5.5	8.0
France	5.4	4.8	2.6	7.8	6.9	4.1
Italy	3.0	3.3	4.5	3.9	5.4	5.7
Great Britain	8.1	6.4	5.2	14.2	9.7	6.7
U.S.A.	15.9	13.3	7.4	7.1	7.4	2.8
Japan	0.4	0.3	0.5	1.2	1.8	1.8
Soviet Union	—	3.2	0.9	—	2.6	0.6

Sources: Statistical Yearbook for the German Reich, 1914, 1930, 1939/40.
*1913 Austria-Hungary.

(B) Federal Republic of Germany

From	Imports				
	1950	1955	1960	1965	1970
Industrialized European Countries	52	51	54	59	63
EEC-Countries	27	26	30	38	44
EFTA-Countries	21	19	20	17	15
Others	5	6	5	4	4
Industrialized Overseas Countries	20	19	19	18	16
Communist Countries	3	3	5	4	4
Developing Countries	24	27	22	19	16
France	6	6	9	11	13
Italy	5	4	6	9	10
Netherlands	11	10	9	10	12
Belgium/Luxemburg	4	6	6	8	9
Great Britain	4	3	4	4	4
Austria	2	3	3	2	2
Switzerland	3	3	4	3	3
Sweden/Denmark/Norway	12	9	9	9	6
United States of America	15	13	12	13	11
Japan	0.3	0.4	0.7	1.3	1.8
Soviet Union	0	0.6	1.6	1.6	1.1
German Democratic Republic*	4	2	2	1.8	1.9

24. *(continued)*

To	Exports				
	1950	1955	1960	1965	1970
Industrialized European Countries	72	65	64	69	69
EEC-Countries	37	29	30	35	40
EFTA-Countries	27	29	28	27	23
Others	8	7	6	7	7
Industrialized Overseas Countries	9	11	13	13	14
Communist Countries	4	2	5	4	4
Developing Countries	15	22	19	14	12
France	7	6	9	11	12
Italy	6	6	6	6	9
Netherlands	14	9	9	10	11
Belgium/Luxemburg	8	7	6	8	8
Great Britain	4	4	4	4	4
Austria	4	6	5	6	4
Switzerland	6	6	6	6	6
Sweden/Denmark/Norway	12	13	11	10	8
United States of America	5	7	8	8	9
Japan	0.4	0.7	1	1	1.4
Soviet Union	0	0.4	1.6	0.8	1.3
German Democratic Republic**	4	2	2	1.7	1.9

Source: Federal Ministry for Economic Affairs, *Leistung in Zahlen,* 1972, pp. 69–81.
  *Intra-German shipments received, as percentage of total FRG imports including intra-German shipments.
**Intra-German shipments made, as percentage of total FRG exports including intra-German shipments.

25. *German Share in World Trade, 1913–1970*

Year	1913	1928	1937	1950*	1958*	1970*
Percent	12.1	9.3	8.3	3.7	7.5	10.0

Sources: Kuznets, Modern Economic Growth, p. 308; Federal Ministry for Economic Affairs, *Leistung in Zahlen,* 1967, p. 68; Statistical Yearbook for the FRG, 1972.
*FRG only.

Index

229

Designer: Al Burkhardt
Compositor: Viking Typographics
Printer: Braun-Brumfield
Binder: Braun-Brumfield
Text: VIP Baskerville
Display: VIP Baskerville
Cloth: Holliston Roxite A50267
Paper: 50lb. P&S offset B32